THE LOVE AFFAIR

THE LOVE AFFAIR

Michael Harper

HODDER AND STOUGHTON
LONDON SYDNEY AUCKLAND TORONTO

All biblical quotes are taken from the
Revised Standard Version.

The author and publishers wish to thank the following for their
kind permission for the use of their copyright material in this
edition:

Northern Songs Ltd., for five lines from 'God' by John Lennon.

Faber and Faber Ltd., for eleven lines from *The English
Auden: Poems Essays and Dramatic Writings, 1927–1939* by
W. H. Auden.

ISBN 0 340 28202 9

Hodder and Stoughton Editorial Office: 47 Bedford Square, London WC1B 3DP.

To Jeanne

In thankfulness to God for our life together
for twenty-five years

CONTENTS

1 Doodles in the dust: an introduction   9
2 The dream is over   11
3 All we need is love?   21
4 Love is the greatest   28
5 All's love and all's law   42
6 Agape   54
7 God is love   65
8 The love of God   75
9 No U-Turns   93
10 Love and sex   107
11 Love or money?   120
12 Agape versus Eros—from apostles to
       reformers   132
13 Agape versus Eros—from reformers
       to pentecostals   151
14 Mrs. Bergmeier's baby   163
15 Self-love, agape or narcissism?   184
16 The indubitable seal   204
   Notes   217
   Bibliography   231
   Index   235

1 DOODLES IN THE DUST

The first ideas for this book can be traced to the near drowning of its author in a lake in New Zealand. On New Year's Eve 1976 I was sailing solo on Lake Taupo when my boat capsized in a sudden and particularly violent squall about a mile offshore. Clinging to the side of the boat and unable to right it, I was rescued after over an hour in the chilly glacial waters. I nearly died of hypothermia.

When I recovered I asked God why he had saved me and what he wanted me to do. The reply came something like this: "I want you to learn how to love people the same way as I do." A few days later I met a chubby Presbyterian called Leonard Evans. Together with Robert Frost we were the speakers at Summer Schools arranged by Christian Advance Ministries of New Zealand. Leonard gave us what he calls 'the love message'. He ribbed us mercilessly. He got us to laugh at ourselves and our spurious pieties. He taught us the true meaning of love, and I have never forgotten those talks.

From then on I have wanted to write a book on this great subject. Many of the most loving people I have met haven't written books. They are too busy loving others to have time to write about it. They find it a full-time job. Maybe, I'm being a little hard on writers. Nevertheless, the greatest lover of all, whose love affair with mankind has no beginning and will have no end, not only wrote nothing about it, but didn't speak much about it either. The greatest verbal statements about love in the New Testament do not come from the lips of Jesus but from the pen of Paul, particularly in the so-called hymn of love in 1 Corinthians 13. Jesus did not have to teach it, because *he was it*.

Every thought of his mind, every word of his mouth and every action of his body were demonstrations of love. A person like that does not need to speak or write about love; you just have to look at them and you get the message.

Actually Jesus did write something. When confronted by the woman who had been caught in bed with someone else's husband, he didn't look at her but simply traced doodles in the dust. In the presence of that man, all writing is mere doodling.

*   *   *

I'm well aware of the fact that I have done scant justice to the many important subjects that fall within the scope of this book. To write fully on love would require at least a library, and so I can only apologise for the inadequacy of my treatment of this great theme.

The main New Testament Greek word for love is *agape*. Whenever in the book I refer to the Greek word itself it is in italics—*agape*. But when I use the word as a kind of code word for 'true love' it is usually printed Agape, especially in contrast to the Greek concept of love—Eros.

I would like to record my great appreciation to Professor C. F. D. Moule for all the trouble he has taken in reading chapters two to eight and fourteen, and his many helpful criticisms, corrections and comments. Also to Professor Paul Vitz of New York University for his similarly helpful comments on chapter fifteen. I should like also to thank Rob Warner, the religious editor of Hodder & Stoughton, for his detailed editorial work, suggested improvements and constant encouragements.

Finally I would like to thank my wife Jeanne to whom this book is dedicated. It was completed within a few weeks of our 25th wedding anniversary. It has been in these years that we have come most fully to know the meaning of true love, and our prayer for this book is that it will help others discover the springs of living waters that never dry up when their source is in God himself.

2 THE DREAM IS OVER

> God is a concept
> By which we measure
> Our pain . . .
> You just have to carry on
> The dream is over
> (John Lennon)

The Dakota is a gloomy, high maintenance gothic fortress overlooking the west side of Central Park in New York. Outside the Dakota that particular December night a man was loitering in the shadows of the entrance to the fortress. Suddenly he fired a revolver at a man entering the building. The victim was John Lennon, and for millions of young people 'the dream was over.' John Lennon spoke to his generation of their sense of helplessness. He expressed their longing for love and peace. "Give peace a chance" and "All you need is love" were perhaps his two most famous songs.

Speaking at the end of his famous series on *Civilisation*, shown on BBC television, Kenneth Clark confessed, "I am completely baffled by what is taking place today." He went on to say, "the trouble is there is still no centre. The moral and intellectual failure of Marxism has left us with no alternative to heroic materialism, and that isn't enough. One may be optimistic but one can't exactly be joyful at the prospect before us."[1]

Others too have expressed their total despair, and yet the world has survived. Aristotle, as long ago as three hundred years before Christ, wrote, "When I look at the younger generation I despair of the future of civilisation," a rather liverish Duke of Wellington towards the end of his life wrote, "I thank God I shall be spared the consummation of ruin that is gathering around us." But neither Aristotle nor the Duke of Wellington were confronted with the possibilities of a nuclear holocaust, the exhaustion of the earth's mineral resources, and a population explosion which makes mass starvation and a world war seem virtually inevitable.

When President Truman confided in Sir Winston Churchill that the first atomic bomb had been exploded in the desert of New Mexico, Churchill, waving his cigar excitedly said, "What was gunpowder? Trivial. What was electricity? Meaningless. This atomic bomb is the Second Coming in Wrath."

For most of us 'the dream is over.' The dream of Chinese communism cost an estimated 26 million lives between 1949 and 1965. Some believe it could have been as high as 63 million. Solzhenitsyn's figure for the Russian dream is around 66 million. Nor are Western dreams doing too well.

The 1930s have been called the black years. The English historian A. J. P. Taylor has called them 'the devil's decade'. Writing about this period he has said, "Its popular image can be expressed in two phrases, 'mass unemployment' and 'appeasement'."[2] It was the decade of the great recession, of unemployment in Britain which exceeded 20% of the labour force in some parts of the country, of the rise to power of the great dictators, Hitler and Mussolini, of the great purges of Stalin in Russia, of the Munich agreement, to become a byword for appeasement, and of the start of the war which was to take the lives of over 50 million people and change the whole course of world history. At Cambridge the sinister recruiting campaign was going on for communist spies, who were to betray their country, men like Anthony Blunt, Guy Burgess, Kim Philby and Donald Maclean.[3]

But the 1930s was also a decade in which there was much writing about morals. In 1932 the English translation of Anders Nygren's famous book *Agape and Eros* was published. Emil Brunner's great book *The Divine Imperative* also came out in this period. Later in the same decade came John Burnaby's *Amor Dei*, more or less a riposte to Nygren's book and a defence of Augustine's ethical teaching. Bonhoeffer was also writing a book on ethics, which was to be published posthumously. He wrote in terms of "the love of God and the decay of the world." So far as the decay of the world was concerned, there was evidence on every hand, but where was the love of God? Those who deserted the Churches after World War 1 never came back again, and the '50s and '60s were to see a mass exodus, a tide which has still not turned. Evil was everywhere, God seemed nowhere. Any idea of a God of love had sunk without trace.

Half a century has passed since Nygren, Brunner and others were writing. Today there are not a few who have detected ominous similarities between the '30s and the '80s. Once again the domestic scene is dominated by the hard realities of unemployment and trade recessions, while the international scene is again faced with the perils of world war, and by the temptations to appease aggressors for the sake of peace at any price. Never has the unthinkable become so thinkable, a nuclear holocaust between East and West.

In 1979 the famous Brandt Commission published its report in which it sought to show a new and even more dangerous polarisation between North and South. Is the East-West confrontation of ideologies going to be superceded by a North-South confrontation on basic human needs—that of food, essential medicines and shelter? The chilly statistics suggest this. Malnutrition in 1974 affected 460 million people, and the figures mount every year. The world abounds with inequalities. One third of the world's cereal harvests are fed to Northern livestock and one quarter of its fish catch. The Peruvian anchovy catches could satisfy the protein needs of the whole of Latin America. Instead it is exported to North America for animal and pet food. Britain's cats and dogs eat enough protein to satisfy half a million people. In the last century Hegel arrogantly said "the earth exists to be appropriated by man." That is exactly what man has done, but he has yet to find a way by which the world's resources can be fairly distributed. The West has gorged herself on the world's scarce resources.

Many Western countries are groaning with superfluous wealth, seemingly oblivious to demeaning poverty. We have accused communism of arrant materialism, but the West has displayed an even greater idolatry of things.

The real foundation of our global schizophrenia is neither to be found in the ideological East-West divide or the economic North-South; rather we must look for it in another direction altogether. Alexander Solzhenitsyn exposed it in his famous Harvard lecture, the common title of which was "a world split apart". Arnold Toynbee once wrote about "the widening morality gap between man's ever increasing technical prowess and the obstinate inadequacy of his social performance." It is that 'morality gap' about which Solzhenitsyn spoke at Harvard, and with which this book is concerned; for the gap can only be spanned by love. For Solzhenitsyn the split in the world has to do with spiritual values, not primarily ideological or economic ones. He sees the division in the world as first caused by its materialistic outlook. Both Eastern communism and Western capitalism are on trial, for both are selfishly materialistic.

There is a sense also that we are in an 'end-time'. Whether this is the end to end all ends, or just an end before a fresh beginning, is open to question. But the general sense of being near the end is almost universal. When we sense the Apocalypse upon us, we all begin to take ethics seriously again. Like the famous description which Dr. Johnson gave of the man about to be hanged, "It marvellously concentrates the mind." Oscar Cullmann stresses the need to take ethics seriously *because we live in an end-time*. "The apocalyptic character of our century," he writes, "makes this imperative."[4]

But the task is a daunting one. Ethical questions have become increasingly complicated. Karl Rahner stresses what he calls "the complications of love." He writes, "It cannot be performed or negotiated . . . it is never simply present, but is always on the way to itself."[5] We have only to take the ethic of war to realise what a dramatic change has taken place in the twentieth century. Never before in world history has war involved on such a massive scale, men, women and children of all ages. It was a comparatively unknown Englishman who helped to change all this. His name was Pemberton Billing and he was the first person in modern times to advance the view that war should be directed indiscriminately against civilians rather than exclusively the armed forces of the enemy. A. J. P. Taylor comments, "By 1945 all attempts to civilise air warfare or to control the effects had been rejected, and the British took the lead in this rejection."[6] The bombing of Dresden on the night of February 13th–14th 1945 was the most glaring example of total war against the enemy, until Hiroshima six months later. That night 25,000 people died, all but a handful civilians, and a beautiful city was burnt to the ground. Altogether around 593,000 German civilians were killed in air raids during World War 2, and there is no evidence that it shortened the war by so much as a single day.

Wars are a tragic example of the departure of man from firm ethical behaviour. The seeds of this disaster have produced a heart-breaking harvest in the fields of sexuality and economics. Love seems to have become irrelevant in these contexts. Instead aggression and self-interest have become the dominant forces in personal and public life.

In the Synoptic Gospels the noun *agape* only occurs twice, which is rather surprising. But in one of these it is highly significant. In one of Jesus' final teaching sessions, describing the end-times, he said, "because wickedness is multiplied, most men's love will grow cold" (Matt. 24:12). Jesus prophesied that evils would predominate and as a result there would be a cooling off of love. We live in such days. There has been a change in the ethical temperature, and a chill wind has been blowing fiercely across the human landscape. In commenting on this passage Ceslaus Spicq writes, "this verb 'to grow cold' has the most baleful meaning. It means to become extinct."[7] It is no exaggeration to say that in many areas of personal and national life the kind of love which was taught and practised by Jesus and the early Christians is practically extinct. The importance

15

of re-discovering the true meaning of the word cannot be exaggerated. Quell and Stauffer in *Kittel's Wordbook* in the section on love see the subject as "central both for theology and for religion *in a disordered world*."[8]

But it is not only the absence of true love which should concern us, but also the false substitutes that have replaced it. Later in the book we shall look again at some of the arguments of Nygren's book *Agape and Eros*. These two words represent quite different ideas of love. When one is dominant, the other tends to be weakened. The ideas of Eros originated in Greece and were passed on later tc the Romans. For Aristotle love began with the pleasures of the eyes. Beauty was definitive. The Greeks were not expected to love or appreciate the unlovely. Our modern synthetic image of beauty, glorified and sensualised by Hollywood and T.V., comes from the same source. Aristotle once said, "Only he who is deserving of love can be loved." The Greeks could not conceive of love which was not a response to something inherently lovely. Plato once said, "Love is for the lovely." Agape love is different, and it is this love not Eros love which the world needs so much.

When we go deeper into this we find that all the philosophies contemporary with Christianity had one aim and object, what the Greeks called *ataraxia* by which they meant 'peace of mind'. John Lennon sings about it in "Give peace a chance." Arndt and Gingrich define it as "being without confusion, being undisturbed." This word never occurs in the New Testament itself, apart from a near synonym in 1 Cor 7: 35. William Barclay in his book *Flesh and Spirit*[9] points out that *ataraxia* can be divided into two component parts expressed by two other Greek words, *autarkeia* and *apatheia*. The first word can be translated 'absolute self-sufficiency or independence' and the second word (from which we get the English word apathy) means 'the inability to feel joy or sorrow, gladness or grief'. William Barclay describes it as "an attitude that cannot be touched by anything that can happen to itself or anyone else. It is the heart insulated from all feeling and from all emotion."

Paul writes of it in the Epistle to the Ephesians, "They [Gentiles] are . . . alienated from the life of God because of the ignorance that is in them, *due to their hardness of heart; they have become callous . . .*" (4:18, 19). If you add to all this the amorality in sexual behaviour which characterised the Greeks, then you have our present Western society all over again. Modern man seeks to achieve peace of mind through isolating himself as much as possible from others, especially in order to avoid trouble, and not to allow his feelings to get the better of him.

Joseph Fletcher has quite rightly pointed out that the opposite of love is not 'hate', but 'indifference'. He writes, "Hate treats the neighbour as a 'thou', indifference as a 'thing'. There is one thing worse than evil itself, and that is indifference to it."[10] The lowest point to which our society often seems to sink is, when it says, "I couldn't care less." Commenting on Matthew 6:24, Spicq says that the opposite of love is to be neglectful of others. The word used is *kataphronein*, which means, "to despise, disdain, set no value on, refuse to consider or to interest oneself." Spicq concludes, "Where God is concerned disdain is vile outrage."[11]

During 1980 a man called George Christie was taken ill on the top deck of a Glasgow bus. As he lay dying the bus carried him back and forth on no less than five journeys before the police were called. He was thought to have been drunk, but in actual fact he had suffered a brain haemorrhage. Passengers reported him but it was three hours before he was handed over to the police, who locked him up for the next seven hours. Only then was he taken to hospital where he died the following day. In the court hearing it was said, "It is a sad indictment that in Glasgow such a thing can have happened." Perhaps an extreme case, but fairly typical of the callousness of a society which gives more protection to a blade of grass in a national park than it does to the human foetus.

But God's love affair with the human race never ceases. It had no beginning, and it will know no end. It hovers over the wastelands of the world's lovelessness. It waits its moment, ready to transform us into people of compassion and concern. God is prepared to wait. Amongst examples of modern graffiti, pearls can sometimes be found. One seen on Camden Town Station read, "The world is fragile, handle it with prayer."[12] The world has seldom seemed so fragile. It appears in danger at any moment of breaking into a billion pieces, blown apart by a nuclear explosion of horrendous size, or of being poisoned and asphyxiated by the sheer density of its pollution and the effluence of its affluence. Man has never before attained to such heights of technical skill nor has sunk so deeply or disastrously into moral chaos and a sense of helplessness.

The cinema has tried in the last twenty years to reflect on some of these ethical quagmires that so many are stuck in. It has tried to demolish, with a certain degree of success and certainly of satisfaction, most of what remains of self-glorification and glamour in war. One of these movies is *Catch 22*, based on a book by Joseph Heller.[13] The hero of the story is an American airman on a bomber station in Italy during World War 2. His name is Yossarian. His philosophy of life is strictly and blatantly egotistical. "From now on," he says, "I'm thinking only of me." Which is at least being honest. Major Danby responds with, "But Yossarian, suppose everyone felt that way." Yossarian answers, "Then I'd certainly be a damn fool to feel any other way, wouldn't I?"

During the action of the film the head of the bomber station, Colonel Cathcart, is talking with Milo Minderbinder, the mess officer, who is running a multi-million dollar racket through the lucrative black market. He calls it M & M Enterprises, standing for Milo and Minderbinder. The & is inserted "to nullify any impression that the syndicate was a one-man operation". The two men are making a business deal as they drive in a jeep along the perimeter track of the bomber base. As they talk a bomber comes in to land. Both its engines are on fire. It skids off the runway and bursts into flames. The crew are incinerated. Both Cathcart and Milo continue their conversation as if nothing has happened.

Right at the end of the film Yossarian's friend Aarfy rapes a woman and then throws her out of the window like a discarded cigarette end. She falls to her death. Yossarian happens to be walking by. Horrified by what he sees he rushes up the stairs of the apartment block and bursts into the room where Aarfy squats in a corner.

"I only raped her once," he says.

Yossarian explodes, "You killed a girl, you're going to be put in jail."

"I hardly think they are going to make too much fuss over one poor Italian servant girl when so many thousands of lives are being lost every day. Do you?" is Aarfy's defence.

Suddenly they hear police sirens and two burly M.P.s burst from the jeep. "They are coming to arrest you," warns Yossarian. Our moral indignation is roused. The police rush into the room and arrest Yossarian for being in Rome without a pass. Before leaving they apologise to Aarfy for intruding.

This is the kind of nightmarish world we live in. We don't seem to know any longer who are the good guys and who are the bad ones. *Catch 22* ends with Yossarian pushing his rubber dinghy off from an Italian beach and paddling to Sweden, where he hopes to find the peace that has so far eluded him.

W. H. Auden expressed in one of his poems this sense of helplessness and the ethical apathy of our century.[14]

> Faces along the bar
> Cling to their average day;
> The lights must never go out,
> The music must always play.
> All the conventions conspire
> To make this fort assume
> The furniture of home;
> Lest we should see where we are,
> Lost in a haunted wood,
> Children afraid of the night
> Who have never been happy or good.

19

Ronald Higgins in his chilling book *The Seventh Enemy* calls our age 'The age of collective insanity.' He goes on, "The cold bright light of objective reason has blinded us to the larger if more elusive truths." But what are the larger truths?

A Swiss dramatist called Friedrich Dürrenmatt once wrote a play called *The Physicists*. It was about a famous physicist who commits himself to an insane asylum to prevent his knowledge from being exploited by unscrupulous and warlike governments. As the play develops one becomes aware that all the patients in the asylum are famous scientists, and most of the staff are famous spies out to discover hiding scientists for their contending governments. The message of the play is clear, there is no way to escape from the moral dilemmas which torture our world. Fantasy today becomes reality tomorrow. Our world is far too divided and broken for anyone to find any human answer to the global schizophrenia which is so evident everywhere.

All we need is love. But how?

3   ALL WE NEED IS LOVE?

We would all agree with John Lennon that love is the answer; but that is not much help to us if we don't, in any exact sense, know what love is.

We are moving towards the end of a century which has seen the shaking of many foundations. The theories of Einstein shattered the Newtonian principles upon which science had stood secure. Freud in a similar fashion shook to its foundations the rational frame of man's mind. But whatever has happened to morals? What does modern man mean when he talks about love?

We must be under no illusions. Vital though our subject is, it is not going to be easy to discover the meaning of love. We are going to have to do a lot of sifting. We shall have to distinguish carefully between fact and fiction. It is the easiest subject in the world in which to make do with superficialities. But many people have come to see that it won't do to leave it there. We have got to break through the tinselled thoughts about love which lie on the surface and get down to foundations. We are going to have to 'think' as well as 'feel'. After all the great commandment to love God tells us to act with our minds as well as our hearts. We make no apologies for looking closely at theology, nor for delving back into the past in our quest for real and genuine love.

It is important from the beginning to see that theology and ethics belong together. Emil Brunner was right to assert that no distinction could be made between them. "The whole New Testament," he wrote, "is an indissoluble blend of ethics and dogmatics."[1] Elsewhere he writes, "Christian ethics is the science of human conduct as it is determined by divine conduct."[2] The apostle John summarised this in one of the most striking statements in the New Testament, "God is love" (1 Jn 4:8). If this is true, then it is impossible to understand the nature of love, without first understanding the nature of God himself.

There is speculation about love today that bears little relationship to the true nature of God, and all too often is based on a false and sentimental view of him. C. H. Dodd makes this same point: "The religious and the ethical moments in Christianity are no longer distinguishable. Ethics reaches out into that which transcends ethics, while at the same time the religious principle which is the foundation of all Christian theology, the definition of the nature of God himself, cannot be stated except in ethical terms."[3]

One is not unaware of the danger of trying to simplify what is extremely complex. But perhaps at this early stage it would be helpful to the reader if there was a summary of the arguments of the book, so that it may be easier to follow and understand them as we go along.

THE MAIN ARGUMENT

The main argument can be summarised in this simple statement:

The main reason why there is an absence of true love in the world is because man has divided what God has united and tried to unite what God has divided.

The Three Divisions (where there should be unity)

1. God and love

Because God is love, we do not discover God from our experience of love, but we discover love from our experience of God. Our knowledge of the true meaning of love depends on our knowledge of God in Jesus Christ. Emil Brunner puts it well, "Only God himself defines love in his action. We . . . do not know what *love* is, unless we learn to know God in his action, in faith . . . Every attempt to conceive love as a principle leads to this result, it becomes distorted

22

either in the rigorist legalistic sense or in the hedonistic sense. Man only knows what the love of God is when he sees the way in which God acts and he only knows how he himself ought to love by allowing himself to be drawn by faith into this activity of God."[4] There are many forms of human care expressed in a variety of ways. But true love, the Agape love of the New Testament is an expression of God's grace. It is because we have divided God from love and love from God that we are both confused and bereft.

2. God and man

The division between God and man is perhaps most clearly seen in the way the two commandments (to love God and to love our neighbour) have become separated. It was Jesus himself who first brought the two commandments together. They occur in two different parts of the Old Testament. When Jesus was asked the question, "Which is the great commandment in the Law?" he answered, "You shall love the Lord your God with all your heart, and with all your soul, and with all your mind. This is the great and first commandment. And a second is like it, You shall love your neighbour as yourself. On these two commandments depend all the law and the prophets" (Matt. 22:36f). They still remain two commandments, but Jesus regarded them as inseparable. In the words of John you cannot claim to love God (who is invisible) if you fail to love your brother (who is visible). But man has found it extremely difficult to hold the two commandments together. Either there is the error of a pietism which glories in God and ignores the needs of men, or the equally false position of pursuing the causes of justice and human rights and dignity whilst ignoring the first commandment to love God. There seems to be an innate tendency in man to polarise into one or other position. Thus love is often emptied of its essential divine quality in the sole pursuit of human goals, or rendered valueless by its concentration exclusively on pious objectives, while people and their needs are ignored.

Hans Kung has put it well. "In the last resort," he writes, "a love of God without love of man is no love at all. And if God must keep his inalienable primacy, then God's love can never become a means or a symbol for love of man, neither can love of man ever become a means or symbol for love of God."[5] There are meant to be no U-Turns in the movement of God's love towards man; what we receive in that relationship we are to pass on to others.

3. God and nature

Another sign of the failure of people to love one another can be seen in the collapse of many marriages. Love and human sexuality have been separated with painful results. The same is true in the field of economics. We have come to tolerate economic systems which are sometimes blatantly unjust. Compassion for the economically deprived seems to some out of place, even dangerous. The death of millions from hunger has sometimes been 'justified' by the system of economics in operation at the time. Sexuality and economics describe man's most basic human needs; his physical life is sustained by food and drink, and propagated through his sexual activity. But when love is separated from these two areas, disaster often follows.

It is tragic when man deifies sex or economics. Whenever they are worshipped as gods they become demons. This happens when we divide God from his creation. Eros and Mammon are attractive to our senses, but they can become hard taskmasters, and in the end destroy those who idolise them.

C. S. Lewis put it well in his book *The Four Loves*, "Nature cannot satisfy the desires she arouses nor answer theological questions, nor sanctify us; our real journey to God involves constantly turning our back on her. This love of nature begins to be a god, and, therefore, a demon. And demons never keep their promises. Nature 'dies' on those who try to live for a love of nature . . . Say your prayers in a garden early, ignoring the dew, the birds and the flowers, and you will come away overwhelmed by its freshness and joy; go there in order to be overwhelmed and after a certain age, nine times out of ten nothing will happen to you."[6] Only when our lives are centred on God is his world safe for us to live in and appreciate to the full.

The Unity (where there should be separation)

We have seen how man has divided what God has put together; we now need to see how man has also united what God has divided. One of the most important theological books on this subject is *Agape and Eros*, written by Anders Nygren and first translated and published in England in 1932.[7] The author went on to become a Bishop in the Swedish Lutheran Church. When I read the book I was surprised that it ended so abruptly with the writings of Martin Luther. So I thought I ought to try to find out if he had written anything further on this subject. I wrote to a Swedish friend Agne Nordlander, who was teaching at the Johannlunds Teologiska Institut in Uppsala. He checked out my question with his professor, Axel Gyllenkrok, who studied under Nygren himself. Apparently he wrote nothing further. In his letter to me Agne Nordlander wrote, "Nygren considered Luther as the climax of Christian thinking. For Nygren, Luther has the same level of authority as the apostle Paul, although he never dared say so openly. But in reality Luther belonged to the canon of scripture."[8]

Nygren had many critics, and some of his book has been seriously questioned by scholars. His excessive bias towards Luther is a valid criticism. He has sometimes exaggerated his arguments in order to make a point. But the importance of the main theme of his book cannot be denied. He has shown clearly the conflict throughout Church history between Agape and Eros. I believe his main thesis is an exposé of this battle, which is of significance for our day. The book itself is now largely forgotten. But its main arguments stand, and remain important.

The danger of syncretism is a constant theme in the Old

and New Testaments. By this I mean the alliance of truth and error, righteousness and sin. Right from earliest days the Christian Church had to battle to preserve the truth from the subtle attempts to add to it some of the philosophy and ethics of the Graeco-Roman world. In the field of ethics this can be summarised in the contest Agape versus Eros. Sometimes Agape has dominated the scene, sometimes Eros. To recover the true meaning of love we have to disentangle Agape and Eros. The New Testament presents a united testimony to its rejection of Graeco-Roman ethics and philosophy. The Church's ethics are derived from Judaism not Greek philosophy. The greatest insult that the New Testament writers could give to that other system of thought and life was to ignore Eros altogether. The word never comes in the New Testament. It was a key word for the Greeks, but Christians totally ignored it.

Eros' comeback needs to be seen in the light of the important influence of gnosticism in the centuries that followed the Apostolic Age. It proved to be Christianity's major thorn in the flesh. The three fundamental dogmas of the Christian Church were challenged by gnosticism.[9] They are—belief in God as Creator, the Incarnation and the Cross, and the Resurrection. These three doctrines stood as bulwarks against the Greek theory of salvation. Christians did not believe that they had to be saved from the material world. Sin was due to disobedience and rebellion, not corporeality. But man is for ever seeking new ways of escape from his human prison. In the Greek world it came through *gnosis* (knowledge). Today men seek release through hallucinatory drugs or alcohol; or possibly through psychiatry. The Christian gospel says, "You don't need to escape, but by repentance and faith you can be set free within that prison (our bodies), which in any case is a temple created by God not a prison." For the Greeks the last thing in the world their gods would have done would have been to take human flesh, as Jesus did; and as far as resurrection was concerned, it was unnecessary. Their belief in the immortality of the soul meant they would rise anyway, once they were able to escape from the prison of their bodies. So there was no great significance in Christ's resurrection, and so far as the resurrection of *the body* was concerned, it was wholly unacceptable; their whole desire was to leave it behind not take it with them, since to them it was a prison not a temple.

It is in this context that Eros thrived. We don't have to look far in the New Testament to see that Agape and all that it stood for was to be locked in a deadly struggle with both the advocates of Jewish Law (Nomos) on the one hand, and Greek ideas of God and man on the other (Eros). All through Church history Eros has muddied the pure streams of Agape and confused whole generations. One of the main reasons why our generation is so muddled about the subject of love is because of its failure to see the distinction between these different concepts.

Our task, therefore, is clear. We must reunite what man has divided, and separate what he has united. But before we can begin to do this we need to look first at the primacy of love over everything else. In theology there is no greater subject, for "God is love." In ethics there is no more important theme, since to love God and our neighbours are the greatest commandments, and to love one another is the only new commandment left us by Jesus Christ. We shall be looking at this primacy in chapter four, with a separate chapter on the relationship of love to law. Then in chapter six we shall be looking at the meaning of the word *agape* before we turn to the main arguments of the book.

4   LOVE IS THE GREATEST

"So faith, hope, love abide, these three; but the greatest of these is love" (1 Cor. 13:13).

In that delightful book *Mister God, This is Anna*,[1] the little girl Anna encounters the Vicar one day in the High Street. The conversation went something like this:

Parson:	Do you believe in God?
Anna:	Yes
Parson:	Do you know what God is?
Anna:	Yes.
Parson:	What is God then?
Anna:	He's God.
Parson:	Do you go to Church?
Anna:	No.
Parson:	Why not?
Anna:	Because I know it all.
Parson:	What do you know?
Anna:	I know to love Mr. God and to love people and cats and dogs and spiders and flowers and trees (the catalogue went on), with all of me.

Fynn comments, "There's nothing much you can do in the face of that kind of accusation . . . Anna had by-passed all the non-essentials and distilled centuries of learning into one sentence—'and God said, love me, love them and love it, and don't forget to love yourself.' "[2]

The world needs to rediscover the primacy of love, and we must ourselves begin the voyage of discovery. Bertrand Russell, who was not a Christian himself, once said, "I can say that what the world needs is Christian love and compassion." He may not have understood exactly what this meant, but he clearly perceived that it was the one thing needful.

Augustine was one of the greatest advocates of the primacy of Christian love. He saw that love was the heart of Christianity. Nygren comments: "There is scarcely a word of the New Testament that he does not use repeatedly in expounding Christian love. Beyond question, here is one of the most important turning points in the whole history of the Christian idea of love, and perhaps the most radical of all, in view of its results."[3] Nygren (as we shall see in chapter twelve) is critical of Augustine's interpretation of love and the results that followed from it. But the facts speak for themselves, that the greatest moments in the history of the Christian Church have nearly always involved a rediscovery of the primacy of Christian love, of which Augustine is only one of many witnesses. "Where love is, what can be wanting?" he asks. "Where it is not, what can possibly be profitable?"[4]

From monasticism to pentecostalism there have been moments when there has been a desire to return to the primitive simplicity of early Christianity and its principle characteristic: divine love experienced in the lives of Christians and overflowing to the entire world. St. Benedict wished to recreate a community of love and prayer in place of the formality and worldliness of the Church of his day. Even the two most divisive movements in the early days of the Church, associated with the names of Marcion and Montanus, were attempts to restore love to its place of primacy in the life of the Church.

The continental Pietist movements sought the same kind of restoration in the eighteenth and nineteenth centuries. One of their most famous exponents was the Anglican John Wesley. In a book called *A Plain Account of Christian Perfection*[5] he answered the question "What is Christian perfection?" with "Loving God with all our heart, mind, soul and strength. This implies that no wrong temper, none contrary to love, remains in the soul; and that all the thoughts, words and actions are governed by pure love."

Quell and Stauffer summarise the teaching of Paul on this subject, "For Paul, as for Jesus, love is the only life

force that has a future in this age of death."[6] Its primacy is
clear to anyone reading the New Testament. According to
Quell and Stauffer, "It was Jesus who first broke down the
old foundation walls (of Rabbinic Judaism) and undertook
the daring task of a complete rebuilding."[7] Jesus demanded
the exclusiveness of love over every other influence in life.
Mankind was no longer to be systematically graded as in
Rabbinic Judaism. Our love is to be inclusive as God's is
(Matt. 5:43–48). It is to embrace our enemies as well as our
friends. Love is to have no strings attached. It was a
revolution of awesome proportions. In the Apostolic Age,
to quote Quell and Stauffer, "the eternal love of God
becomes a world-changing event." They point out that
Paul always uses the verb in the aorist (e.g. Rom. 8:37,
2, Thess. 2:16, Gal. 2:20, Eph. 2:4, 5:2). The aorist use of
the verb in Greek describes an event rather than a continuing action, but an event which has significant repercussions
in an on-going sense. For Paul, as we shall see again and
again, the key to understanding and experiencing love is in
the past action of God, particularly in the action of the
crucifixion of Jesus; and this divine event, finished and
completed though it is, has an eternal effect on all those
who believe in Christ, the crowning glory of which is the
experiencing of the love of God oneself and the free
bestowal of that love on all those around us. Christ changes
us all into Good Samaritans. For Augustine love was the
one infallible sign of real Christianity.[8]

There would be few who would dispute the centrality
of love in Christian theology and ethics. Nygren writes
of it, "Agape sets its mark on the whole of Christianity.
Without it nothing that is Christian would be Christian."[9]
Later on he writes, "Love is the central and governing
idea of Christianity."[10] A more recent writer, Rudolf
Schnackenburg, has written about the teaching of the
apostle John, "He raised it (love) to be the ruling principle
of Christian morality throughout all ages."[11] Ceslaus Spicq
describes the love of God and our neighbours as "the
foundation on which man's entire religious and moral

conduct rests as a door rests on its hinges."[12] J. L. Houlden writes of the command to love as "a key principle, a touchstone, by which moral action and all other commands are to be judged."[13]

When we turn to the history of the Christian Church its greatest moments have usually been demonstrations of this divine love. There are many names one could mention. There are the monastics like Benedict and Francis of Assisi, mystics like Bernard of Clairvaux and John of the Cross, Bishops like Augustine and Chrysostom, and those who have cared for the poor and needy like William Booth and Mother Teresa of Calcutta. In the eighteenth century the Wesleys stand out as men whose lives and message were governed by the primacy of love. The greatest movements in the history of the Christian Church have usually been concerned, at least in part, to restore love to its proper place in the life of the Church, and, alas, the darkest moments have been when the Church has most obviously departed from this touchstone. There have also been not a few who have gone down in history either as heretics or unbalanced fanatics, and yet who have sought this same goal. There is no sadder case than that of Marcion, whose efforts at restoring love to its proper place in the life of the Church led him into heresy and confrontation with the leadership of the Church. Yet Harnack, the famous Church historian, once described Marcion as "The most significant religious personality between Paul and Augustine."[14] Marcion was one of the first in the Church to see the difference between Agape and Eros, and tried to deliver the Church from the influence of Eros. Marcion saw love as the very centre of Christianity. God to him was love and nothing but love.[15]

We need now to see the primacy of love in relationship to what we may call its 'underlings'. When Paul tells us in 1 Corinthians 13 that love is the 'greatest', he specifies its superiority over other qualities; in this he shows the uniqueness of Christianity, and where it so fundamentally differed from the Roman and Greek worlds of his day.

31

1 Corinthians 13 is a crucial passage, not only for what it teaches us about love, but also because of its historical setting. The atmosphere in which the Corinthian Christian lived was heavy with the Greek concept of love—namely Eros. Here for the first time there occurred a meeting of the ideas of Agape and of Eros, or more accurately, between Agape and Gnosis.[16] In this chapter, usually called 'the hymn of love', Paul stresses the superiority of love over everything else, especially as it turns out those things which the Greeks prized so highly.

KNOWLEDGE

"And if I have prophetic powers, and understand all mysteries *and all knowledge*, and if I have all faith, so as to remove mountains, *but have not love, I am nothing*" (v. 2).

Paul here is not against knowledge as such, any more than he is against speaking in tongues, prophecy or faith. He is simply saying that if we don't have love with it, *we* are nothing. Even if our heads and intellects are stuffed with all the knowledge of the universe, the absence of love makes it valueless to us. Thus love is primary over knowledge. Knowledge, in other words, is one of love's underlings.

This is not the first time in this epistle that Paul raises this question. In the Greek society of Corinth, knowledge (gnosis) was primary. Paul is at pains to contradict this throughout the epistle. In the first chapter, for example, he makes plain that we don't come to know God through wisdom. Or again, that the Cross was folly to the Greeks but to Christians the power of God and the wisdom of God. Very few of the Corinthian Christians were wise in the worldly sense, yet God chose them to put to shame the wise (1:27). In a particularly terse but pregnant phrase, Paul writes, "Knowledge puffs up, but love builds up" (8:1).

There you have it in a nutshell. Knowledge and intellect without love simply boost man's ego. It is only Agape love which builds people up.

The place of intellect and reason in the life of the Christian is important, but never primary. You cannot reason your way to faith. Only the child-like can enter the Kingdom of Heaven. Richard Holloway puts it well, "Intellect is a secondary element (after experience), it follows after the original experience as an attempt to order and explicate that which has been given . . . reality is there before our apprehension of it and it makes itself available to our senses, *all* our senses."[17] Augustine put it another way, "God is not *reason* but love, and he employs reason as the instrument of his love."[18] Paul in this passage leaves no doubt in our minds that knowledge can be an instrument of blessing in our lives. But it must be ruled by love.

ENTHUSIASM

"If I speak in the tongues of men and of angels, but have not love, I am a noisy gong or a clanging cymbal" (v. 1).

Enthusiasm has always been a problem in the Church. The pattern of the Corinthian Church and its immaturity regarding charismatic gifts has been repeated in the Church to this day. The first major movement which caused serious trouble in the Church was Montanism in the latter half of the second century. From then to Pentecostalism in the twentieth century enthusiasm has often threatened the Church. Bishop Butler called the enthusiasm of the Methodists 'a horrid thing', and clearly thought it did not belong in the Church of England. Even that most orderly churchman, Charles Simeon, incurred so much obliquy from his congregation in the early days of his long pastorate of Holy Trinity Church, Cambridge, that the Church had cast on one of its bells the words, "Glory to God in the highest and damnation to enthusiasts."

There has been for many years a popular exposition of this passage which sees Paul as replacing the charismatic gifts with love. Love, they say, was what he was really after.

If you love people then you can ignore the charismatic gifts. If you take that view then you must logically dispose also of faith and church offerings! Paul never suggests in 1 Corinthians that love and gifts are alternatives, and that you are free to take your pick. This is made clear by what he says in 1 Cor. 14:1, "Make love your aim *and* earnestly desire the spiritual gifts." It is also important, in our study of love, to realise that love is not a charism of the Holy Spirit. Paul calls it a fruit (in Gal. 5:22), but never a charismatic gift. J. P. M. Sweet has written, "It is worth insisting that Paul does not call love a *charisma*. Certainly it is *given* by God . . . but he uses the term *charisma tou pneumatos* (gifts of the Spirit) for activities and powers in which Christians may differ, not for qualities which all Christians should possess or at least cultivate. Love and glossolalia, like mercy and sacrifice, are words of different logical level, and it is misleading to treat them as alternatives."[19] In a footnote he adds, "In 1 Cor. 13 love is not alternative to tongues, prophecy, etc. but a *sine qua non*. Love cannot exist unless expressed in activities, any more than faith can (see James 2:18)." In other words Paul is saying here, "If you love your brother, you will give him gifts."

What is more important for us to see, especially in the light of the modern resurgence of spiritual gifts in the pentecostal and charismatic movements, is that these gifts are secondary to love—that is, they are underlings. Love should govern them and their exercise, not vice versa. If this principle had been applied more thoroughly in these movements they might have commended themselves to more people more quickly. There is a brand of Christianity which caters for the sensation-seeker, and the pursuit of love is not always on that horizon. When love and gifts flow together, as Paul obviously intended they should, then all is well. Even then a carnal or faithless Church will not accept them easily.

SACRIFICE

"If I give away all I have, and if I deliver my body to be burned, but have not love, I gain nothing" (v. 3).

It was George Bernard Shaw, perhaps the greatest cynic of the twentieth century, who said, "Martyrdom is the only way in which a man can become famous without ability." There have been times in the history of the Christian Church when this was true. The Church has had its kamikaze martyrs, who believed that martyrdom was the quickest and surest way to heaven. But sacrifice is another of love's underlings, and a life sacrificed other than from the motive of love is a life wasted. Many civilisations and ideologies have regarded the surrender of life as the finest act of all. The Greeks regarded the soul of man as imprisoned in the body so that death was the ultimate way of ensuring its release. If life was surrendered for a noble cause, that added a premium of inestimable value. But Paul says love is primary, sacrifice secondary. When Jesus said to his disciples, "Greater love has no man than this, that a man lay down his life for his friends" (Jn 15:13), he is not absolutising the sacrificial element, nor is he defining true love in terms of sacrifice, as if to say that the end (sacrifice) justifies the means.

It has always been part of man's religious instinct to imagine that sacrifice is the way to please God. The most primitive religions still make their offerings to placate or bribe their gods. Saul, that most carnal of Jewish kings, tried this one on the prophet Samuel when he told him that he had preserved some of the Amalekite cattle and sheep, "to sacrifice to the Lord our God".[20] But Samuel was having none of that. His answer was devastating: "Has the Lord as great delight in burnt offerings and sacrifices as in obeying the voice of the Lord? *Behold, to obey is better than sacrifice*, and to hearken than the fat of rams" (1 Sam. 15:22). In other words sacrifice is all right provided it is done in obedience to the Lord: sacrifice is not acceptable to God in the place of obedience. Obedience to God is absolute, sacrifice is always relative to it.

Returning to what Jesus said in John 15:13 about laying down our lives for our friends, we need to see that here too Jesus is speaking in the context of a love which is obedient. In the very next verse Jesus said, "You are my friends if you do what I command you." Earlier in the same discourse Jesus had said, "If you love me you will keep my commandments,"[21] and, "If a man loves me, he will keep my word."[22] So true love issues in obedience to God; if that obedience calls for the supreme sacrifice, the laying down of our life, then that will be the most loving thing we can possibly do, for there is nothing greater that we can give than our life or do than to lay it down in sacrifice. But sacrifice itself, without an obedience which springs from love is, as Paul says in 1 Corinthians 13, useless.

LOVE'S SUPERIORITY

In the later part of this famous chapter Paul very simply explains why love is greater than the knowledge of the intellectual, the enthusiasm of the charismatic and the sacrifice of the martyr or ascetic.

Love is Permanent

In verse eight Paul writes, "Love never ends." Everything else that he has spoken about is transitory and will pass away, but love will remain. Arnold Bittlinger comments, "Love belongs already to the coming world and consequently does not have to undergo any metamorphosis. Every Christian act, clothed in love, is already anticipated in that which continues."[23] One of the qualities of divine love is that it never wavers. Jesus' love for his disciples never gave up. It is said of that love, "having loved his own who were in the world, he loved them to the end."[24] God's love is always like that.

The gifts of the Spirit are temporary gifts from God. They serve our temporal needs. But at the coming of Christ they will have served their purpose. There will be no need for speaking in tongues to help bridge the communication gap between God and man; there will be no need for healing in a society delivered entirely from pain and illness; there will be no need for the discerning of spirits after Satan and his agents have been utterly destroyed. But love will remain for eternity.

Love is Perfect

In this chapter Paul stresses the inadequacies of charismatic gifts and knowledge. "Our knowledge," he writes, "is imperfect and our prophecy is imperfect." He then goes on to speak of the perfect coming. This has often been taken to refer to the coming of Jesus Christ who is the Perfect Man. But in the context it is more likely to refer to a world once and for all rid of all sin and error. This will, of course, only happen at the coming of Christ, but when it does happen there will be the perfect reign of the love of God, the perfect expression of it, not only in the Perfect Man himself, Jesus Christ, but in all his people. In this life knowledge is partial. Paul says, "Now I know in part." The only thing that is absolute is love; everything else is relative. Even faith and hope pale into insignificance in the face of love. W. Meyer has written, "Faith is the outstretched hand with which we take hold of the grace of God. Hope is the holy perseverance with which we take a firm hold on the grace of God. Love is the grace itself."[25] Arnold Bittlinger summarises this part of the chapter with the words, "Love is the greatest of the three, for love is not only for the now but for all eternity—even after faith has become sight and hope become fulfilment. Love still remains as love. Love is already the fulfilment and therein lies its unsurpassable greatness.[26]

All these then are underlings. Knowledge, enthusiasm and even sacrifice cannot match the primacy of love. It is easy to use knowledge and charismatic gifts to achieve kudos in the sight of God and people. Many a person has used them as the pathway to power and success. They are self-achievement orientated. They are ego intensive. There is an incipient individualism in the pursuit of knowledge, spiritual gifts and sacrifice. They are ways by which we can score points off one another. Only when love is the master, and they are underlings, are they safe in our hands to be used for constructive rather than destructive purposes. When knowledge and gifts are no longer practised in a spirit of love, they are not only useless, but positively harmful in their effects. As Arnold Bittlinger says, "They are counterfeits which offer my neighbour nothing, but positively deceive him."[27] God reveals knowledge and gives men gifts for the purpose of serving others, and not as ego boosters. Love, therefore, is the essential companion of both knowledge and gifts.

LOVE AND JUSTICE

There are many today who regard justice as a synonym for love. Joseph Fletcher, for example, in his book *Situation Ethics* makes it one of his major propositions: "Love and justice are the same. Justice is love distributed, nothing else."[28] Tillich also maintains this in his book *Morality and Beyond*.[29] He writes, "Love, *agape*, offers a principle of ethics that maintains an eternal, unchangeable element, but makes its realisation dependent on continuous acts of a creative intuition . . . love alone can transform itself according to the concrete demands of every individual and social situation without losing its eternity and dignity and unconditional validity." For Tillich, justice and love were inseparable. "Justice," he wrote, "is immanent in love."

That there is a closeness between love and justice is undoubtedly true; but to say that they are the same is confusing. It is possible for example to dispense justice without love, just as it is possible to prophesy or sacrifice your life without it. What J. P. M. Sweet says about the difference between charismatic gifts and love would apply just as much to justice and love. They are words of different logical level and it is misleading to treat them as the same. Justice is altogether laudable. God is a just God. The word justice and the word righteousness come from the same source. But justice or righteousness and love are not only different words, they open up quite different horizons. One could say that an unjust act is an unloving act; but one cannot say that all just acts are loving. It is possible to be a just person, but at the same time to be cold and calculating. God's call to us is to be both just and loving, because he is both just and loving; but the words and concepts are different.

This is particularly relevant today when for some 'justice' is all important. I have spoken to white South Africans, who have risked imprisonment and even their lives for the sake of a just society in their country, but who find that they are cold-shouldered and treated with disdain by Christians when they come to Britain. This seems to me an example of a situation in which the cause of justice has become so imbedded in the minds of people that they have neglected the commandment to love one's fellow Christians whatever the colour of their skin. At its worst here is apartheid in reverse. Love and justice are not the same thing, and in some senses justice is love's underling.

LOVE AND TRUTH

It is difficult to understand the relationship between love and truth. In the New Testament they are often linked and seen as partners. In Romans 12:9 Paul says, "Let love be genuine." In 2 Cor. 6:6 he writes again about 'genuine love', and in 8:8 he urges the Corinthians to prove the genuineness of their love. In describing the power of Satan, whose chief weapon is deception, we are told in 2 Thess. 2:10 of those who are to perish, that they "refused to love the truth". In Ephesians Christians are urged to speak the truth in love to one another (4:15).

It is in John's epistles that the relationship between the

two is most fully developed. In 2 John 1, for example, John writes to "the elect lady and her children whom I *love in the truth*." The word that John most freely used for truth in the epistles and in his gospel is 'light'. The opposite of light is darkness, and that is the word he uses for error. Thus the relationship between Christians is described as being 'in the light' when they are walking in love with each other. Truthfulness is a qualification for love between Christians (see 1 John 1:5f). John Stott in his commentary on the Johannine epistles has summarised this: "If we are Christians we are to love our neighbours and even our enemies; but we are bound to our fellow-Christians by the special bond of truth. Truth is the ground of reciprocal Christian love . . . we do not love one another because we are temperamentally compatible, or because we are naturally drawn to one another, but because of the truth that we share."[30] He goes on to warn Christians in our ecumenical age of the dangers of compromising the truth supposedly for the sake of love. "If Christian love is founded on Christian truth, we shall never increase the love which exists between us by diminishing the truth which we hold in common. In the contemporary movement towards Christian unity we must beware of compromising the very truth on which alone true love and unity depend." We are to love not only enemies but heretics and schismatics. But true love only thrives when it is established on the bedrock of truth.

It is popularly thought today that woolliness and so-called 'tolerance' are synonyms for love. To forsake truth for the sake of love is to lose both. Peter moves very naturally from truth to love for one another in 1 Peter 1:22: "Having purified your souls by your obedience to the truth for a sincere love of the brethren, love one another earnestly from the heart." Obedience to the truth should lead naturally to love for one another in the Christian family. Alas, Church history is littered with examples which belie this. There seems so often to be love without truth and truth without love. Their divorce is a tragedy, their marriage a blessing beyond description.

We must never forget that in the same epistle that John said "God is love," he also said "God is light" (1 John 1:5), and the two are closely related together. Dr. James Packer in his book *Knowing God*[31] says, "The God who is love is first and foremost light, and sentimental ideas of his love as an indulgent, benevolent softness, divorced from moral standards and concerns, must, therefore, be ruled out from the start. God's love is holy love." We must also add that God's love is *in the truth*, for God is the truth.

We live in days when lies and distortions of the truth are the order of the day. In Russia no published map is allowed to be accurate. Every river, city and town must be moved slightly from its actual location.[32] The two main newspapers are called *Pravda* and *Izvestia*. The first word means 'truth' and the second 'news'. A wit has said about the Soviet press that "the truth isn't news and the news isn't true."[33] But the East is by no means the only culprit. The whole educational system of the West and the cultural pattern of life in which the majority have to live is not always concerned about the pursuit of truth. G. K. Chesterton once remarked that when people cease to believe in God, "They do not believe in nothing, they believe in anything."

Love is prostituted without truth. Dietrich Bonhoeffer in his book *Ethics* (published posthumously), pointed out that love and truth do not conflict.[34] "Love and truth," he wrote, "are *not* mutually conflicting—nor should priority be given to love as the personal principle over truth as the impersonal principle—thereby coming into direct contradiction with St. Paul's saying that love 'rejoiceth in the truth'. For indeed love knows nothing of the very conflict in which one seeks to define it. A love which violates or even merely neutralises truth is called by Luther 'an accursed love,' even though it may present itself in the most pious dress. A love which embraces only the sphere of personal human relations and which capitulates before the objective and real can never be the love of the New Testament."

But perhaps the most crucial question is the relationship between love and law; and that requires a chapter to itself.

5   ALL'S LOVE AND ALL'S LAW

I spoke as I saw:
I report, as a man may of God's work—
    all's Love and all's Law.
                              (Robert Browning)

The relationship between love and law is an indispensable
theme of Christian ethics. Helmut Thielicke calls the Law
'gauze in the wound,' because although it does not heal the
wound, the gauze does not let us forget it.[1] Paul used the
analogy of a 'custodian'.[2] Law does not save us, but it does
help us to come to the one who does. In the same book
Thielicke uses the illustration of a sheepdog. Anyone who
has seen a sheepdog in action will know what he means. All
is well with the sheep so long as they are doing as they are
told. But if they move out of line the dog makes their life
most uncomfortable.

But not everyone will agree with Thielicke or his illus-
trations. There is the 'new morality' school of thought,
popularised by John Robinson in his famous book *Honest
to God*, and linked with what Joseph Fletcher calls 'situation
ethics'. Dr. Robinson in another book has written, "The
Christian ethic can never honestly be presented as law plus
love, or law qualified by love, *however much safer that
would be*. There is no question that law has its place, but
that place is at the boundaries and not at the centre . . .
Jesus' teaching was not a reform of legalism but its death."[3]
What the 'new morality' does in effect is to replace law with
love. Joseph Fletcher denies that he is an anti-nomian. He
allows that in making ethical decisions the Law should be
considered as part of the information and knowledge which
help us make those decisions. But in treating Law in this
way, Fletcher is not treating it as law at all.

On the opposite side to Dr. Robinson we could place
Dr. James Packer, the well-known Anglican evangelical. In

his book *Knowing God*, he quotes Ps. 119:151, "All thy commandments are true" and comments, "Because they [the commandments] have stability and permanence as setting forth what God wants to see in human lives in every age, and because they tell the unchanging truth about our own nature . . . a working definition of true humanity . . . we are only living truly human lives just as far as we are labouring to keep God's commandments; no further."[4] Dr. Packer sees God's laws as being part of the permanence of revelation; Dr. Robinson sees these laws as only 'having a place' in God's schemes.

We might give another example from the controversial question of homosexuality. Norman Pittenger has written about sexuality: "Let me say frankly that I believe that any and all sexual activity, genital or otherwise, is good—provided that it does not violate the intentional understanding of each other human as a person and not simply and solely as a *thing*. Some of us would be prepared to say that the 'one night stand', for instance, cannot be called evil in itself; there is genuine goodness there, in so far as loneliness is overcome, some slight sense of companionship is given, strong desire is released and to some degree satisfied."[5] This may be an extreme example, but it is fairly typical of the view that anything done in 'love' is O.K. Contrast that with the comments of Professor Lovelace on homosexuality, "The Scripture nowhere commends homosexual behaviour and condemns it in every place where it is mentioned. If we can interpret scripture to endorse homosexual acts among Christians, we can make it endorse anything else we want to do or believe, and our faith and practice are cut loose in a borderless chaos." Who is right, Pittenger or Lovelace?

First of all we need to recognise that it is not a new problem. The 'new morality' is as old as the New Testament Church! Paul had to grapple with this issue, and the Epistle to the Galatians is mainly written with it in mind. In the opening chapters of Romans he seeks to deal with the legalism of the Jews on the one hand, and some of his

43

opponents who accused him of anti-nomianism on the other. Jesus himself was constantly being asked questions about the place he gave in his life and teaching to the Law. In the Sermon on the Mount he speaks about the relationship of his 'new morality' to the existing Law—"You have heard it said . . . but I say . . ." Paul's strongest battles were fought not against the Roman authorities, or even the orthodox Jews of his day, but Christians within the Church who were enforcing the Law in a way that he thought made void the gospel. They were called Judaisers and there are several mentions of them in the Acts of the Apostles, and Paul's controversy with them is frequently recorded in the Epistles. It is no surprise to find that Christianity, cradled in Judaism, had from the beginning to relate the gospel of Jesus Christ to the deeply imbedded reverence that Jews had for the Torah. Much of the New Testament is about this.

But the first century does not see the end of the matter. One of the first major schisms in the Church was caused by this same issue, and Marcion was the man who caused it to happen. He is thought to have been the son of a Bishop and lived in the second century. He could see no way of accepting both love and law, and opted for love. He found many difficulties in his way in the Old Testament, so he taught that Jesus had come to rescue us from the God of the Old Testament. But he also found difficult passages in the New Testament, so he produced his own edited version with the passages that seemed to support the concept of law skilfully deleted. One of Marcion's most famous opponents was Irenaeus, whose answer to Marcion's splitting of Law and Gospel to find room for love, was that it is precisely *love* that binds them together, for in both the Old and New Testaments *love* comprises the chief commandments.

There are not a few who have seen Jesus Christ as one who came to overthrow the Law and reconstruct a new kind of morality on the basis of love. But a close look at the New Testament will show that this was far from Christ's intention. In the Sermon on the Mount Jesus said, "Think not that I have come to abolish the Law and the prophets; I have come not to abolish them but to fulfil them" (Matt. 5:17). Some of Marcion's followers actually had the audacity to change the verbs round to read, "I have come not to fulfil the Law but to abolish it." It would seem from the opening words of this verse that there were people in the audience who were saying, or had heard it said, that Jesus was abolishing the Law. Maybe his actions regarding the sabbath had been taken to mean that he was intending to sweep away law altogether. But in this passage Jesus is clear in what he says. He does not duck the issue. He makes it quite clear that he is not abolishing the Law, for not even the least of the commandments was to be relaxed (v. 19), nor is he endorsing them in a literalistic fashion (as the scribes and the pharisees did) but he is fulfilling them. As Chrysostom expressed it, "His sayings were no repeal of the former, but a drawing out and filling up of them."

As we shall see there were different kinds of laws, and some of them had been misused by the pharisees, and there had been many additions which were man-made rather than from God. Nevertheless Jesus himself was a law-abiding Jew. When it came to his trial his accusers could find nothing wrong with him and had to hire false accusers to get him condemned. "He had nothing to add to the commandments," was Bonhoeffer's comment, "except this, that he keeps them."[6] John Stott writes, "His purpose is not to change the Law, still less to annul it, but to reveal the full depth of meaning that it was intended to hold."[7]

The apostle Paul has also been regarded by some as one who, like Jesus, had little place for the Law, and regarded love as replacing it. "Love is the fulfilling of the law" (Rom. 13:10), is often cited as conclusive evidence. In Galatians he is at pains to point out that 'the works of the law' are not the grounds of man's salvation. He writes also about 'the curse of the law' from which Christ has 'redeemed us' (3:13). He describes the Law as a 'custodian' until Christ came. Does he imply, therefore, that with the coming of Christ the Law passed away?

When attempting to interpret Paul we need to take the

whole of his writings into consideration, not just a part, or we shall be like Marcion and his followers who mutilated the works of Paul for their own ends. To call Paul anti-nomian is to misunderstand him. Quite obviously there were some amongst his contemporaries who regarded him as such. His arch-enemies the Judaisers would have accused him of this very thing. In Romans Paul asks himself the imaginary question, "Why not do evil that good may come?" (3:8). Some people, he writes, have slanderously charged him with saying this very thing. His conclusion? "Their condemnation is just." When we look at the whole Pauline corpus, to charge Paul with overthrowing the Law and replacing it with 'love' is a distortion. The Marcionites would have been much more sparing in their mutilations if this were the case. Paul's letters are full of the strongest ethical content. In 1 Corinthians he condemns in no un-certain terms the immorality of the Corinthians and their weakness in dealing with it. In Romans he lists the sins of that nation, including homosexuality, and says that the wrath of God is against all ungodliness and wickedness. The last three chapters of Ephesians are full of specific ethical exhortations related to the Ten Commandments— deceitful lusts, falsehood, unbridled anger, stealing, evil speaking, immorality, covetousness etc. In Galatians he lists 'the works of the flesh' and says that they are "plain" or unambiguous. In Ephesians he tells the children to "honour your father and mother." You cannot read Paul's letters without being vividly aware that, although salvation and the gift of the Spirit do not come as a reward for keeping the Law, for they are free gifts of God, there are clear ethical standards which are related to the Law of the Old Testament and are not to be set aside. Here Paul's teaching parallels and complements the teaching of Jesus.

The key to understanding the ethical teaching of Paul, and where it is different, though not contradictory, to the teaching of Jesus, lies in his understanding of the work of the Holy Spirit. Oscar Cullmann has drawn this out in his book *Salvation in History*. He sees Agape as the principle for applying Christian ethics, and also as linked with the Holy Spirit.[8] He then goes on to speak about *sarx* (the flesh) as Paul uses it, that it is impossible to love our neighbour as ourself except through the operation of the Holy Spirit. "Only the latter (Spirit)," he writes, "can offset the deadly power of the *sarx* . . . In Paulinism the Law is not abolished as the formulation of the divine will. But its radical fulfilment is possible for the first time only through the *pneuma* which is received in faith and which impels us to love our neighbour . . . It is the Spirit that enables me to fulfil the Law."

The love which Paul speaks about is for him a fruit (probably *the* fruit) of the Holy Spirit. According to Paul, God's love "has been poured into our hearts through the Holy Spirit which has been given to us" (Rom. 5:5). In Ephesians 3:14f Paul's famous prayer interlocks the two themes of the Spirit and fullness of God with the knowledge of and grounding of God's love. Perhaps most striking of all is his phrase in Romans, "the law of the Spirit of life in Christ Jesus" (8:2). He goes on to explain that it is as we live "according to the Spirit" rather than the flesh that "the just requirement of the law" is fulfilled in us (vv. 3, 4). Victor Furnish is surely right when he says, "Paul rejects the Law as a way of salvation but he does not reject it as a norm for the conduct of one's life. It remains for him an instrument of God's will and purpose if it is correctly interpreted."[9]

When Paul is dealing with ethical questions he assumes an ethical structure which has divine origins and is non-negotiable. There is mercy for the repentant law-breaker, but the Law remains. He is particularly concerned with the Gentile world of his day for which no such structure existed, a world very like our own. Paul might have been tempted to soft-pedal the Law in such a situation; but on the contrary he is all the more insistent on it. He sees love as the way by which we keep the Law, and love as derived from an experience of the Holy Spirit. But the Law remains.

We need next to try to understand what 'the Law' is. Misunderstanding here can cause us to miss the point altogether and lapse either into pharisaical legalism which is self-destructive, or a form of ethical anarchy which is equally lethal. We need, then, to see law from three different perspectives.

LAW AND NATURE

Certain laws are observable in our world. The law of gravity and the law of thermo-dynamics are examples. Man has not created gravity or thermo-dynamics, he has only discovered their secrets. Our world is, basically, an orderly place. It is so orderly that man is able to say exactly when the tide floods or ebbs, and is able to calculate accurately what the tide was doing when Julius Caesar landed in Pevensey Bay over 2,000 years ago. No one complains about these laws until they are broken, when it can be painful, even deadly. These laws have been implanted in nature by the Creator for his own purposes. In Psalm 75:3 we read, "When the earth totters, and all its inhabitants, it is I who keep steady its pillars." God takes care of his universe and reigns over it.

What is true of the creation is also true of ethical behaviour. I once saw a cartoon of Moses standing in front of the people, with the people saying to him, "Will you please put it in writing." The Ten Commandments are part of the 'putting in writing' of God's law, but the writing part is simply the expression of the fact that God's ethical laws are part of the very nature of God himself. They can no more be abrogated than the law of gravity can. God cannot deny himself. Larry Christenson has put it well, "Morality is not something *demanded* by God, in its primary sense, but is something *created* by God. The Law in its ultimate sense, does not describe how things ought to be, or how God would like things to be, but ultimately how things *are*. At root the Law *is*; only in a secondary sense does an *ought* come into the picture."[10] He goes on to explain that the *ought* of the Law is there because another part of the creation is the freedom of man to choose, that is, individual moral freedom. Larry Christenson illustrates this from the law of gravity. There is an *ought* factor, when, for example, we teach children about the danger of falling from heights. But for an adult it is plainly silly to say "You ought to obey the law of gravity," since we have no other option. If we don't it is not the law of gravity that we break, but we who are literally broken by that law. What is true of the law of gravity is true also of the Ten Commandments. If you have any doubts—try it out and see what happens. Work for seven days a week for a year and see if you survive. Steal a few times and see what happens. Larry Christenson writes, "A man who steals, murders, or profanes the name of God is *in the very doing of it* broken—though the brokenness may not be readily apparent, since the moral law is spiritual, and, therefore, the brokenness can only be spiritually discerned."

In the teaching of Jesus Christ we find many ethical laws introduced which are of the same kind. Often these are based on the laws of nature. The parables of Jesus are a good example, in which he not only illustrates spiritual principles from natural analogies, but declares spiritual principles which are akin to the natural. For instance Jesus spoke about the grain of wheat falling into the ground and bringing forth fruit. It will produce no fruit until it is hidden in the ground. The seed has to be sown to produce a crop. So it is with us—because the natural law has its spiritual counterpart. 'Give and it will be given you,' is the same principle. It is true of nature and of man created in the image of God. It is an immutable divine law.

There is nothing wrong with the Law as such; the main problem is that we can't or don't keep it. Thus the Law reveals to us our weakness and sinfulness. It is a custodian to bring us to Christ. Christ forgives us when we break his laws, justifies us through his grace and blood shed on the Cross, writes his laws on our hearts and gives us the Holy Spirit to enable us to keep his laws. It is natural for us to blame the Law for our problems and that is exactly what man has done in the twentieth century. He has rebelled against God's laws with frightful results. The thing that shouts at us is man's failure to keep these laws. The answer is not to overthrow the Law and substitute love, for man is as incapable of loving as he is of keeping God's law. And in any case, love which is not righteous love is not true love.

LAW AND SYMBOL

Our whole world is full of symbols, and symbolical actions form a regular and important part in our lives. Religious acts also are highly symbolical. The sacraments of Baptism and Holy Communion use the symbolism of water and bread and wine, and there are many symbolical gestures involved in these ceremonies. Secular ceremonies also have their symbolism. But the symbol is never more than the outward sign of the thing signified. As Christians we are both commanded to be baptised and to eat and drink bread and wine of the Eucharist 'until he comes again'. But the mere reciting of words and the undertaking of rituals are meaningless if the thing signified is not honoured. Baptism without a commitment of life to the Lordship of Jesus is to miss the whole point of the symbolism.

Now there is a whole area of law in the Old Testament which is symbolical. All the rituals concerning sacrifice and the place of the Temple in the life of God's people were symbolical. The prophets again and again attacked God's people for concentrating on the symbol and missing what it was really all about. It is no good making symbolical gestures in terms of sacrifices for sins if you are not repenting and living a true life. There was then a whole area of law in the Old Testament which found its fulfilment in Christ and so the 'shadow' was done away with. Jesus himself was the fulfilment of all these laws. He was the Temple; he was the High Priest; he was the Sacrifice itself. Symbols, therefore, are not eternal laws; but what they signify in terms of God's nature and actions are eternal.

LAW AND LIFE

One of the themes that Paul grapples with is the relationship between the Law and spiritual life. He combines the two words together in that important phrase in Romans 8:2, "The law of the Spirit of life in Christ Jesus." But in 2 Corinthians 3:6 the contrast is developed. He writes categorically, "The written code kills, but the Spirit gives life." He describes two dispensations, the one of the Law and the other of the Spirit, one of condemnation, the other of righteousness, the one having faded away, the other being permanent. But again we need to be careful to see that Paul is not abrogating the Law—he is only saying that as a principle of life it had only a temporary purpose. It could never give life, only direction to life. With the coming of Christ and the Holy Spirit the Law remained, but its role and purpose changed radically. Pannenberg has a good way of putting it in his book *Theology and the Kingdom of God*, "Love effects that unity among men which expresses itself in legal forms but which is always more than those forms. Love fills the legal forms with life and thus achieves true justice."[11]

LAW AND LEGALISM

We need finally to establish that there is a difference, which is not always recognised as it should be, between law and legalism. Jesus was against legalism, but not against law. No society can eventually stand the strain of too much law. The Jews of Jesus' day had to contend with 613 commandments, 365 of which were prohibitions, one for every day of the year. No wonder when Jesus condemned this excessive making and enforcing of law that his words fell on ready ears and attracted large crowds.

The Church has often suffered from the same legalistic policy. At times it has been too much for people to bear, and has led to a reaction of anti-nomianism as harmful as the legalism which preceded it. Henry Miller has a good phrase to describe the worst features of this approach, 'the immorality of morality'. H. G. Wells, one of the greatest secular prophets of the twentieth century, once described moral indignation as 'jealousy with a halo'.

Jesus quite obviously wanted to preserve his Church from the harmful effects which follow from the multiplication of laws. To the list of 613 commandments, Jesus added only one, "A new commandment I give to you, that you love one another; even as I have loved you, that you also love one another. By this all men will know that you are my disciples, if you have love for one another" (Jn 13:34, 35). It is a sad commentary on the history of the Church that whilst strenuous efforts have been made to enforce and keep a multiplicity of laws, many of them entirely man-made, the Church down the centuries has signally failed to keep the one new commandment that Jesus gave to his people. In fact, if the one new commandment had been kept, a great many of the other commandments would have proved unnecessary.

SUMMARY

Law and love are vital partners, and they come from the same source, for the same God who is love is also the one who has created a law-abiding world for law-abiding citizens. It is impossible to do justice to the New Testament if we separate law and love. Law without love becomes legalism, and Jesus came to deliver us from it. But love without law becomes soft and sentimental. It lacks depth, direction and content, and Jesus came to deliver us from that also.

Love itself is a law, and, according to Paul, is the fulfilling of the Law itself, which it never abrogates. Jesus said, "This I *command* you, to love one another" (Jn 15:17). Or again, "If you keep my *commandments*, you will abide in my love" (Jn 15:10). In John 14:15 he says, "If you love me, you will keep my *commandments*." In other words, love always leads to the keeping of the commandments, and the keeping of the commandments is the way to abide in God's love. Love is both the fruit of the Holy Spirit and the root of obedience. Love and law are bound eternally together, and to attempt to separate them is to make shipwreck of both theology and ethics.

Karl Barth had a fine way of describing Christian ethics. "It is not one disputant in debate with others," he writes, "it is the final word of the original chairman, only discussed of course in Christian ethics, which puts an end to the discussion and involves necessarily a choice and separation."[12] We need less discussion of ethical questions, and more listening to the final words of the original chairman.

6 AGAPE

"We have every right to say that the idea of Agape is not merely a fundamental idea of Christianity, but *the* fundamental idea *par excellence*. The idea of Agape is a new creation of Christianity."

Anders Nygren in *Agape and Eros*, Part I, p. 32.

Kathleen Bliss tells the story of someone at the World Council of Churches Assembly at Evanston who kept on hearing the word 'agape' being used, but had no idea what it meant. Eventually in his frustration he looked it up in an *English* dictionary only to discover that it meant 'with mouth wide open'. Of course he should have looked in a *Greek* dictionary, he would then have discovered it means 'love', and a study of the New Testament reveals that it is the word most frequently used by the writers to describe what we call love. I was tempted to call this chapter 'with mouth wide open', because it does at least describe what our reactions should be to the divine Agape.

The word *agape* was used infrequently in conversational Greek at the time of Christ, although it was used in the Greek version of the Old Testament (the Septuagint). But it became the most commonly used word to describe what we call 'love' in English, and the New Testament is flooded with references to it. There are few words in the English language more in need of redemption than 'love'. It is equated today with sex, or is used, mostly by those living in the North of England, as others would use the word 'sir'. "Do you take sugar in your tea, love?" is how a waitress will address you in Bolton or Leeds, and she's not trying to get familiar with you. The word is more than ever used as a synonym for 'like'. "I love strawberries" is far more commonly said than "I like strawberries."

We are embarking on a perilous voyage in trying to define such a word. "Love is swampy" is how Joseph

Fletcher describes the problem.[1] James Packer, in commenting on the phrase 'God is love' states that "False ideas have grown up round it like a hedge of thorns."[2] Nevertheless he thinks it is essential "to cut through this tangle of mental undergrowth." Paul Tillich was so aware of the problem, especially as the word was used in such a confused way in his day, that he suggested we ought to use the word Agape to describe God's true love, and to abandon the word love to the secularists. Another suggestion he made was the clumsy formula 'C—love' to describe what Joseph Fletcher calls 'agapeic love' (which sounds to me like a disease). Personally I think we should abandon all such attempts and work all the harder on redeeming the word love from its corruptions. After all, in the final analysis it will not be the words we use, but the people we are, that will be the best description of love. It is significant that the synoptic gospels never use the noun 'grace' (*charis*), and very seldom the noun 'love' (*agape*). When they are used, it is in a random and unsystematic manner. But the Son of God *is* full of grace and truth and he *is* love incarnate. To know him is to know love.

In attempting to get to the meaning of this word, we need to look first at some of the mistaken notions that people have had. One of C. S. Lewis's most popular books is *The Four Loves*. It is, like his other books, brilliantly conceived and written. It deals with four Greek words, *storge*, which Lewis translates 'affection', *eros* meaning 'sexual love', *philia* meaning 'friendship', and *agape* meaning 'charity'. But the book is written by a classical scholar rather than a theologian, a master of the English language rather than of New Testament Greek. So a whole generation has grown up believing that there are four loves. *The New Testament makes it plain that there is only one*. It is also confusing to place all these words together. They don't really come from the same stable as we shall see. The book ends on a hesitant note. "With this," he writes, "where a better book would begin, mine must end. I dare not proceed."[3] He then makes the startling statement about *agape*: "God knows, not I, whether I have ever tasted this love. Perhaps I have only imagined the tasting." It may be that in following Augustine's teaching so closely C. S. Lewis has mistaken our love *for* God (Augustine's emphasis) for his love *of* us. But there is a sense of having missed something vital in the concluding chapter of this book. Be that as it may, we need to examine more closely these four words.

Storge

The word that C. S. Lewis translates 'affection' is only used in a compound form in the New Testament. It perhaps best describes the love or affection which exists in family life. It is natural love. But it is important to notice that neither the Old nor the New Testament have a word to describe it. The word is only used in the compound, and then very rarely.

This is not to say there is no sense of family in the Bible. Far from it, there are copious references to the importance of family life. But when Paul comes to define the relationship between parents and children he tells children to 'obey' their parents and parents to bring their children up 'in the discipline and instruction of the Lord'.[4] This is not to say there is to be no affection between them. This is assumed as natural, and condemned when there is a lack of it (e.g. Rom. 1:31, 2 Tim. 3:3). It comes out beautifully in the words of Jesus, "If you then, who are evil, know how to give good gifts to your children . . ."[5] Jewish family life has always been strong and well defined. And so far as love is concerned, family life ought to be an example of agapeic love. If love extends to our enemies, how much more to our natural family. We will have to see that there is nothing exclusive about the word *agape*. It is not selective. In that sense it can be applied in the family setting. We do not select our parents, neither can our parents select us. They may decide not to have children; or through abortion deny life to them, or today even decide the sex of their children, but the child itself, and its capabilities, weaknesses and personality are not capable of selection. So in that sense *agape* does have a real application to the family situation.

We hear a great deal about the generation gap. Many parents are finding it increasingly difficult to relate happily with their children, especially when they go through the traumas of adolescence. The gap widens as the years pass. Natural affection is not enough. It is Agape which bridges the generation gap as well as every other kind of separation between human beings. We sometimes hear parents protesting about the lack of consideration their children give them, as if they have the right to be considered. But Agape is not about rights. It is not demanding love. It only survives when it breathes the air of freedom. A truly loving relationship is a free and spontaneous one. Equally children sometimes make exorbitant demands on their parents; but the growing child also needs to learn how to love parents with Agape love. *Storge* is inadequate for the stresses and strains of modern family life, in which nothing can be taken for granted.

Obviously there are special responsibilities, especially in the field of instruction and discipline, which parents and children have; but there is always a temptation to worship the family. At its most extreme it can be seen in Confucianism. Agape breaks down artificial barriers and puts to death natural affections which so easily degenerate into self-love. Agape stands like a guardian angel over family life to prevent it from turning in on itself. C. S. Lewis brilliantly exposes the false kind of family love in the character of Mrs. Fidget who 'lived for her family'. When she died her family 'brightened up'. C. S. Lewis writes about her death—"Mrs. Fidget is now at rest. Let us hope she is. What's quite certain is that her family are."[6]

Philia

This word does come fairly frequently in the New Testament. It is often used as a prefix, and some of these words have come over into the English language (e.g.

philosophy, philanthropy etc.). But the word is not always used in a good sense. For example *philaguros* is an adjective from the noun *philaguria* (meaning love of money) and is translated 'covetous'. *Philia* and its compounds are used about a hundred times in the New Testament (as compared with 320 times for the word *agape* and its verbal form).

But this word is usually in strong contrast to *agape*. Friendship is of necessity selective on both sides. One can only have a strictly limited number of friends. Spicq brings this out when he writes, "In demanding love of enemies, Jesus radically distinguished love of charity from love of friendship. Friendship is founded on mutual liking, it is by nature reciprocal. Charity is neither passionate nor ordinary liking. It is a pure and spiritual desire for the good rooted deep in the heart . . ."[7] There is nothing in essence wrong about friendship. It is good for us to have friends and to select them carefully. Also our love for them should be agapeic. Perhaps the distinction we need to make is between *who* we love and *how* we love. So far as *who* is concerned, friendship cannot be described as agapeic, and can be positively harmful, as for example, when a larger group is divided into cliques of those who have a special regard for one another. But when it comes to *how* we love, we should love our friends with Agape love as well as our enemies. So we see that there is really only one word to describe true love—*agape*, and that word needs to be applied differently in each situation.

It does need to be observed that the words *agape* and *philia* are used apparently interchangeably in St John's Gospel. Sometimes, when referring to Jesus' love, *philia* would seem to refer to his love as 'friendship', as, for example, his love for Lazarus (11:3 and 36) and the unknown disciple (20:2). But only once is the word used of God's love for us (16:27) and the Father's love for the Son (5:20), apart from the famous dialogue with Peter, when the two words are used interchangeably (John 21:15f).

Eros

We have already drawn attention to the fact that *eros*, one of the most important words in the Greek language and definitive of so much of the substructure of their life and thought, is absent from the vocabulary of the New Testament. We shall be treating in greater detail the conflict between *agape* and *eros* in chapters twelve and thirteen. But for the moment we need to establish one important truth. *Eros does not mean in an exclusive sense 'sexual love'.* C. S. Lewis has encouraged this confusion, which has now become almost complete in popular literature about sexuality. For instance Lewis Smedes in *Love Within Limits* writes, "Romantic love, *of course*, is eros" (italics mine). And "Within marriage eros demands exclusive sexual love."[8] It is true that the Oxford Dictionary defines Eros as 'sexual love', and the words erotic and eroticism are firmly placed in the English language to mean just that. But *eros* in its original use and in its religious and philosophical sense means much more than that. It covers the ground of sexuality, but also a lot else besides and its primary and causal meaning is of great significance. To talk, as many Christians do of Eros as sexual love and, thereby, to legitimise it, is to be misleading when we need to be clear.

C. S. Lewis is too good a classical scholar to make this mistake himself. Although *The Four Loves* is written with a popular readership in mind he writes, "That Eros includes other things besides sexual activity, I take for granted."[9] Unfortunately these days we cannot take anything very much for granted. But C. S. Lewis goes on from this statement to distinguish between Eros and what he calls 'Venus', by which he means what is obviously sexual. In a strangely confusing manner he uses Eros to distinguish human sexuality within love from all other brands including that of the animal creation.

What is important for us to grasp is that the Christian view of love grew out of the Old Testament and from the revelation of that love in the life and death of Jesus Christ the Son of God, and owes nothing to Greek or Roman thought.

In other words for Christians the word Eros is inappropriate to describe love of any kind—be it sexual, filial, or any other variety. Yet it is constantly being done. William Barclay, for example, who is usually very careful in his use of words, speaks of Eros as "characteristically love between the sexes".[10] Hans Kung takes the same line in his book *On Being a Christian.*[11] He argues for the mutuality of *agape* and *eros*, while it is one of the purposes of this book to show they are *mutually exclusive*. They are based on different religious ideas and should not be confused. The only basis on which Hans Kung argues such a position is on Eros being sexual love. Sexual love and Agape should belong together. But the Christian understanding of sexuality does not derive from Plato, Aristotle and other Greek philosophers (who saw it in terms of Eros) but from the Hebrew concept. We will develop this more fully in chapter ten.

Here we need to observe something else of importance. Just as C. S. Lewis is forced to distinguish between Eros and Venus, so Plato himself distinguished between what he called vulgar Eros (*pandemos*) and heavenly Eros (*ouranios*). I suppose what C. S. Lewis calls Venus, is roughly what Plato called *pandemos*.

Thus heavenly Eros for Plato describes a whole religious system of thought which begins and ends at different points from that of Agape. The attempt to join together *agape* and *eros* was later to prove disastrous to Christianity.[12] The baneful fruit of this union still deeply afflicts Western Christianity. Plato knew nothing of Agape. Whenever the two have been blended down the centuries the vigour and purity of Agape has been weakened. The difference between Agape and Eros is not one of degree but of kind. Eros was Agape's most dangerous enemy. The story of their conflict, which we shall be elaborating later, is, according to Anders Nygren, "A drama full of tension and the plot of the drama is the inner history of Christendom, for the history of Christianity is the history of love."[13]

In case there should be misunderstanding, Nygren is using the word Eros correctly in the sense that Plato and other Greek writers did and some of the Church Fathers (notably Origen). Eros is a word which summarises a religious system alien to Christianity, whereas Agape is the basis of a true understanding of Christianity, and stems from Judaism, was reinterpreted by Paul and others, but incarnated in the Son of God and demonstrated through his death. Like Eros it includes sexuality, but approaches it differently. Nygren is not denying the God-given nature of sexuality and its proper expression in the lives of men and women. The plea that I would make is that we should not think about or discuss Christian sexuality in the pagan terminology of Eros. Rather we should site it firmly in the territory of Agape. Canon Quick has put it well in distinguishing between the two, "*Whereas in Eros desire is the cause of love, in Agape love is the cause of desire.*"[14] The story of Eros, strictly speaking, is not the story of sexual love, but the story of 'religion'. Eros in the correct sense is religious love, and as such is often confused with Christian love (Agape). We need constantly to be reminded that Jesus Christ was a layman who came as the Son of God to set us free from religious systems. He did not come to make us more religious. One of the tragedies of history is that the Church has constantly been rebuilding what Jesus Christ came to destroy. Eros is part of that false understanding of religion from which Jesus came to free us.

Agape

We must now examine the word *agape* itself. In recent years there has been renewed interest in the origins of this word and its place in the New Testament. Much of the controversy has revolved around the writings of two men. Father Spicq is a French Dominican who taught at Fribourg in Switzerland and has devoted much of his life to the study of the use of the word *agape*. *Agape dans le Nouveau Testament*[15] is the most extensive work ever done on the subject. Written in three volumes it is a remarkable piece of writing with a deep insight into the meaning of the word and its importance for Christians. Spicq tends to take an Augustinian view of love and, therefore criticises Nygren in several places. His work is a devotional classic as well as being accurate in its scholarship. The other writer is a Belgian classicist, Robert Joly, one of whose aims in life seems to be to demonstrate that there is nothing really original in Christianity. He has written a slim book entitled, *Le Vocabulaire Chretienue de l'amour est-il original? Philein et agapan dans le grec antique.* [16] The book seems to show that key Christian concepts, in this instance *agape*, can be found in previous or contemporary writings. Thus he tries to disclaim what Father Spicq affirms in his book.

Spicq, as the title of his book suggests, concentrates on the references to *agape* in the New Testament. Obviously the word *agape* does not exhaust the meaning of love in the New Testament. For example the word *agape* is not used once by Luke in the Acts of the Apostles, which nevertheless abounds in references to Christian love. Peter's attitude to the crowd at Pentecost and his willingness to forgive, and Stephen's attitude to his murderers are two examples. An over-concentration on a word study can be limiting. Joly is right to challenge the claims that some have made that *agape* was a new word which the Christians invented. I am indebted to Paul Lebeau, a Belgian Jesuit, for helping me here. He knows Joly personally and wrote in a letter to me, "There may be some truth in this (Joly's disclaimer). After all, the early Christians created very few new words. What, however, Joly does not see is the fact that they usually infused a new meaning into the old words in order to express the uniqueness of the 'Christ-event' in human history. This is obviously the case for *agape*." [17] J. B. Skemp in a review of Joly's book in *Gnomon* sensibly points out that the theological exposition of *agape* may not really rest on these language studies even when it is made to appear to depend on them." [18]

It is clear that *agape* was in use in the Greek language at the time of Christ because of its inclusion in the Septuagint, though it had a vague and variable use. It was mostly, it seems, employed as a substitute word. But there is hardly any use of the noun in pre-biblical Greek other than in the Septuagint. One example is found in the small coastal town of Thornis in Egypt, where Isis was worshipped. Apparently the name Agape was substituted for Isis. What does seem to have happened is that the writers of the New Testament were in need of a word to describe the indescribable. If they had wanted to be trendy they would have needed to look no further than *eros*. That would have made the Greeks sit up and take notice! It would have had a contemporary ring about it. But the apostles and others were much more concerned with truth than with popular appeal. Popularity lasts only for a moment. Fashions come and go. But truth endures for ever. William Barclay is not strictly accurate when he writes about *agape* that it was "a *new* word to describe a new quality."[19] Nor was R. C. Trench when he describes *agape* as "a word born within the bosom of revealed religion." If one is strictly accurate one could say it was 'adopted'. After all, words are only ways of expressing the truth. It's the truth that ultimately matters. Thus *agape* was adopted and invested with new and striking honour. It is a Cinderella story. Just as God's very life was veiled in the weakness of human flesh, so weak and feeble that he was 'despised and rejected by men', so Christians took one of the most insignificant words in the Greek language and made it the most important word of all.

Strachan in his *Commentary on St John's Gospel* writes, "The early Christians chose the most colourless word for 'love' in the Greek vocabulary in order to express the new moral demands of the Christian faith."[20]

Eros was humiliated. Its place was taken by Agape. From henceforth Agape not Eros would describe the very nature of God and his final revelation of himself to man in Jesus Christ. So far as we know the New Testament writers used the word *agape* uniquely to describe such a revelation.[21]

Its new usage was and still is uniquely Christian. Only in Christ can we understand and experience true love.

At this point I want to pause in order to comment on the text which has come to be called by some 'the golden rule', Matt. 7:12. "So whatever you wish that men would do to you, do so to them; for this is the law and the prophets." This text has been taken from its context and given a place disproportionate to its importance. In so doing people have lost sight of and at times distorted the true meaning of love. Bultmann called the so-called golden rule "Morality of a naive egotism,"[22] and Tillich, "Calculating justice". Victor Furnish contrasts the golden rule with the disinterestedness of true love. "Love is not just an attitude but a way of life . . . and love is not guided in its course like an anti-ballistic missile by something inherently attractive in its object. It is empowered and guided rather by its own inherent rightness as a response to human need."[23] Furnish rightly interprets the so-called golden rule in the light of the context in which the words occur. Spicq also rejects the idea of the golden rule—"It would apply," he writes, "much better to the 'be perfect as your heavenly Father is perfect.' To act towards others as we would like them to act towards us is simply a rule of ordinary decency found over and over again in profane, Old Testament and other religious literature."[24] Surely these writers are correct in rejecting the so-called golden rule.

Word studies can be helpful, but they have their limitations. It is not fundamentally in them that we shall begin to understand the meaning of love. 'Flesh and blood' will not reveal it to us, only our heavenly Father. Our need is for a revelation of God himself, and particularly the meaning of the Cross. It is in him and at Calvary that the reality of love can become plain to us.

7   GOD IS LOVE

"Only he who knows God knows what love is."
                                   (Dietrich Bonhoeffer)

There is a story told about Charles Spurgeon. He noticed one day a weather vane on the roof of a farm building which bore the phrase 'God is love'. "Do you think God's love is as changeable as that weather vane?" he asked the farmer. "You miss the point, sir," replied the farmer. "It is on the weather vane because no matter which way the wind is blowing, *God is still love*." There is much truth in what the farmer said. We know that love is eternal because God himself is eternal. Love never changes because God never changes, love is rooted and grounded in the nature of God, and we can only know love and be loving as we know and relate consistently to God.

We sometimes think that we first discover love and from that point come to know God. But that is to see God in our image, and will distort our understanding of the true nature of God and of love itself. Both go together. The reason why we know so little about love is because we know so little about God. One of the most common questions asked by sceptics is, "How can a God of love allow such and such to happen?" Whatever else may be behind the question, it assumes that God is a God of love. If there is a God at all he should be a loving God. But the question usually indicates that the person knows little about the God whose morality they are questioning. Bonhoeffer puts it clearly when he emphasises the word God rather than the word love. "God is love," he writes, "that is to say not a human attitude, a conviction or a deed, but God himself is love. Only he who knows God knows what love is . . . love, then, is the revelation of God."[1]

Dr. James Packer makes an interesting contrast in two statements he makes about 'God is love'. First of all, he says that 'God is love' is not the complete truth about God so far as the Bible is concerned. "It is not an abstract definition which stands alone, but a summing up from the believer's standpoint of what the whole revelation set forth in Scripture tells us about its Author. This statement pre-supposes all the rest of the biblical witness to God." Secondly, he says that 'God is love' is the complete truth about God so far as the Christian is concerned. "God is love means that his love finds expression in everything that he says and does." For instance in Romans 8:28 Paul is declaring "that every single thing that happens to him expresses God's love to him and comes to him for the furthering of God's purpose for him . . ."[2]

This is an important distinction to make, and we shall make shipwreck of our understanding of the multi-faceted nature of God, and, therefore, of the true nature of love, if we do not grasp it. John's statement "God is love" does not call in question the biblical understanding of the severity of God's justice. We must not argue that a loving God cannot punish and condemn the disobedient. Rather John is speaking of that very God. Paul calls upon us to behold "the goodness and the severity of God". If we see only one aspect of God's nature we are not seeing God. And God is not only loving in the area of his goodness, he is also loving in the area of his severity. Many have found the doctrine of election hard to stomach. It seems inconsistent with their view of a loving God. But Paul finds no such contradiction. In Ephesians 1:5 he writes, "He destined us *in love* to be his sons through Jesus Christ according to the purpose of his will." We will discover what love is all about, only when we allow ourselves to be divested of all assumed concepts which may have come from non-Christian sources, and seek to know God and find in him and his actions the real meaning. Packer writes of the sentimental ideas of this love as an indulgent benevolent softness divorced from moral standards and concerns . . . God's love is holy love. The God whom Jesus made known is not a God who is indifferent to moral distinctions, but a God who loves righteousness and hates iniquity.''[3] How many people there must be who principally identify God with the Santa Claus of their childhood fantasies. We are to avoid what Bob Mumford has called "sloppy agape", which is not true agape at all.

Helmut Thielicke makes this point when he writes, "To look at some Christians one would think their ambition is to be the honeypot of the world. They sweeten and sugar the bitterness of life with an all too easy concept of a loving God . . . but Jesus did not say 'you are the honey of the world,' he said 'you are the salt of the earth.' Salt bites, and the unadulterated message of the judgment and grace of God has always been a biting thing.''[4]

We have already shown how important it is to see that God's moral laws are expressions of his very nature and, therefore, of his love; and how vital it is not to set against each other law and love. But it is also important to notice that love is not simply one attribute of God. 'God is love' is a far more basic statement than simply that God is a loving God. This is seen also in the Old Testament. The Hebrew word *Ahebh*, which is the one most commonly used in the Old Testament, is an intensely personal word. Quell writes, "Everywhere in the Old Testament God's love implies his personality.''[5] But what is implicit in the Old Testament becomes explicit in the New. Leon Morris puts this point strongly, "We should not regard love as simply one of the attributes of God among a list of others. It is the very central thing. Without it God would not be God—God *is* Love.''[6]

C. H. Dodd states this clearly in his commentary on the Johannine epistles.
"Love is not just one of his activities . . . but all his activity is loving activity. If he creates, he creates in love; if he rules, he rules in love; if he judges, he judges in love.''[7] For Martin Luther love was nothing other than God himself. The man who abides in love is one who becomes 'one cake' (ein Kuchen) with God.

One of the purposes of this book is to show how we need

to hold together *all* our understanding of the nature of God with *all* our understanding of love. There is nothing that can be claimed to be true love which does not originate in the nature of God, and there is nothing in the nature and actions of God which is outside the scope of love. All of God is love, and all *true* love is of God. C. H. Dodd argues for the holding together of God's nature and the ethical aspects which come from that nature. "The definition of the nature of God himself cannot be stated except in ethical terms: 'God is love'. The thing we have to guard against is the danger of converting that proposition simply, and saying 'love is God', making the ethical primary and subordinating the religious to it. If we do that we are making it impossible ever to understand the thought of the New Testament either on its religious or its ethical side. For John there is no possible separation of gospel and commandment. The theme of both is *agape* . . . and both together constitute 'the word of life'."[8]

But the fullest and clearest expression of true love was manifested in the life and death of the Lord Jesus Christ. 'The word was made flesh' so that love might be seen, heard and touched. For just thirty-three years a small corner of the world saw perfect love manifested. That life was recorded faithfully by those who witnessed it. Wicked men tried to destroy that life. But Jesus Christ rose from the grave and in the Holy Spirit bequeathed that same life and love to all those who would believe and obey him. From the one epicentre of Bethlehem and Calvary a seismic shock wave of divine love has continuously shaken the world. That is what Christianity is about.

Strachan in his commentary on St. John's Gospel has written about this: "The New Testament concept of love . . . is delivered from all saccharine or merely emotional interpretations by the fact that its character is determined by the Christian belief in God and its pattern fixed in the example and teaching of Jesus."[9]

We need to hold together with equal emphasis the manifestation of the love of God in the *Person* of Jesus Christ and in his *work* on the Cross. Emil Brunner and Dietrich Bonhoeffer in two sections of their books on ethics have beautifully tied them together. Emil Brunner writes, "In the Cross of Christ, here alone is the meaning of the word 'love' disclosed, for here alone is it possible to distinguish between *eros* and *agape*, *amor* and *caritas* . . . love which has no limits and makes no conditions is love 'in Christ'. . . before Christ love was one commandment among others and unconditional love was not understood. It could not be understood until God himself had defined its meaning . . . in the Cross of Christ. *Only God himself defines love in his actions.*"[10]

Emil Brunner, together with many others, sees love in the actions of God. But we need to balance this by looking at the other side of the coin. It is all too easy to leave love entirely in the area of an activism which can depersonalise it. Dietrich Bonhoeffer puts the other side for us in his book, *Ethics*, "Only he who knows God knows what love is . . . love is the revelation of God . . . love has its origin not in us but in God . . . love is inseparably bound up with the name of Jesus Christ as the revelation of God. The New Testament answers the question 'what is love?' quite unambiguously by pointing solely and entirely to Jesus Christ. He is the only definition of love . . . love is not what He *does* and what He *suffers*, but it is what *He* does and what *He* suffers. Love is always He Himself . . . love is always the revelation of God in Jesus Christ."[11]

We are not to set one aspect of divine love over against the other. To place the Incarnation and the Atonement in such a relationship that they compete with one another is mischievous theology. Both Brunner and Bonhoeffer are right. The Cross does show forth as no other event in world history the nature of true love; but that love is divine love because it is God incarnate who is suffering and dying at that place and at that time. To deny, as a number of modern theologians do, the deity of Christ is not only destructive of incarnational theology, it also renders ineffective the reality of the Cross. Just as his enemies mocked Christ and suggested he might come down from the Cross to save himself, so there are those who want to deny that the one who was suffering there was God's only begotten Son. Both bringing Christ down from the Cross and denying his divine nature demolish the foundations of God's salvation, since both aspects are declarations of the love of God in action and demonstrations of the same.

The weakening of the Church's faith in the effectiveness of the Cross and the deity of Christ, the uniqueness of Christian revelation as the truth about the only true God, have inevitably led to distortions of our understanding of love. Distort your understanding of God and your understanding of love will likewise suffer. But we can see something else which compounds the damage which has been done. There has been also an increasingly distorted view of man. Original sin is no longer accepted by some, and it is ironic that in a century in which wickedness has multiplied and mankind has sunk lower than at any other time in its history, man has continued to entertain the most optimistic notions about his destiny and proud thoughts about his achievements.

The truth of the matter has been put sublimely by Paul in Romans 5:8, "But God shows his love for us in that while we were yet *sinners* Christ died for us." In other words alongside the statement that only those who know God can know true love, we can also say, only those who know the reality of human sin can fully appreciate the reality of divine love. Paul does not mince his words. In Romans chapters one and two he catalogues the sins of his day, which are a mirror in which we can see ourselves. "We were enemies," he says (5:10) and "still weak" (v. 6). A far cry from our smug self-satisfaction. But it was for sinners that Christ died and thereby his love was demonstrated. *Agape* means undeserved and unmerited love, and in this it is totally different from *eros*. Here is one of the major cleavage points. *Eros* is love for the beautiful. *Agape* is love for the ugly as well as the beautiful. *Eros* is love for the good. *Agape* loves the bad and evil also. *Eros* is love for the friendly. *Agape* is love also for one's enemies. *Eros* arises within man himself, distorted by original sin, and so can be self-deceiving. *Agape* arises within the heart of God and has its only source in him, and so is pure and uncontaminated by the pride of man.

So we see that it is not only the One who died, who through that particular death declares, demonstrates and enacts the nature of true love, but the fact of *who he died for* that puts the seal on the whole matter. It can be summarised in the words, "Christ died for sinners." That is the only revelation of love that we can really go by. Paul's testimony comes simply to us in his Letter to the Galatians, "the Son of God, who loved me and gave himself for me" (2:20). Because of this Paul was not going to allow the Galations to "nullify the grace of God" by a works salvation which never works.

The Cross marks the end of selfdom. Later on we shall be considering some of our modern ethical systems. Two of these are situationalism (what has become known as situation ethics or the new morality) and selfism or personalism. What is striking about much of the approach to ethics followed by these two popular systems is that they have very little to say about the Cross. It is noticeably absent from much modern Christianity, which presents in many instances a sugar-coated gospel. It is, like many modern foods, 'processed'. In the Western world most people eat processed bread. This means that some important and healthy ingredients are removed (such as the wheatgerm) and artificial and unhealthy ingredients substituted (such as preservatives). We have processed the gospel in the same way by removing healthy parts of it and substituting others which don't really belong and can be harmful.

One of the main missing ingredients is the Cross, and one of the main 'artificial' substitutes is a 'bless-me' theology which can be seen in the sugar-coated gospel of today all the way from an evangelicalism which promises salvation without cost, to a sacramentalism which promises baptism without commitment to Christ, to a radicalism which offers social justice without grace and to a pentecostalism which offers spiritual experience and blessing without pain or responsibilities. The sugar-coated gospel appears to be the gospel of love, but it is no such thing—for it does not present the whole truth, the whole gospel or the whole Christ. It picks the more palliative aspects, often for fear of offending those to whom it is addressed. The result has been a cosy kind of Christianity which knows little of the real deep love of God for people—and does little to activate Christians to be the kind of people whose love reaches to all, including their enemies. To know love we need not only to know God but to know ourselves. It is the real person Christ loved and died for on the Cross, not the unreal person masked by sham pretentiousness. Spicq has put it well in describing the uniqueness of Christ's demonstration of love: "Jesus alone was qualified to interpret and fulfil the divine oracles of the former Covenant. It was in the name of this love for God and man that he would let himself be crucified, a gift no precept of the Law ever prescribed."[12]

We could easily think that this is the end of the story. The Son of God has died and is now risen and ascended. The message is clear. Love has been seen and known. The world lies ready to be told the message. But the Church can still forget or underestimate the importance of Pentecost. In the same passage in which Paul describes the Cross as the ultimate demonstration and action of God's love, he also writes, "God's love has been poured into our hearts through the Holy Spirit which has been given to us" (Rom. 5:5). Paul uses here the same verb (*ekcheo*) as Luke twice uses in the Acts of the Apostles to describe the experience of the Church at Pentecost (Acts 2:17, 33). Paul describes this experience of the Holy Spirit as 'love poured into the heart', the implication being 'in abundance', for God is often lavish and never mean with his gifts. Pentecost was for the Church, amongst other things, a fresh experience of the love of God. This surely is the main explanation for the speaking in foreign languages which was given so dramatically to all the Church that day. They were, according to the bemused onlookers, "telling in our own tongues the mighty works of God" (Acts 2:11). Therefore, to complete the picture we see and understand love not only by knowing God and his dying love on the Cross, but also by experiencing it through the action of the Holy Spirit in our lives. To divorce Pentecost from the Cross is as spiritually debilitating as to separate Christ's person from his sacrificial action. One of the few modern theologians to grasp the importance of this is Oscar Cullmann in his book *Salvation in History*. He sees *agape* (as the principle for applying Christian ethics) "anchored in terms of salvation—history in the love God showed us in Christ as the decisive climax of all his saving activity."[13] He sees the practice of *agape* as founded on this love and finds in it the possibility of unqualified realisation. He goes on to say, "therefore *agape* is linked also with the Holy Spirit who typifies *the period in which we live*." Cullmann clearly sees the Holy Spirit as the divine actualiser making the realisation of divine love possible in us and our fellowship in the Body of Christ.

Cullmann then turns to the practical fulfilment of this love in the commandment to love our neighbour as ourselves. He stresses the impossibility of doing this because of our being driven by the flesh (*sarx*). But he says "this has already been made possible through the Spirit (*pneuma*)". He goes on to say categorically that only the Spirit "can offset the deadly power of the *sarx*, which is already vanquished by the *pneuma* and yet is still not vanquished. The *sarx* can only drive us to self-love, and this means to mutual destruction. The *pneuma* must motivate us to love of neighbour." He sees also that only in the Holy Spirit can the Law be radically fulfilled. "It is the Spirit," he writes "that enables us to fulfil the Law."

What Cullmann does in linking the action of the Holy Spirit with the experience of divine love, Victor Furnish further underlines. "Paul's identification of the Spirit and love shows that for him the power of the new age is the power of love. For him love is not just an abstract ideal or one quality among others which make up the Christian life. *It is the new aeon itself, powerfully present and active in history.*"[14] Thus like Cullmann, Furnish sees the experience of love in Jesus Christ and its effect in our lives through the work of the Holy Spirit as that divine force which makes God's mighty acts real and contemporary. He comments, "No better title for Paul's theology can be devised than his own formulation in Gal. 5:6, 'faith working through love.' Love is both the context and content of faith; *God*'s love makes faith possible and *man*'s love gives it visibility and effect in the world."

The contemporary Church seems to be chronically allergic to the Holy Spirit. Its failure to trust in him, and its inability to know how to abandon itself to his inspiration and power, constitutes one of the greatest tragedies of our present situation. The substitution of man-contrived institutions and structures to fill the gap causes more ulcers than it does spiritual fruit. Institutionalism not only quenches the Holy Spirit, it creates the kind of climate in which the plants of divine love wither and die.

We began by saying that man has divided what God has put together and that this is one of the reasons why the experience of love is so rare in our world. God and love are indivisible. You cannot know one without the other. And the God who is love chose to become flesh so that we could see in him what love is and receive it by faith. The climax of his self-giving was at Calvary; here we see in its fullest glory the love which emanates from God's nature and which comes from no other source. All this, and more too, comes to us and is demonstrated and given to the world through us by the power of the Holy Spirit. We know that 'God is love' by faith in Jesus Christ. We receive the out-pouring of that love when we are filled with the Holy Spirit. Only God truly loves us; only in Jesus Christ is that love fully seen; only in the Holy Spirit is that love freely manifested in us.

8 THE LOVE OF GOD

The love of Jesus what it is,
None but his loved ones know.
(Bernard of Clairvaux)

In his famous hymn Bernard of Clairvaux is expressing the
fact that the love of God is something that comes to us by
revelation and experience rather than theological research.
It is to do with celebration rather than cerebration. Charles
Wesley, in many ways following the tradition of Bernard of
Clairvaux, wrote a few centuries later an equally famous
hymn beginning with the line:

Jesu, lover of my soul

This was too much for many of his contemporaries and
Bishop Wordsworth in the nineteenth century once said it
was 'inexpressibly shocking', and should not be sung in
Westminster Abbey. John Wesley, Charles' brother, was
sensitive enough to this kind of criticism in his day to
exclude it from the 1780 Large Hymnbook, and in other
hymnbooks 'lover' was altered to 'refuge' or 'saviour'.

It is right that we should beware of a mushy kind of
sentimentalism, which has not been wholly absent from the
Church down the centuries; this not only processes the
Cross out of Christianity and the suffering which is its
hallmark, but injects an artificial kind of emotionalism into
the consideration of the love of God. The English version
of Bernard of Clairvaux's hymn is not an exact translation
of his words *expertus potest credere quid sit Jesum diligere*;
which literally should be translated, "Only he who has tried
to love Jesus knows what love to Jesus is." There is rather
more in the original than in the popular English translation,
which, though not strictly accurate, nevertheless conveys
an important truth with simplicity.[1]

In the last chapter we were thinking around John's phrase 'God is love' and seeing that true love is understood and experienced only in relationship to the nature and activity of God, particularly in the life and death of Jesus. In this chapter we need to look more closely at the nature of God's love. What is 'the love of God'? When considering the love of God we shall be dealing entirely with God's love for us rather than our love for God, which we will be considering in the next few chapters.

God's Love is Spontaneous

God's love does not in the final analysis depend on who we are or what we may be doing. It is not earned or merited. God does not accept bribes. God's love is eternal not only in the sense that it knows no end but also that it has no beginning. It has always been and it will always be.

In *Agape and Eros* this truth plays an important part. In Nygren's handling of the subject he shows that it is the Eros type of love which is to be seen here in marked contrast to Agape love.[2] Since the days of Ritschl it has been usual to speak of 'the infinite value of the human soul' as one of the basic ideas of Christianity, and to associate it with 'God's fatherly love'. Nygren believes this belongs to 'the religion of Eros' rather than Christianity. It suggests that there is something inherently good and lovable in each human being. Thus God's love is not necessarily spontaneous; rather God is drawn to love, in a sense, his own. I believe Nygren is right to draw our attention to this further undermining of the truth about God's love, which is its essential spontaneity. As we saw in the last chapter, it was *'while we were sinners'* that Christ died for us, thereby commending his love. It is entirely uncaused on God's side and undeserved on ours. God's love always takes the initiative. We can only love God because, in John's words, "He first loved us." God's love does not depend on the worthiness of its object. This truth had already been revealed in the Old Testament. In Deut. 7:7, 8, for example, God's love is described as disinterested and spontaneous. It was not because of the size or the importance of the nation that he had chosen them. In fact they were "the fewest of all peoples".

Martin Luther defends the same position in contrasting the love of God with the Law.[3] The Law only commands. The Law enforces its precepts through fear of punishment and the desire for reward, and so cannot be spontaneous. He calls these 'servile' and 'mercenary' and 'counterfeit' in contrast to what he calls 'liberal, gratuitous and blithe'.[4] Luther calls the people of God 'Nedaboth', which he derives from the Hebrew word *nedabah*. It is used quite frequently in the Old Testament to describe what is done freely, voluntarily and willingly. In Hosea 14:4 God says, "I will love them *freely*," and this is the word used. The whole story of Hosea is in itself a graphic illustration of the spontaneous character of God's love. The prophet, with remarkable tenderness, loves his adulterous wife, as a sign of the love God has for an adulterous people.

Luther, in a famous phrase, describes God's love as 'overflowing love' (*eine quellende Liebe*)—as a stream or river which flows eternally and does not depend on whether one is good or bad, for that divine love "is not drawn from thy goodness as from an alien spring, but from mine own well-spring, namely from the word which is grafted into my heart."[5] Again Luther describes the love of God, in an interesting phrase, as 'a lost love' (*eine verlorene Liebe*). He means that it *is* the opposite of rational calculation. He writes, "It is the nature of love to suffer betrayal, since it is exposed to all the uses and the abuses of all men, the general servant of good and bad, faithful and unfaithful, true and false alike."[6] God's love is poured out upon those who reward it with ingratitude. Only one of the ten lepers returned to thank Jesus. For the rest it was a 'lost love'.

When we return to Hosea we see this 'lost love' more clearly than perhaps anywhere else in the Old Testament, and it is a high water mark in the progressive unfolding of the nature of love. The tide was not to rise higher again until the tidal surge of the coming of Christ was to flood everything that had gone before and send the waters of divine love to inundate everywhere. Quell has an interesting insight into the message of Hosea. He sees the prophet as "pulling down the theory of the Covenant, in order to expose God's love as its foundation," and then to "build up again with righteousness, judgment, loving-kindness and faithfulness."[7] What we see in Hosea so explicitly can be seen implicitly in all the scriptures, namely that the foundation of all God's dealings with his people is his love, and that our understanding of 'covenant' needs to be built on it. There is no doubt a juridical meaning to God's covenants with his people. But that element is secondary, love is primary. God loves us because he loves us. We can say no more than that.

The clearest and most penetrating teaching on this aspect of the love of God comes, as we might expect, from Jesus himself in the parable of the Good Samaritan. This must have shocked his hearers, as, indeed, much of his teaching did. A Samaritan would have been the last person on earth the Jews of Jesus' day would have held up as an example of God's love. Spicq comments on the story, "Love is characterised by its *spontaneity* and *promptness*."[8] He loved the suffering Jew disinterestedly. There were no strings attached. The love was personal, active, effective, practical and compassionate. There in a nutshell is the love of God.

God's Love is Compassionate

It is almost universally accepted today that love is not emotional. Joseph Fletcher in his book *Situation Ethics* emphasises this in many places. Love, according to many moralists, is what we *do*, rather than how we *feel*. In Alan Richardson's *Theological Word Book of the Bible* the New Testament verb for love (*agapao*) is described as having neither the warmth of *phileo*, nor the intensity of *erao* and refers to "the will rather than the emotions". Many eminent writers seem to have concurred in this. Stephen Neill, for example, speaks of love as "the steady directing of the

human will towards the eternal well-being of another."[9]
H. R. Niebuhr wrote that "Christ's love is not an inner
feeling . . . it was the *work* of love which was his life."[10]
C. H. Dodd wrote "love is not primarily an emotion or
affection, it is primarily an active determination of the will;
that is why it can be commanded as feelings cannot."[11] So
one could go on.

One naturally hesitates before attempting to fly in the
face of this 'cloud of witnesses'. There are a number of
reasons why people advocate a passionless love, but the
biblical evidence, however, seems to point in the opposite
direction. Christianity is still dominated by Western thought
forms and cluttered with its cultural baggage. One part of
this is the typical Anglo-Saxon renunciation of emotion
and almost neurotic fear of emotionalism. It was Father
Bull of Mirfield who once said of the English clergy that
emotionalism was not their chief peril. It is true that most of
us have at least some painful memories of people who have
been excessively emotional without being too practical at
the same time. We have also passed through a period in life
in which the world scene has suffered major disruptions
through the mass exploitations of nations by men, such as
Adolf Hitler, who have scientifically manipulated people's
emotions while at the same time deliberately by-passing
their intellects in order to achieve their wicked goals. No
one would advocate emotion for its own sake, but one
cannot seriously examine the Old and New Testaments
without coming to the conclusion that the love of God is a
warm and passionate affair, but at the same time vitally
linked with dynamic action and practical concern for people.

When we consider the key Hebrew word for love (*ahebh*)
we see a word which conveys deep feelings. Quell writes
about it, "Love in the Old Testament is fundamentally a
spontaneous feeling which impels to self-sacrifice or the
grasping of the object which awakens desire. Love is an
inexplicable personal force."[12] Love in the Old Testament
has to do with 'heart, soul and might' as well as with the
mind and action. It is intensely personal. It is not concerned

with things but with people. Quell points out that it is always a person-to-person affair when the word is used in a religious sense in the Old Testament. He writes, "Everywhere in the O.T. God's love implies his personality."[13] It is always a strong expression, for which the word passion is often appropriate. There are also strong sexual overtones at times and these are particularly prominent in Ezekiel, Hosea and Jeremiah. But we need to remember that sexual behaviour in the Old Testament is carefully regulated. Thus Israel's conduct with idols is often likened to a spiritual adultery.

It is impossible to think of a healthy sexuality which is devoid of passion. So it is difficult to understand love in the Old Testament without seeing it as intensely emotional, affecting the heart as well as the mind and the will. Quell sees the dominant position given to the idea of love as constituting "The great glory of O.T. ethics". Love in the O.T. is inseparable from humanity.

But when we come to the New Testament it is even clearer that the love of God is to do with warmth of feeling as well as consistency of action. This is seen supremely in the life and ministry of Jesus Christ. No word more clearly reveals this than the word commonly translated 'compassion' (*splanchnizomai*). It is used frequently to describe Jesus' own feelings towards those in need (e.g. Matt. 9:36, 14:14, 15:32, 18:27, 20:34 etc.). It is also used significantly in two of Jesus' most famous parables, the Prodigal Son and the Good Samaritan. Both Matthew and Luke amongst the synoptics are eager to convey to us something of the intensity of feeling that characterised Jesus' ministry, and they could not have used a more powerful word. Moulton and Milligan believe that the word was coined during the time of the Jewish dispersion, a time that was a deeply emotional experience for the Jews.

Father Spicq's great work *Agape in the New Testament* exudes constantly this same warmth. He seems to have grasped the significance of this aspect of divine love, which others are so ready to discard for a colder and perhaps more strictly pragmatic form of love. There are two places where he draws out this important aspect of love with compelling force. In Matt. 24:12 we read, "And because wickedness is multiplied, most men's love will grow cold." Spicq concludes, rightly I believe, from this statement that if *agape* grows cold (in times like those described) then *naturally* it is warm or hot. The verb suggests a change of temperature—a chilly wind of change. Spicq writes, "*Agape* is like a fire, and to love is to burn (see Song of Songs 8:6–7)."[14] This is in keeping with the word compassion. The noun *splanchana* describes our 'innermost being'—our bowels, the seat of our affections and desires. In no way could the life force of Jesus, the Son of God, be more clearly designated as emotional than by the use of this word.

Spicq teases this point out most wonderfully in the attention he draws to an incident in the ministry of Jesus. In Mark 10:21 we are told about the rich young ruler that Jesus "looking upon him *loved him*". Spicq calls this young man 'fortunate' to have had the privilege of being asked to sell everything in order to follow Jesus! He then goes on to point out that Jesus in fact *did nothing* for this young man. In other words here is a clear example of Jesus loving someone and yet that love not issuing in any concrete action. From this example we can see that love does not always issue in action, as if that action is definitive of the love. Sometimes there can be love without action— suggesting that the feelings and emotions are prior to that action, which may or may not be present. Spicq comments "there must have been a very noticeable show of affection, of loving sweetness, not only in Christ's look, but also in his voice and in his whole attitude."[15] Spicq does not care for the idea that Jesus embraced him, but rather suggests that there was *both* respect and delight in that look. "*Agapan* often has a nuance of spontaneous delight," he writes.[16]

In another part of his book Spicq beautifully describes the love of Christ. "Compassion," he writes, "is a *feeling*

81

profoundly suited to the Saviour. It is a physical emotion experienced in the face of grief, pain or misery in others. Jesus never resisted it; it explains his miracles . . . and compassion is an integral part of love."[17]

I think we need to watch carefully in case our assessment of love is being conditioned by those counterfeit alternatives which present themselves in our present society. It may well be that part of the reason why the Church has tended to retreat from the reality of the love of God as warm and personal is because of the subtle invasion of her life by the ideas and culture which can be said to be characterised by Eros rather than Agape. Emil Brunner speaks of "the relation of reason to another person" being always "cold." He goes on, "But love is both 'pure' and 'warm'."[18] Socialism is one way in which we seem to have divorced this warmth from our actions. It appears to have become established in the thinking of people that the whole duty of man is to do good to others irrespective of whether we feel anything towards them, or are able to convey the affection which so many people crave for. Our society has become depersonalised. But this is what some Greek thinkers regarded as a goal worth achieving. As we have seen *apartheia*—absence of feeling—was something to be desired and appreciated by the Stoics. It is interesting that Paul speaks of this as a mark of the degenerate Greek society of his day. In Eph. 4:19 he writes, "They have become callous . . ." The word callous is a translation of the Greek word *apalgekotes* which means to cease to feel pain. The A.V. translates it 'past feeling'. This is in strong contrast not only to the word compassion but also to sympathy from the Greek word *sympatheo*, translated in Hebrews 4:15 "touched with the feeling of" (A.V.).

It is vital that we confront the Eros concept of love, which often lacks feeling, with the Agape, in which our emotions play a vital part and which is touched and moved to action by the needs of people around us. There is no doubt which kind of love motivated Jesus. We need to derive our understanding of love from its Hebrew rather than

Greek sources. The Greek gods were on the whole cold and calculating in their relationship to ordinary men. It was up to men to seek and yearn for them. But God's love is totally different. He did not wait for us, but came down to us—and constantly through both Old and New Testaments revealed the intensity of his love and desire for us. That is the nature of God's love, and in the measure we ourselves receive that kind of love as fruit in our lives will be the measure to which we shall love others with that same kind of warmth and affection.

God's Love is Righteous

We have seen how confusion reigns when one of God's attributes is separated from the others, and even set against them. Nowhere is this confusion more rife today than in the separation of God's love from his righteousness. We shall be looking particularly at situation ethics, which is the most popular modern example of this misrepresentation of both God and his love. The gods of the Greek and Roman world were totally different from the God of Israel. They were amoral, and frequently immoral. They had no particular standards. But the God of Abraham, Isaac and Jacob was a righteous God whose people were to be righteous like him. His love, then, was a righteous love. Both the Old and New Testament unitedly testify to the fact that God acts consistently in a righteous fashion. He is, as some have rather clumsily put it, 'a covenant-keeping God'. He keeps his word and never acts inconsistently with his nature.

We have already seen that we cannot define love except in terms of the love of God. Neither can we define the love of God, or begin to understand it, in contrast or opposition to his righteousness. Just as his love is a righteous love, so his righteousness is a loving righteousness. The Old Testament writers expressed this not only in their accept- ance of God's Law, but in their love for it. This comes out most strikingly in Psalm 119. "I find my delight," the

Psalmist writes, "in thy commandments, which I love. I revere thy commandments which I love" (vv. 47, 48) and "Oh how I love thy law! It is my meditation all the day" (v. 97). We see this vital connection also in Hosea, which is a rich mine of understanding about the love of God. In 10:12 the prophet writes, "Sow for yourselves righteousness, reap the fruit of steadfast love." Thus righteousness and love are seen in the relationship of seed to fruit.

Many modern moralists stress the ambiguity of decision-making in the field of ethics. While there is substance in this, as we shall see when we come to study situation ethics, it has been exaggerated. Reading the Old and New Testament the general impression one gets is that God's righteous standards are on the whole plain and verifiable by any genuine and sincere seeker after righteousness. Paul says about the works of the flesh that they are "plain", or, in the N.I.V. translation, "the acts of the sinful nature are *obvious*" (Gal. 5:19). The constantly reiterated call to repentance in both Old and New Testaments presupposes that one knows what one has to repent of, and that such behaviour in thought, word and deed is sinful. Of course, there needs to be some moral education and the right sort of powerful human example. Unfortunately, some modern moralists do not see 'education' as a genuine part of their approach to ethics, with the result that people are increasingly having to grow up and live in an amoral and often immoral atmosphere, and those who attempt to adopt Christian standards are accused of being legalistic. But such an attitude is the inevitable result of dividing God's love and concern for us from his righteous nature.

The importance of relating God's love to his righteousness is critical. If we fail to do so we make shipwreck of both love and righteousness. Love becomes sloppy and sentimental without righteousness. Righteousness becomes legalistic and harsh without love. Both belong together, for both are part of the very nature of God.

God's Love is Universal

Nowhere is this more clearly stated than in Jesus' teaching in the Sermon on the Mount. In Matthew 5:43–48 Jesus raised the question of loving our enemies. The old Law (at least as understood by his contemporaries) said, "You shall love your neighbour and hate your enemy." But Jesus told his listeners to love one's enemies and "Pray for those who persecute you." This, Jesus says, is what being a true son of God is all about. Then he said these vital words: *"for he makes his sun rise on the evil and on the good, and sends rain on the just and on the unjust."* In other words, prosperity is not necessarily a sign of God's favour and human goodness. God blesses the evil as well as the good. The converse is also true, that adversity is not necessarily a sign of God's disapproval. The Book of Job is a splendid example of this in the Old Testament. God sometimes withdraws his blessings, at least for a time, from the righteous. But the main lesson Jesus gets across in this passage is the universal nature of God's love. He loves his enemies as well as his friends. He is not spiteful or vindictive. All his actions towards friends and enemies alike are governed by the principle of love as well as righteousness.

Bonhoeffer sees the love of enemies as "the supreme command". He writes, "Through the medium of prayer we go to our enemy, stand by his side and plead with him to God." [19] Chrysostom saw this responsibility to pray for our enemies as 'the very highest summit of self-control'.[20] Jesus' prayer for the forgiveness of his tormentors, "Father, forgive them; for they know not what they do" (Luke 23:34), is in the imperfect tense which suggests that he repeated it several times.

John Piper in his book *Love Your Enemies* stresses that we are not to take the command to love our enemies as "the over-arching norm" but rather as "one command in tension with others under the norm of love."[21] In the same passage John Piper sees the context of the 'enemy love' passage in terms of the contemporary tension of the eschatological situation. Our own situation has many similar features. When Christians are faced with persecution and the moral problems of belonging to two Kingdoms at the same time, as many do today, this passage has a new ring of truth about it. He writes, "The content of the command of enemy love is determined by the tension of the eschatological situation. The inbreaking of the powers and blessings and demands of the age to come has created a situation of ambiguity and stress for the person who knows himself both grasped by this new in-breaking power and yet bound 'in the flesh' in this new age. He is called, as it were, to live in two worlds whose rules are not the same." The dilemma which many Christians face in the situation of being a persecuted minority is illuminated by this passage from St. Matthew's Gospel and the clear declaration it makes of God's universal love. And when Jesus went on to press his followers to imitate this love, he was indicating that this is one area in which it is possible for our love to bear fully the divine mark. "You, therefore, must be perfect as your heavenly Father is perfect," Jesus said. It is impossible for any human love to be perfect like God's in quantity or quality. But we can love perfectly as God does by loving *everyone*—our enemies as well as our friends, those who speak evil of us as well as those who speak well, and God will give us grace for this.

We live in a world in which the commandment to love our enemies is all too relevant. We have noticed how John Piper describes this tension in the original context in which the words were written. Bonhoeffer, of course, realised this as he witnessed the rise of Nazism in pre-war Germany with a dismay which few of his contemporaries shared. Bonhoeffer quotes a man called Villmar who wrote in 1880, "This commandment . . . will grow even more urgent in the holy struggle which lies before us . . . Christians will be hounded from place to place, subjected to physical assault, maltreatment and death of every kind. We are approaching an age of widespread persecution . . . soon the time will come . . . when we shall pray for these very sons of perdition who stand around and gaze at us with eyes aflame with hatred, and who have perhaps already raised their hands to kill us . . . Yes, the Church which is really waiting for its Lord, and which discerns the signs of the times of decision, must fling itself with its utmost power and with the panoply of its holy life, into this prayer of love."[22] Such words will be increasingly relevant in the coming years.

God's Love is Unilateral

God's love is not only *universal*—he loves all people; it is also *unilateral*—he does not wait for human initiative nor does he depend on the responses of those who are his beneficiaries. Martin Luther saw love in the Christian sense as primarily God's own love. According to Luther, man is so wholly governed by sin that he *cannot* love properly.[23] Man's love can never fully be a love which 'seeketh not its own'. In the Heidelberg Disputation of 1518 there was no mention of the Agape and Eros categories which Nygren sees as the vital issue at that time. Nevertheless, the reformers were concerned to overthrow some of the presuppositions of the ethical system which had been built so skilfully by St. Augustine. Thus in the Heidelberg Disputation human love is described as acquisitive love and so created by the desirable nature of its object, whereas God's love is creative: "it makes something of that which is nothing." The reformers, as in other areas under dispute, were concerned to confront what they saw to be false in the Roman system—particularly the concept of human merit, the seeming ability to save oneself, which in its more popular forms of expression was a contradiction of the doctrine of grace so rightly cherished by the reformers. It is perhaps true that theirs was an over-reaction which did not allow for a theological understanding of man as created in the image of God and, therefore, after baptism and salvation (and even *before* to some extent) capable of loving with the same quality of love as God's, since it comes from the same source. Nygren takes Luther's side uncompromisingly. Spicq challenges Nygren on this point and bluntly says that he is "incorrect" in saying that there is "no way going from man to God, only a way from God to man."[24] His assertion is based on his exposition of Luke 7:36–50, the story of the sinful woman who washed Jesus' feet with her tears. Spicq comments, "The love of the sinful woman proves what was already clear in the Septuagint that *agape* can ascend from man to God." It is true that Jesus said "Her sins, which are many, are forgiven, *for she loved much*." But it would be wrong to deduce from this (as some have) that she was forgiven because she loved. The next words suggest something quite different—"He who is forgiven little, loves little." Here the implication is that forgiveness is primary, the human response of love secondary. The preceding six verses bear the same meaning. This must be so if there is any consistency in the whole background to the doctrine of divine grace. It would seem for the sinful woman (as for all sinners) it was the unilateral love of Jesus for her—a truly forgiving and accepting love, which drew her to him in the first place, and so her own great love for Jesus was a response to his rather than the other way round. As Bishop Ryle puts it, "Her love was the effect of her forgiveness, not the cause, the consequence not the condition, the result not the reason, the fruit not the root."[25] But perhaps Nygren and Spicq are closer to one another than it first appears. Both in their efforts to defend a position seem to go further than they should. Both stress the spontaneity and unilateral nature of God's love, Nygren stressing the Godward initiative of that love, Spicq (at least in this example) the human response to that divine initiative.

If the universal and unilateral love of God is most clearly expressed in the teaching of Jesus in the Sermon on the Mount in Matt. 5:43–48, it is most lucidly exemplified in the life of Jesus during the events immediately preceding his death on the Cross. Here are expressions of unilateral love which are seen in an almost unending chain culminating in the words forgiving his executioners, "Father forgive them, they know not what they do." Jesus constantly during this period takes the initiative with those whose words and actions were anything but loving. He gives the favoured sop to Judas the betrayer; he appears privately to Peter, the one who three times denied him; he washes the feet of those who a few moments before were insensitively discussing which of them was to be the boss. Never once is there a trace of revengefulness or vindictiveness. He quietly and with no fuss or ostentation loved everyone without partiality. He never waited to be loved, but spontaneously and unilaterally, without self-consciousness, poured out his life for others, whoever they may have happened to be. But at no time did he compromise truth or righteousness. He never pandered to the schemes of Pilate, and remained silent in the presence of the charlatan Herod. Love and righteousness were in perfect harmony and balance.

Karl Barth has a beautiful description of this kind of love. "It is identification with a person's interests in utter independence of the question of his attractiveness or what he has to offer, of the reciprocity of the relationship or repayment in the form of a similar self-giving. In *agape*–love a man gives himself to another with no expectation of a return, in a pure venture, even at the risk of ingratitude, and of that other person's refusal to make a response of love."[26] Barth uses one of his favourite words to describe this kind of unilateral love—*Einsatz*—which literally means 'stand surety for another person'.

This kind of love, perfectly portrayed in the character and life of Jesus, is in stark contrast to the limitations on love imposed by the narrower grasp of truth seen in the Old Testament. Not only could the hatred of one's enemies be construed as justifiable at least in the Rabbinical traditions if not in the Old Testament itself, but the salvation plans of God were limited also to God's own people, the Jews. Quell may be exaggerating when he writes that nowhere in the Old Testament does the love of God reach out beyond Israel.[27] In the concern expressed over and over again for the sojourner or the stranger—or as we would say 'the overseas visitor', there is at least in embryo the revelation to the Jews of God's concern and love for the whole world. In Psalm 146:9 we are told that "The Lord watches over the sojourners," and in Deut. 10:18 that he "loves the sojourner". It goes on, "Love the sojourner, therefore; for you were sojourners in the land of Egypt." The prophets also saw God's ultimate purpose as one of universal blessing throughout the entire world. The whole earth was one day going to be full of the knowledge of the Lord "as the waters cover the sea" (Is. 11:9).

God's Love is Excessive

The love of God is seen not only as universal (directed to all men), unilateral (dependent on nothing in anyone) but as excessive—an unfathomable sea. Paul tries to grapple with this aspect in the Letter to the Ephesians and finds words incapable of expressing God's love adequately. He talks about "the riches of his grace" in chapter one, and in chapter three about "the breadth and length and height and depth, and to know the love of Christ which surpasses knowledge . . ." (vv. 18, 19). Martin Luther talked of the 'abyss of eternal love' (*ein Abgrund der Liebe*). He spoke of it as *quellende Liebe*—'overflowing love'. Spicq beautifully sums up this divine love and our response to it: "To love as God loves is to love with the same breadth in objects, the same ingenuity in activity, the same purity in intention. To love with God's love is the goal of love, in the light of this goal simple human love changes in nature and is transmuted into *agape*. It gradually takes on a divine mode of behaviour. Although no one can be assimilated entirely to this divine mode here on earth, everyone can discover its essential qualities of gratuitousness, generosity and universality and everyone must tend increasingly to approach it as an ideal."[28]

God's Love is Creative

We need also to see that God's love is *creative*. Here again we can see the stark contrast between Agape and Eros. Nygren criticises the Ritschl idea of the 'infinite value of the human soul'. Nygren dubs this "Eros". Ritschl and others have seen this as that which calls forth God's love. But the real meaning of Agape, which leaves Eros at this point standing, is love for the unworthy; or we might say the worthless. Some imagine that contrary to man's condemning gaze, God sees the good in us and his love is directed at that. Some say rather piously that God sees Christ in us—as if God is looking at us as a mirror and only seeing himself, a kind of divine narcissism. Such may be true of Eros but not of Agape. God sees us as we often are—mean, selfish, narrow-minded, lustful, proud, lazy, self-righteous and carnal. He loves these sort of people. Jesus demonstrated this in his ministry. To use the hackneyed phrase, Jesus loves the sinner but hates their sin. Eros was essentially love for the beautiful and the good. It is egocentric love— self-interested rather than disinterested.[29] It is always *caused* by the value of its object. Eros is need love. So we are not surprised to find that in some Greek thought the gods do not love human beings, since they do not need them. Love is, therefore, impossible for the gods. They can only be the objects of love. Thus love belongs exclusively to man's side of the relationship. Eros seeks for happiness and glory. It moves down a one-way street—man to God; never God to man.

No wonder Eros is never mentioned in the New Testament! It is anathema to the whole concept of Agape. Agape begins and ends in God. He is its author and finisher. He is the only initiator. He loves the ugly and the un-lovable; in this sense his love is creative. It brings love to birth in man. The one who is loved learns to love. The one who is accepted learns to accept. The beauty of Christ, which surpasses all the concepts of beauty which the Greeks cherished and which our society longs for, is planted in ugly human soil and produces its own unique blooms.

9   NO U-TURNS

"The chief good which the Christian lover will seek to realise for the loved is to make him also a lover."

(Hastings Rashdall)

The ultimate purpose of God's love is not that those who are the objects of his love should return it (though they obviously will), but that they should themselves become instruments of his love to others. God wants us to pass on his love; he wants us to be lovers also.

Having looked at the way in which love has been separated from God himself, we need to see how the two commandments have been separated from each other with unfortunate consequences. When Jesus was asked by the lawyer, "Which is the great commandment in the law?" his answer was, "You shall love the Lord your God with all your heart, and with all your soul, and with all your mind. This is the great and first commandment. And a second is like it, You shall love your neighbour as yourself. On these two commandments depend all the law and the prophets" (Matt. 22:34f). Both these commandments are to be found in the Old Testament, but in separate places; the first in Deut. 6:5, and the second in Lev. 19:18. Jesus, in answering the lawyer, was underlining an important part of the revelation of the nature of God in the Old Testament, namely that the love of God and love for our neighbour belong together. But we need to see that the two commandments not only belong together, *they remain two and not one or three*. It is in the disruption of the balance of the two commandments that much damage has been done. Put simply, men have either tried to dissolve the two and make them one; or to make three commandments out of them rather than two. Pietism has tended to stress the first commandment and to subsume love for one's neighbour under love for God; Christian radicalism (one part of which has found expression in so-called situation ethics, which we shall be looking at in chapter fourteen) tends to see God in one's neighbour, an idea which Nygren asserts, "has no basis in gospel teaching".[1]

Then there are others who have found a third commandment hidden in the other two. The commandment to love our neighbour *as ourselves* has been taken to mean that there is also a commandment here to love oneself. Nygren takes issue with those who have either reduced or added to the two commandments. "It is fatal to merge the two commandments into one. It is important to observe that Jesus presents them as two commandments because subsequent history is full of attempts to make them into one. In general the procedure has been to subsume love to one's neighbour under love to God . . . to show how love to one's neighbour is really directed not to him but to God . . ."[2] Later in the same passage he comments on the so-called 'third commandment', "The two commandments are two only, and no third can be added to them."[3] He goes on to show that the idea of self-love is alien to the New Testament and has grown up out of a wholly different soil. "If there had not been a desire on other grounds," he writes, "to include self-love among the ethical demands of Christianity, there would be no motive for seeking to find it in the New Testament commandment."[4]

Before we go on, it is important to see that there is much good in all three approaches. Those who have stressed the love of God at the expense of love for one's neighbour have sometimes been called pietists. In standing for the foundations of the gospel of the grace of God their witness has been important. Others, who have stressed neighbour love, sometimes to the exclusion of divine love, have also made an important contribution—a corrective to a false kind of pietism. While those who have unearthed the 'third commandment' have helped to free many from self-hatred and despair. All three, in different ways, have tried to restore love to its primacy in Christian belief and ethics. But all three have at times distorted the true meaning of love—not by what they have asserted, but by what they have neglected to assert. In varying degrees their contribution is unbalanced.

Perhaps the most tragic feature of modern Christianity is the way in which Christians seem to polarise so easily faced with these two commandments. It seems to have often occurred in the history of Christianity, but probably never more so than today. In the Roman Catholic Church Cardinal Suenens has for many years sought to bring the two love commandments together. In a written dialogue with his close friend Cardinal Dom Helder Camara of Brazil he expresses his concern about what he calls the horizontalist tendency (which leaves out God), which he sees as a reaction against a disembodied Christianity of the pietist type.[5] He sees a double pitfall—a disembodied Christianity (the first commandment only) and a Christianity without the risen and living Christ. They both in their dialogue see the Cross as the meeting point—where the vertical and the horizontal converge. They write, "The desertion of the world in the name of God is just as unacceptable as the neglect of God in the name of temporal commitments."[6]

We shall be looking at the meeting point of the two commandments—in the sanctuary *and* the poor ghettos of our world—in a later chapter. For the moment we are concerned to establish how important it is to unite the two commandments without confusing them. One of the most important sayings of Jesus in this respect is Matt. 5:23: "So if you are offering your gift at the altar, and there remember that your brother has something against you, leave your gift there before the altar and go; first be reconciled to your brother, and then come and offer your gift." Here we see the two commandments held together.

In this particular text Jesus is standing in the shoes of some of the Old Testament prophets. Isaiah, for example, prophesied that God is not interested in the 'trampling of his courts', and "cannot endure iniquity *and* solemn assembly".[7] His soul hates "appointed feasts". Instead he urges his people to "Seek justice, correct oppression; defend the fatherless, plead for the widow." Amos in a famous passage says the same thing, "I hate, I despise your feasts, and I take no delight in your solemn assemblies . . . Take away from me the noise of your songs . . . But let justice roll down like waters, and righteousness like an everflowing stream."[8]

For the prophets, as for Jesus, love for God and love for our neighbour are not options. To love one's neighbour is *not* to love God, nor is loving God the same thing as loving one's neighbour. *Both* are commandments to be obeyed. The man who is coming to the altar unreconciled to his brother, must not only seek that reconciliation but also bring that gift. There is a brand of Christianity that seems blind to the material and social needs around it, impervious to the cry of the poor and destitute. There is another brand of Christianity that is so immersed in the sea of human need and so out of touch with the divine source of power and inspiration that it can neither save itself nor anyone else. A non-swimmer cannot rescue someone drowning in deep water.

The tragedy of so much of the history of Christianity is that it has constantly been doing U-Turns, where U-Turns are not permitted. Leonard Evans, who has preached what he calls 'the love message' all over the world, has said this about love, "The Kingdom of God is where the love which the Father has for the Son has been implanted in our hearts through the Cross, imparted and invigorated by the Holy Spirit so that you and I can love one another like the Father loves the Son and the Son loves the Father."[9] There are no U-Turns here. The Father loves the Son. The Son, of course, loves the Father also; but that love, to use another metaphor, is not to be short-circuited. It is not monopolised by the Trinity. The Son loves us. He loves us so much, he died for us. We, of course, love the Son. But again there is to be no short-circuiting. The Church gathering is not to be simply the venue for a glorious love-in between Jesus and his people. We are also to love one another. Nor does it stop there. We are also to love the un-Christianised world.

Only then is the circuit completed. Then it all flows back again to God. But the trouble is that the Church has been guilty of U-Turns. There has been a pietism which simply returns God's love to God himself, instead of lavishing it on people. There can also be a selfish form of Christianity which concerns itself with making the Church into a cosy kind of club—a members only or closed shop mentality, which neglects the unreached masses outside the Church. When the flow of divine love is stopped, it becomes stagnant. No wonder Jesus spoke of the outpouring of the Holy Spirit from our innermost beings as 'rivers' and not as 'reservoirs' (John 7:37).

Leonard Evans' definition, which helps us to see this flow of love within the Trinity, to the Church and to the world, is also a definition of the Kingdom. One does not normally associate the concept of the Kingdom with love. The words seem totally different, even antithetic. Kingdom suggests rule, authority and power. Whereas love suggests care and concern. Love is more gentle, even tender in its application. But on the contrary it would seem most important that the two words are closely and carefully related to each other. Like truth and righteousness the word kingdom is part of what love is all about. For the kingdom we should be concerned about is the Kingdom of God, and since God is love, presumably the Kingdom will be the Kingdom of his love. Victor Furnish puts this well, "The rule of God is the rule of love. Love is the law of life in the Kingdom . . . love is . . . the power and the purpose of God's coming and reign. So in Jesus' teaching love is not just *commended* as a prudent or noble way of life, it is actually *commanded* as the rule of the Kingdom."[10]

It is very easy for us to think of love and Kingdom as two different concepts. But the Kingdom without love becomes harsh and legalistic. It resembles the barrack square with the sergeant-major barking out his orders. On the other hand love without the Kingdom as the context in which it operates, easily becomes anaemic and sloppy. The Roman Catholic writer Michael Scanlon has written, "The life of the Kingdom consists of loving one another and that love is a sure sign to others that what has been preached to them is true."[11] Spicq sees access to the Kingdom of Jesus "in proportion as he is really united to God and to men by a love both interior and active."[12] He goes so far as to define a Christian as "a person who loves".

Now the whole weight of the New Testament argument flows out of the insistence by Jesus, and the Old Testament for that matter, that altar gifts are unacceptable when our brother has something against us. The flow is normally one way—from God to men and then men to one another. For instance in 1 Peter 1:22f we read that the purification of our souls and obedience to the truth is *for* a sincere love of the brethren. It goes on—"Love one another earnestly from the heart." We are then told about our being 'born again'. This is immediately and naturally followed by the exhortation to "put away all malice and all guile and insincerity and envy and all slander," which are sins against people. To be 'born again' means one should have a different attitude towards others, and one's behavioural patterns will also be changed. Belief and behaviour, especially towards other people, belong together; the one should flow naturally into the other.

This important link between the two commandments is perhaps seen at its clearest in John's first epistle. He writes that it is impossible to be truly 'in the light' with God, if one still hates one's brother (2:9). The one who does not love his brother is not a child of God but a child of the devil (3:10). It is the sign that we have passed "out of death into life" (3:14). Belief is intrinsically linked with loving one another (3:23). It is the one who loves who is "born of God" (4:7). God so loved us that our principal response should not be to love him back, but to love one another (4:10, 11). The pious statement "I love God" is unacceptable if we do not love one another. The reason is plain—"He who does not love his brother whom he has seen, cannot love God whom he has not seen" (4:20). The message is clear. The two commandments belong together. You cannot truly obey one without the other.

From the very beginning the love that Christians had for one another was one of the clearest distinguishing marks of their profession. This is not surprising when we remember that Jesus Christ said, "By this all men will know that you are my disciples, if you have love for one another" (Jn 13:35). This was a remarkable word of prophecy when you remember it was spoken at the Last Supper just after Jesus had washed his disciples' feet and just before his betrayal by Judas. The disciples were anything but loving to him or to one another. But Calvary and Pentecost were to change these men. Love was to grow until it became the principal mark of Christianity in the first two centuries. Tertullian was to make his famous remark, "Look . . . how they love one another."[13] A Roman called Minicius Felix wrote a letter about the same time to a fellow Roman about the Christians he was meeting. He accused them of what he calls 'a vile abomination'—"They fall in love almost before they are acquainted." Lucian of Samosata, writing in the first century, describes a man called Peregrinus who was in prison and seems to have claimed to be a Christian, though he was probably a bit of a fraud. Apparently the Christians visited him conscientiously. "They show," Lucian writes, "incredible speed whenever such public action is taken, for their first law giver (Jesus) persuaded them that they are all brothers of one another."

Nygren is suspicious of the apostle John because he refers in both his gospel and letters to our love for God as well as God's love for us.[14] There are times when it would seem Nygren is pressing his case unnecessarily strongly, and this is perhaps an example. In pursuing his main thesis he is critical also of the mystical tradition of the Church. But he surely takes his argument too far when he accuses John of being the first deviant from the straight path, the first person to reintroduce Eros alongside Agape.

Nevertheless, in the New Testament most of the references to love concern God's love for us, and our love for one another, and there are few references even in John to our love for God. John says so little about our love for God that it is difficult to understand why Nygren takes such strong exception to these few references. After all the first commandment is to love God. Actually the most common response in John's Gospel to the love of God is *obedience* rather than a reciprocity of love. Jesus said, "If you love me you will keep my commandments" (Jn 14:15). This seems the typical response in the fourth Gospel.

Some have raised problems with John's teaching, and have suggested that the universal scope of love, so clearly taught by Jesus, taking in as it does enemies as well as friends, is seriously restricted again by John, so that it becomes the love of the Christian ghetto. Ernst Kasemann finds a severely restricted view here, a kind of 'brotherhood of Jesus' rather than love of the world.[15] Furnish's response to Kasemann is to quote John 4:42, 3:16, 8:12, 16:33 and 16:8,11. He writes, "Love for one another is neither a softening nor a repudiation of the command to love the neighbour, but a special and indeed urgent form of it."[16]

The important thing about John's teaching is that he repudiates the notion that you can get away with just one of the commandments. Both are in God's statute book. Perhaps John's answer to Kasemann might be something like this: "Yes, we are to love all men. But it is easier to love those you have not seen than those you are seeing all the time; if you can love those you do see and live in close proximity to, then there is a better chance that you will be able to love those who are distant from you." A true Christian witness to divine love has to be seen, and the only love which is visible is the love we have for those who are close to us. The love of Christian for Christian is not to stop there, but to flow on to embrace all men everywhere. But if Christians are not able to love their brothers and sisters in Christ in a practical and wholesome fashion, how can they begin to love the rest of the world and particularly their enemies? Down the centuries Christians have not always shown the love they should for one another and there are many examples of religious conflict between Christians which has been distasteful. Love must not stop at the level of Christian brotherhood; but there is no other place where it can start.

Nygren's case is much stronger when we turn to Paul's writings. Here there are very few references to our loving God. Nygren is surely right when he sees *faith* as the Pauline response to the Agape of God.[17] One of the very few texts in Paul that refer to our love for God is Romans 8:28, "We know that in everything God works for good *with those who love him*, who are called according to his purpose." But even in this text the response of love is qualified somewhat by the addition of the words, "who are called according to his purpose". Paul's message is full of references to Agape love, God's love for us and our love for one another. But there is little place for U-Turns. According to Paul there can be no sound relationship in which love for God shuts out our brother. Paul follows the teaching of Jesus Christ in emphasising that the two commandments belong together.

There have always been those who have set the Gospels and the teaching of Jesus over against the teaching of the rest of the New Testament as if Paul and others polluted the pure teaching of Jesus and spoilt it all for us. This is not the time to go into this in detail, except to say that, concerning the teaching in the New Testament about love, it seems clear that Jesus' teaching and the apostles' is one and the same. What Jesus said Paul reiterates. For the apostle the Second Commandment was crucial as well as the First. In Romans 13:8 he writes, "Owe no one anything, except to love one another; for he who loves his neighbour has fulfilled the law." Paul sees this commandment as a summary of the Law. Again in Gal. 5:14 he writes, "For the whole law is fulfilled in one word, 'You shall love your neighbour as yourself'." Here there is no soft-pedalling of brotherly love in favour of loving God. If you say you love God, then you should express this in your love for your neighbour. We need to look again at what Victor Furnish has written about Paul's theology: "No better title for Paul's theology can be devised than his own formulation in Gal. 5:6 'faith active in love'. Love is both the context and content of faith; *God*'s love makes faith possible and man's love gives it visibility and effect in the world."[18] He goes on to show how for Paul both the sacraments of Baptism and Holy Communion are 'social' in their effects (see Gal. 3:27, 28 and 1 Cor. 10:16–18).

Quell and Stauffer emphasise this point in their book on the word love. "The purpose of divine love is not that we should return love to God, nor that we should obtain freedom for our own sakes; it is that he who is called should put himself, in love and freedom, at the service of his neighbour."[19] Rightly too, in spite of Nygren's fears, they see John's emphasis in the same direction: "In John, love to God or Christ takes second place after love to the brethren which springs from God and has its prototype in Christ." It is as if the Lord wants to tell his people, "Please don't take time to love me. I know that you love me—now take my love for you and pour it on your fellow human beings." So the way our love for God is to be expressed is not so much in returning that love, whatever that means, but in obedience to God (Jn 14:15) and caring for others. In John 21:15 Jesus asks Peter if he loves him "more than these". When the answer was in the affirmative, Jesus told Peter to "feed my lambs" and "tend my sheep". In other words, the way to love the Lord is to care for those whom he loves.

Perhaps the simplest presentation of this truth is found in James 1:27, "Religion that is pure and undefiled before God and the Father is this: to visit orphans and widows in their affliction, and to keep oneself unstained from the world." Professor Tasker writes in his commentary on James, "The externals of religion, however punctiliously performed, are quite unacceptable to him unless accompanied by a genuine desire on the part of the worshipper to render sympathetic and practical service to his fellow-men."[20] Thus the Christian has a two-fold task in the world, to care for its needs and to reject its spirit.

It is clear from the Old and New Testaments that worship has played an important part in the life of God's people. The great moments of redemption and deliverance in the life of Israel as well as the Christian Church were occasions for paeans of praise. Thus Moses on the shores of the Red Sea sang a song to the Lord, "I will sing to the Lord, for he has triumphed gloriously . . . The Lord is my strength and my song, and he has become my salvation; this is my God, and I will praise him . . ." (Ex. 15:1, 2). Many years later the angels announced the birth of Jesus Christ with shouts of, "Glory to God in the highest, and on earth peace among men with whom he is pleased" (Lk. 2:14). Later the start of the Church's missionary task (at Pentecost) was inaugurated with praise, and the Acts of the Apostles reverberates with it, not least when the Church is suffering.

It might be thought that this in itself is an example of a U-Turn. Surely praise and worship are ways by which God's people return his love. Of course this is one way of seeing the worship of God. But there is another way of looking at it. It should also be seen as an assertion of *faith*, of confidence in the Word of God and the presence and power of God. It would seem that this is the predominant meaning of worship in the Bible. At Pentecost, for example, the Church's response to the coming of the Holy Spirit in power was to speak in tongues. What were they saying? According to Acts 2:11 they were "telling . . . the mighty works of God". Later, in Acts 4:24, the worship of the Church is a declaration of God's power and authority. It is an assertion of faith rather than love. Their worship begins with the words, "Sovereign Lord, who didst make the heaven and the earth and the sea and everything in them . . ." Both the worship of the Psalms and the heavenly company in the Revelation are expressions of the truth about God rather than declarations of men's love for God. Although there is much richness in the Church's mystical tradition, Nygren has something important to say about it when he criticises its absorption in expressions of love for God, compared with the biblical emphasis in which worship is a declaration of the love of God and his other attributes, and a confident assertion of faith in him.

In his book *The Four Loves*, C. S. Lewis quotes Denis de Rougemont, "Love ceases to be a demon only when it ceases to be a god." Lewis goes on, "Every human love at its height has a tendency to claim for itself a divine authority. Its voice tends to sound as if it were the will of God himself."[21] In a strange way we can try to make God into God, which is quite unnecessary because he is God anyway. The pietist can be so concerned about God that he tends not to let God be God. The devotee of social action is just as much in danger of making a god of his neighbour. But all love which becomes divorced from the very nature of God himself becomes a form of idolatry sooner or later. By caring for our neighbour we are not worshipping God; and if we do it without a rich relationship to God it will soon degenerate into idolatry. But to worship God and lay claim to love him and obey him, and at the same time to ignore the needs of the world, is not true worship either; and in fact is another and more subtle form of idolatry. For to worship 'God' and to ignore the needs of our neighbour reveals that we don't really know the true God, and our worship being ignorant is idolatrous. The 'God' we are worshipping is not the true God at all, but another god, and, therefore, an idol. No wonder the final words of St. John's epistle are, "Little children, keep yourselves from idols."[22]

Joseph Fletcher in his book *Situation Ethics* raises another important question concerning our love for our neighbour. Speaking about what he calls 'agapeic love' he says that it is not a 'one-to-one affair'.[23] This he calls either eros-love or philia-love. "Love," he goes on to say, "uses a shotgun not a rifle . . . love is not only for people one at a time." There is some truth in this, but Fletcher misses something of importance. Quell and Stauffer point out how little the Old Testament speaks of God's love for a particular person; only collective objects of love are mentioned.[24] From the Old Testament it would seem that God reveals his love for people in general rather than one-by-one in particular.

But the New Testament emphasis is quite different. Jesus Christ reveals a new dimension to the love of God. One of the most striking characteristics of Jesus' love, as revealed in the Gospels, is its winsomeness. When relating to individuals he does so personally and intimately. It was said of the rich young ruler, as we have seen, that Jesus "loved him". The parables often reveal God's concern for the individual, so that the shepherd leaves the ninety-nine and seeks the one that is lost, the woman looks for the one lost coin, and the father for the one lost son. The Good Samaritan is about a one-to-one situation, as is Dives and Lazarus. Jesus took his disciples through a dangerous storm on the lake to an unfriendly shore for the sake of one madman, whom society had banished to the town cemetery. And in some ways most poignant of all, there is the story of the woman who touched Jesus in the crowd. Jostled by thousands, Jesus knew the difference between the general and the particular. He knew when a person needed him. Then there was poor blind Bartimaeus on the roadside near Jericho, crying out to Jesus in his desperate need. We are told simply but dramatically that "Jesus stopped". Nor should we forget the phrase in the fourth Gospel "the disciple whom Jesus loved". You could not have anything more particular than that. Jesus often stopped for the individual and singled some out for special attention. An indiscriminate spray of shotgun pellets is an inadequate description of the love of God. God's love in the aggregate is the sum of his love for each person. The love of God is for people—*one-by-one*. There are many people today who feel lonely in the crowd. So much of our modern social concern is of the shotgun variety; blanket charity. But the individual needs to be loved for himself, not as an insignificant part of the human race, a number on a social security card. Neighbour love, if it is to be like the love of God, is to include love for the individual. Ron Sider has defined true Christian fellowship as "an unconditional availability to and unlimited liability for the other brothers and sisters, emotionally, financially and spiritually."[25] Our neighbour, in the first instance, is the person nearest us in need. If we don't care for that neighbour, it's no good our priding ourselves on caring for anyone else.

But U-Turns take on a tragic complexion when we look at the state of marriage and our economic systems. Eros is no substitute for Agape in the area of sexuality. God's love must be allowed to flow on into these areas of life. The only way in which our sick society can experience the healing it so desperately needs will be when the Agape love of God reaches into it; then healing and restoration can begin to take place.

10 LOVE AND SEX

"Fynn, is church sex?" I was awake, very much so!
"What do you mean is church sex?"
"It puts seeds in your heart and makes new things come."
"Oh."
"That's why it's Mr. God and not Missus God."
"Oh is it."

(Mister God, This is Anna[1])

The irrepressible Anna in her conversation with Fynn raises all kinds of questions. Whatever connection there may be between church and sex, most people equate the word love with the word sex. We need to examine carefully the connection between these two words, and in the next chapter to look at how love and economics relate to each other. Here are the two basics of human life. Without sex and food the human race would die out. It can survive without almost everything else. The two strongest inherent human drives are sex and hunger. It should not surprise us that these two areas are the ones which are most open to corruption. Lust and greed are vices capable of causing immense damage. How important, therefore, that true love acts constantly in these two areas. Love should be both the dominant motive and the purifying principle that governs men and women in their relationship to each other. Jesus said that we should not "live by bread alone", and he went on to say, "but by every word which proceeds from the mouth of God".[2] It is God's viewpoint that is crucial in man's sexual and economic life, and it will often differ from human standards and expectations.

We have already seen how man has tended to separate what God has joined, and this is certainly true when we look at man's sexual life. What is worse still is that Eros dominates this subject, and is usually assumed, even by Christians, to have a rightful place there. But Eros was the

Greek word for love, and as we have seen the Christian concept of love is quite different.

So two evils have been committed, God's true love has been separated from man's sexual life, and a false concept has been substituted, namely Eros. Jeremiah, speaking in a wider context, said, "My people have committed two evils: they have forsaken me, the fountain of living waters, and hewed out cisterns for themselves, broken cisterns, that can hold no water.''[3] Thus Agape love has been neglected and a leaking cistern substituted. Eros can never be the basis for lasting happiness and stability in a marriage relationship.

One of the best known examples of the identification of Eros with sexual love is in C. S. Lewis' book *The Four Loves*. However, it needs to be made clear that in dis-associating Eros from Agape love, I am not saying that there is anything inherently wrong with sex itself. It is one of God's most wonderful gifts. But sex is not love, nor is love sex. Sex is sex and love is love. Like all God's gifts sex can be enjoyed in accordance with the principle of Agape love. So again we see how important it is to define the meaning of love, and God alone can show us how to do that.

Some people still think that Christianity is anti-sex. Perhaps this stems from the false idea that Christianity exists to take away our pleasures because they are by definition sinful, and that we are not meant to enjoy life, and if we do, there is something wrong with us. Since sex is pleasurable then it must be wrong. The German philosopher Nietzsche once wrote, "Christianity gave Eros, the god of love, poison to drink; he did not die of it, it is true, but he degenerated to vice." In other words he blames Christianity for corrupting sex. If only Christianity had accepted sex, all would now be well. Eros should have been welcomed, not assassinated.

Now it has to be admitted that there is a brand of religion which has sometimes emanated from distorted forms of Christianity, which tends to regard sex as impure or un-wholesome, something to be either avoided altogether or indulged in furtively and guiltily, and certainly never to be talked about. That is as false a form of Christianity as Eros is a false form of love. What I am saying is that sex is not wrong in itself, but like everything else is safe and healthy only when exercised in love and that love should be Agape not Eros.

We have already emphasised how important it is to separate initially the words sex and love. They should belong together, but unless we understand what love is we cannot understand the meaning of sex. It is love (truly understood) which helps us to understand sex, not sex the nature of love. Many have turned to sex in the pursuit of love, but it has only brought frustration and even despair.

Sex can be examined in a variety of ways. Sociologists, anthropologists, psychologists, and biologists will all say something different about it. But the word love, unexplained and detached from our understanding of God, cannot adequately describe sex. Yet the word is constantly being used to do just that. Thus we talk about falling in love and making love and having a love affair. Our love life means our relationship to the opposite sex. The widespread identification of the word love with sex indicates that most people think that sex ought to be an experience of love. Of course it can be, and rightly understood ought to be, but it need not be and sometimes decidedly isn't. And that is where the frustration comes in. People feel cheated because sex has not delivered the goods.

When we read the Old Testament we encounter a rich understanding of sex and discover that the writers associated it closely with God himself. There is no trace of prudishness in the Old Testament. They were vividly aware of the dangers of sex and that it possessed a power that could easily be corrupted. They were not afraid to admit that sometimes it did lead to disastrous acts of infidelity and lust even in the lives of some of their national heroes, like King David. But they are not afraid to use the same language when talking about their relationship to God as they used to describe their sexual relationships. Quell points out that the word most commonly used in the Old Testament for love is *Ahebh* which is "rooted in the sex life, a love which finds its proper objects in persons."[4] Perhaps the most striking example of this important dual use of language is 'to know', which is used to describe the sex act as well as our experience of knowing God. In other words both Old and New Testaments are not ashamed to use the same language to describe both these relationships. And Paul shows his acceptance of this when he writes, "Husbands, love (*agapao*) your wives, as Christ loved the Church" (Eph. 5:25). Bishop John Robinson, when he gave evidence in the famous 'Lady Chatterley's Lover' trial at the Old Bailey in 1960, spoke of sex as 'holy communion'. In the context of D. H. Lawrence's novel it is an improper association of ideas, but in the context of true marriage it is wholly biblical, rooted in both the Old and New Testaments. One has only to read Hosea or Jeremiah to see the connection; and most dramatically of all in the love poetry of the Song of Solomon.

To link sex with God in this way is not blasphemous. We can only have true sexual fulfilment when we understand love, and the only perfect model of love is God himself, who is also its only source. Sexuality is, in its essence, divinely created and inspired. It is 'made in heaven'.

Untold pain has been caused to the human race because that most sacred and wonderful of gifts has become for some so degraded and corrupted. This is all the more reason why we should be careful with our language and especially over the use of the word Eros. Philip Sherrard in his book *Christianity and Eros* not only fails to accept this distinction, but argues for the joining of the two together. He writes, "We tend to distinguish between the love of God and the love of one person for another, to distinguish between Agape and Eros, and to regard the second as a rather debased form of the first, if not as directly opposed to the first and only indulged at the expense of the first. In a secularised sacramental love there is no such distinction."[5] This is also what Hans Kung says, "When Eros and Agape are regarded not only as distinct but as mutually exclusive, this is at the expense of both Eros and Agape . . . when Eros is depreciated . . . Agape is overvalued and dehumanised. It is desensualised and spiritualised . . . vitality, emotion, affectivity are forcibly excluded, leaving a love which is totally unattractive."[6] But the New Testament uses the same word (*agape*) to describe God's relationship to us as our relationship to one another, including that of husband and wife. There are not two words for love, one describing what we do sexually (Eros) and one for everything else (Agape); what we do sexually and what we do economically and what we do spiritually should be Agape. It is largely because Agape has been left out that sexuality has become so corrupted.

In the light of the sharp rise in the number of broken marriages, it is easy to forget that there are still many that do succeed, and that there are divorcees who make successful second marriages. Nevertheless standards of morality have changed drastically in the last twenty years. After the Miss World 1980 crown had been placed on Kimberley Santos' head she remarked that she was 'a good girl'. Patricia Roberts of the *Daily Mail* discussed in her column what it now meant to be 'a good girl'.[7] "Twenty years ago everyone would have known what she meant. It was clear and simple: good girls didn't . . . But today? The world has moved on, through the era of the permissive society, and clearly good does not equal chaste any longer." Apparently it now means being faithful to one's boyfriend. Heather Jenner, who runs a marriage bureau, said that forty years ago a 'good girl' meant a virgin, "but nowadays a good girl isn't necessarily one who has never slept with a man but one who is very selective and makes love only to a man she really cares about. Girls are no longer expected to be virgins." Leslie Kark, the Principal of a Modelling School, says that a 'good girl' today means 'faithful'.

There are some signs that a reaction to the permissiveness of the last twenty years is already setting in. Barbara Cartland, who writes her romantic novels at the breathless pace of over twenty a year, believes that the pornographic novel has passed its peak, and that people want to read about old-fashioned standards of faithfulness. To her a 'good girl' is "one who doesn't go to bed with her man until she's got the ring on her finger. Always has been, always will be." The success of her novels suggests there are a growing number of people who would support her in this. It is interesting to note the continuing success of the film *Brief Encounter*, which tells the story of a man and a woman, both married, who meet casually in World War 2. They are both 'good' in the old sense of that adjective. This old black and white film is still appearing at least on American screens. Perhaps audiences are tired of seeing the faithlessness of their screen gods and goddesses, and believe that there is something more heroic to see, which enhances masculinity and femininity, namely old-fashioned self-mastery and faithfulness in the face of sexual temptations.

There is an important aspect of this we need to consider. Contrary to popular opinion our modern Western society is not *generally* permissive. We are living at a time which is rife with moral absolutism in almost every area *apart from sexuality*. All that has really happened is that the absolutism which once was applied to sexual morals has been withdrawn from that area and is now applied with just as much moral indignation to other areas. Nations, political parties and Churches which were once dogmatic about sexual behaviour are now equally dogmatic about matters like race, human rights, social action and nuclear disarmament. Dr. Ralph McInerny, a Roman Catholic Professor at the University of Notre Dame, has written: "In certain selected areas, it is fashionable to disallow any possible exceptions to quite circumstantial precepts. In matters of civil rights, discrimination on a purely racial basis is widely seen as universally and always wrong. The harridans of Women's Liberation flourish any number of prohibitions admitting of no exceptions. And in the case of the most notable scapegoat of recent times, it seemed quite generally believed that not even God could forgive President Nixon."[8] He goes on to contrast this with sexual morality. "In the area of sexual morality, there has been a noticeable tendency to relativise, to question absolutes, to create a miasma of confusion." Far from living in a permissive society, the world is becoming increasingly dogmatic. We find this in the fields of science, the media, politics and education. Why then is sexual behaviour the exception? Much attention has been drawn by Church leaders to the attacks on injustice which come so frequently in the writings of the Old Testament prophets. But why do not these Church leaders draw our attention also to the denunciations of sexual misconduct which are equally prominent in the words of the prophets? Why is the accolade of 'prophet' conferred on those who speak out against social evils, while those, like Mrs. Mary Whitehouse and Malcolm Muggeridge who attack sexual permissiveness, are either ignored or treated with disrespect?

Love between the Sexes

1. In marriage

We have already noted that Paul sees the husband's relationship to his wife in terms of Agape love (Eph. 5:25). In the Old Testament one of the important Hebrew words for love is *chesed*. Norman H. Snaith prefers to translate it 'covenant love'.[9] Hosea says that God desires "steadfast love and not sacrifice" (6:6), and this is particularly striking in the light of the prophet's call to marry an unfaithful woman, and his insistence that God's people have been unfaithful to him. In Micah 6:8 the prophet declares what God requires of man, "To do justice and to love kindness (*chesed*)." God's love for his people is not fickle but faithful. The relationship into which God calls his people is a covenant relationship. There is nothing casual about it. I do not want to go into the controversial matter of divorce and remarriage; suffice it to say that, whatever case may be made out for certain exceptions to the general rule, Jesus taught that marriage is a covenant which is intended to last one's lifetime, and that once married there is required of both husband and wife a faithfulness to one another which precludes sexual relations with anyone else.

It is important for us to realise that marriage does not legitimise sex. In other words, just because a man and a woman are married it does not mean that 'anything goes' within that relationship. Agape love is to be the governing factor in every aspect of that marriage, not least the physical side of their sexual life. They are not to make selfish demands upon each other.

Self-control is to govern married life as well as our life before we are married. It is possible for a man to treat his wife like a prostitute and the fact that they are one, legally and spiritually, does not automatically legitimise all that may take place within that marrriage. Unfortunately, because the truth of this is universally accepted, it has been assumed that the converse is also true, namely that it is possible to have a truly loving relationship outside of marriage. On the contrary, sexual intercourse is part of the *chesed*, or covenant love, in the Old Testament, so that it is impossible to think of it as loving except when those involved are married to one another. True love is always Agape love, and that love comes from God who is faithful and righteous; so every expression of that love should conform to that righteousness. Another important aspect of Agape love is that it is for others not for oneself. A marriage is never just a private affair between two people. When children are born they need to be considered, and a stable home life is important for a growing family. Also society in general has a stake in that relationship. Wholesome family life is an asset to any society. Bad family life has a debilitating effect on the rest of society. Children growing up in a home where there is little or no love will not understand discipline, and will tend to develop into antisocial personalities, who can become a menace to society.

Paul paid marriage the highest compliment possible when he compared the relationship between husband and wife to that between Christ and his Church. People do find it difficult to understand the meaning of Agape love. One of the chief ways in which it can be demonstrated is when a man and a woman relate together in faithfulness and love for a lifetime. Marriages like this are the finest examples of Agape love available, and so are of immense importance and so worth cultivating, however hard the road to success may be.

2. In friendship

One of the revolutions of this century has been the emancipation of women, and their release to work and serve in the world at large, so that there are today very few jobs which women cannot do alongside men. This means that men and women have to relate to one another at many more levels than before. They see much more of one another, and society seems to have taken the line that men and women should be integrated at every level.

We have already looked at the differences between love (Agape) and friendship (Philia). While we cannot select whom we love, it is natural to be selective when it comes to friendship. But that does not mean to say that Agape love is irrelevent to a relationship between friends. Every relationship we have should be controlled and motivated by Agape love.

Here is where a modern phenomenon cuts into our subject—the mixed community. The Church has had communities for many centuries, and many of them have been successful. They have been beacons of hope in dark days when human relationships have been breaking down all around them. But in most instances they have been either for men or women, who take vows of chastity; however, today we are seeing many mixed communities emerging, for men and women, marrieds and singles, celibates and non-celibates. Obviously there are dangers that marriage bonds will be weakened in these kinds of communities (but it is equally true that some marriages have been deepened and some saved from the divorce courts in this sort of situation). Perhaps the greatest danger lies in the temptation to lose sight of the unique elements in a marriage which obviously cannot be duplicated in other relationships within the community. Singles, for example, can make demands on those marriages which can weaken or even cause them to break down. They can claim 'equal rights' in a community, when it is obvious that a married couple have something unique which they cannot fully share in the community, but which because of its preciousness the community needs to support and nurture rather than endanger. This does not mean to say that marrieds should treat singles as second class citizens. But neither does it mean that marrieds should have an attitude of 'all things in common', nor should be made to feel guilty if they maintain, as they should, something of their independence as husband and wife. Some communities seem to have worked this through, others haven't and it can be a constant source of strain.

3. Between homosexuals

Alongside the emancipation of women in Western society there has also been the emergence of the modern 'gay movement', which has sought to free homosexuals from the social and moral stigmas which have attached to them in the past. For example, they have been called faggots, because in the Middle Ages the best way of dealing with them was to bind them together and burn them.

Society has come a long way since those days, but it is only in the last few years that the law in Britain has been repealed that made homosexual practices between consenting males a criminal offence; in some Western countries the law is still on the statute book. Today love between members of the same sex is becoming almost universally accepted as a valid alternative to heterosexual relationships, and this is being said by some within the Churches as well as secular society. In many Western countries there has been a rapid increase in the number of male and female homosexuals, some of which can be accounted for by aggressive

gay proselytising, and some by the increasing breakdown of
family life and the growing psychological diseases of our
Western society. The Church too can be blamed for this,
for it has contributed to the lowering of moral standards
through its failure to discriminate between healthy and
unhealthy sexuality.

We can be thankful for the growing sensitivity of people
to those who are homosexual, and the desire to accept
them as people rather than single them out for censure.
Sometimes homosexuals have been condemned for their
sexual deviations, when heterosexual deviations have been
condoned. But our Churches and society are at grave risk
when they fail to distinguish between the state of homosexuality and homosexual practices. Bland assumptions are
made today with little supporting evidence. It is often, for
example, said that some homosexuals are born that way. It
is much more likely that all homosexuals are made homosexual, either by the failure of their parents or the influence
of other homsexuals. The virtual absence of homosexuality
in many parts of the world (especially Africa) would suggest
that it is largely a Western disease caused by the failure of
family life, particularly confusions of roles between parents
and their relationship to growing children, a disease that is
being spread by militant gay groups.

Both the Old and New Testaments declare that homosexual acts are wrong. In spite of this there have been
modern attempts to disregard or discredit the biblical
records. For instance some have suggested that the sin of the
men of Sodom was not homosexuality. However, the text
could not be clearer. The men of Sodom ask for 'the men'
and then demand that they be brought out to them, 'that we
may know them'. When Lot offered them his daughters
they were not interested. The British Council of Churches'
report, *God's Yes to Sexuality*,[10] actually suggests that "the
Sodom story is more concerned with breach of hospitality
than with homosexual acts." How silly can one get when
attempting to evade the plain meaning of Scripture?

The Old Testament law forbade homosexual practices

(Lev. 18:22, 20:13) and so did Paul in Rom. 1:26–27. In 1 Cor. 6:9, 10 he reminds the Corinthians that homosexuals will not inherit the Kingdom of God. He goes on "Such were some of you." It would seem from these words that part of their Christian commitment had been to give up homosexuality.

Without exception the Church, until late in the twentieth century, has consistently taught that homosexual practices are wrong. Those Church leaders who now want to allow homosexual practices are advocating something which has been always condemned by both Scripture and the Church. They are leading the Church into a dangerous compromise.

The Changing Climate

In 1966 the British Council of Churches published a report entitled *Sex and Morality*. It caused a storm. It received sensational coverage in the popular press. The first print sold out overnight. The second run sold 60,000 copies. For months it was a constant talking point. The Chairman of the Working Party that produced it, Dr. Kenneth Greet, appeared on nearly all radio and television networks in the Western world. The main reason for the popularity of the report was its refusal to lay down any clear-cut principles, leaving people to make their own decisions on sexual matters. In 1980 the same Council of Churches produced another report entitled *God's Yes to Sexuality*. This time the Chairman was Basil Moss. Here was a much more radical statement of Christian ethics. They rejected, for instance, "the idea that marriage is the normative pattern of relationship against which all other possibilities are to be measured."[11] It even allowed that adultery was justifiable in certain circumstances. But this time the report passed almost unnoticed by the media. It caused hardly a ripple in the Churches. The doves seemed to triumph over the hawks. It led Douglas Brown to ask the serious question, "What is there specifically Christian about this report? Has this post-World War 2 climate entirely permeated erstwhile concepts?

And if so, where do we go now? And is there anywhere distinctly Christian to go to?"[12] So in fourteen years the climate of permissiveness has almost completely triumphed in both Church and State.

It was William Barclay who used to say that the one new virtue which entered the ancient world with the Christian Church was chastity. It entered a world where virginity before marriage was considered impossible, where divorce was commonplace, where fourteen out of the first fifteen Roman emperors were practising homosexuals. In his book *Ethics in a Permissive Society*, William Barclay wrote, "There is no way of making Jesus a supporter of a permissive society. If we support sexual intercourse before marriage or outside marriage, then I do not see how we can continue to call ourselves Christian and flatly contradict the teaching of Jesus Christ."[13] David Edwards writes about this. "Although our merciful Creator always says yes to our sexuality, the Christian says no to extra-marital sex even when saying no to sex means saying yes to the Cross. Do not the saints tell us that?" Here is a crucial battleground. A good marriage, in which both husband and wife delight to give each other pleasure, and thereby reassure one another of the love that they have for each other, does more for the re-establishment of Agape love than almost anything else. On the other hand our 'throw-away' generation, that discards marriages as freely as it discards its cans and plastic bags, has created for itself a climate of confusion in which many young people grow up without any working models of true love. Most Churches have added to this confusion by their cheap compromises. The recovery of the experience of Agape, rooted and grounded in God himself, is the only way by which sexuality can be rescued from the hands of the false moralists in both the Church and secular society.

11   LOVE OR MONEY?

"Justice, raw justice, is the *shekinah* of government."
(The Earl of Shaftesbury, 1825)

Lord Shaftesbury was only twenty-four when he wrote these words in his diary, and he was to spend most of his life trying to inject politics and economics with a strong dose of Christian compassion. By way of stark contrast, Nelson Rockefeller, when he was Vice-President of the United States, put things bluntly in a speech in Dallas, when he warned his audience against the continuing dangers of compassion. "One of the problems in this country is that we have this Judeo-Christian heritage of wanting to help those in need. And this, when added to some political instincts, sometimes causes people to promise more than they can deliver."[1] It is this separaton of the ethics of love from politics and economics which is causing so much harm to our modern society. I believe that God wants us to restore love as *the* motive of economics and political life.

Many leaders today believe that the world is heading for economic disaster and that many people are refusing to recognise it. The famous Brandt Report has clarified for us the world situation. Yet a number of Western governments have virtually ignored it. In the United States only 6,000 copies were sold in the first year and the report was almost totally ignored by the American press. According to the World Bank's 1979 Report on World Poverty, "about 800 million people still live in absolute poverty, with incomes too low to ensure adequate nutrition, and without adequate access to essential public services." The Brandt Report figures show that 17 million children under five die every year from malnutrition. Willy Brandt, the ex-Chancellor of West Germany, commented that these facts constitute "the greatest challenge to mankind for the remainder of the century."

In the spring of 1980 I was driven by a friend through the beautiful Canadian countryside north of Toronto. We travelled for several miles through prime agricultural land. I commented on the beauty of it. "Yes," my friend answered, "but in three years' time all this land will be covered by houses." In March of the same year *The Times* produced figures from a document entitled *World Conservation Strategy* to show that about 1,200 square miles of prime agricultural land is being lost every year to urban sprawl.[2] The same report noted that Japan lost about 7% of its agricultural land to buildings and roads in the 70s. At present rates a third of the world's arable land will have disappeared by the year 2000. But in the same period the population of the world will have about doubled to 6 billion. Another ominous factor is the way deserts are increasing in size by no less than 23,000 square miles a year, the equivalent of two Belgiums. As we mull over the statistics of human misery we must remember that the whole trend, some would say it is irreversible, is towards a worsening rather than improving situation. The worst famine areas are in Africa where the population is increasing more rapidly than anywhere else in the world, but where the per capita production of food has been declining for the past two decades. The future prospects are not good at all.

Jesus told a parable about economic inequalities. It was about two men, the one called Dives, who had more than enough, and the other Lazarus, who was poor and destitute. John Stott comments on the parable, "There is no suggestion that Dives was responsible for the poverty of Lazarus either by robbing or exploiting him. The reason for Dives' guilt is that he ignored the beggar at his gate and did precisely nothing to relieve his destitution. He acquiesced in a situation of gross economic inequality, which had rendered Lazarus less than fully human, and which he could have relieved. The pariah dogs that licked Lazarus' sores showed more compassion than Dives did. *Dives went to hell because of his indifference.*"[3] We need to remember that the opposite of love is not hate but indifference.

In order to understand what has gone wrong we need to go back to the so-called Renaissance and Reformation, to the break-up of the old order when the Church dominated the economic as well as the spiritual life of Europe. There has never been a perfect society; nevertheless this period marks a watershed. With all their faults, European leaders before the Reformation did attempt to relate their Christian ideals to the principles of economic life and to show concern for the material as well as the spiritual needs of all people. Love did have a stall in the market-place. One of the interesting differences between now and then can be seen in attitudes to riches and poverty. Today, in our Western society, increasing riches are regarded as a mark of God's favour and of human spirituality. If you are rich you must be a good person. But in the fifteenth century it was the other way round. According to Wycliffe a man must be wicked who is poor yesterday and rich today, since the only way this could have happened was at the expense of others.

A brilliant exposition of this subject is *Religion and the Rise of Capitalism* by R. H. Tawney.[4] He writes, "The most fundamental difference between medieval and modern economic thought consists in the fact that whereas the latter normally refers to *economic expediency* . . . for the justification of any particular action . . . the former starts from the position that there is a *moral authority* to which considerations of economic expediency must be subordinated."[5] For hundreds of years the principle of 'economic expediency' has ruled the roost. But it is important to remember that there was a time when people treated one another economically as if there was a God in heaven, who knew something about economics, and that there are some basic economic principles to practice, and that moral anarchy is not meant to be the *modus operandi* in economic matters. One of the clearest examples of this in economic practice is the use of interest or usury. In the medieval period it was considered immoral to lend money at interest, partly because the Bible forbade it, and partly for natural reasons. In an agrarian society the main reason why a person needed to borrow money was because he had experienced some misfortune (like the failure of his crops). To lend such a person money and charge him interest would be taking advantage of his misfortune and, therefore, un-Christian. How attitudes have changed! One can hardly imagine such a thought ever crossing the mind of Lord Keynes, or Milton Friedman. To use the well-known phrase of Schumacher, medieval economics was "economics as if people mattered".[6] R. H. Tawney wrote over sixty years ago, "Medieval thinkers insisted that society is a spiritual organism not an economic machine, and that economic activity . . . requires to be controlled and repressed by reference to the moral ends for which it supplies the material means."[7] He goes on to write prophetically, "So merciless is the tyranny of economic appetites, so prone to self-aggrandisement the empire of economic interests, that a doctrine which confines them to their proper spheres, *as the servant not the master* of civilisation, may reasonably be regarded as among the pregnant truisms which are a permanent element in any sane philosophy."

The trouble with our world is, to quote Emerson, "Things are in the saddle and rule mankind." Economic theories have been followed as if they were some kind of divine revelation, to be obeyed to the letter. They can easily be angels of light which deceive millions, and can cause havoc in the world. The only unmistakable sign of divinity is love, and that has been largely ignored by economists since the science of economics was first developed by Adam Smith. David Ricardo, for example, was compassionless towards the poor. For him labour was there as an end in itself and so need only be minimally nourished. Ricardo taught that the state should seldom intervene in economic affairs. His theories were based on the pursuit of self-interest. Wages were to be kept at subsistence levels. One of the most terrible results of this economic theory was the Irish Potato Famine of 1845, which cost the lives of over a million people, and caused over 1½ million to emigrate (mostly to the United States). Out of the bitterness of this shameful affair came eventually the Irish Republican Army. We are now reaping a terrible harvest from what the economists insisted on. At the height of the Irish Famine, when men, women and children were dying like flies, their bodies lying unburied in the fields and streets, not only did the English stop the giving away of food to those who were starving, but food was actually being exported from Ireland. It was economics gone mad.

In Highgate Cemetery there is one of the ironies of history. Everyone knows that the grave of Karl Marx, the father of communism, is there; but few know that the grave of Herbert Spencer, his arch-enemy, is also there. It was Herbert Spencer who invented the phrase 'the survival of the fittest', one of the cruel concepts of laissez-faire economics. According to Professor Galbraith, Herbert Spencer did for economics what Charles Darwin did for anthropology. He 'discovered' the principle of the 'ascent of the privileged classes'. What Marx did in the field of economics to eliminate class, Herbert Spencer did to draw the distinctions even more sharply.

Another strange quirk of history is that the famous economist John Maynard Keynes was born the same year that Marx died. Keynesian economics has done more than anything else to buttress capitalism and save it from the fate that was prophesied by Marx. But Lord Keynes was in the same tradition as the great economists who preceded him. In 1930 he wrote, "The journey the Western world is on can only be accomplished with the help of false gods; for at least another hundred years we must pretend that fair is foul and foul is fair; for foul is useful and fair is not. Avarice and usury and precaution must be our gods for a little longer still. For only they can lead us out of the tunnel into daylight."[8] Well, Lord Keynes is not alive to know that we are still not out of the tunnel into the daylight, and if anything we are further into the darkness than ever before. Nor is it any good pinning our hopes on the present popularity of the monetarism of Milton Friedman.

The trouble with all these economic systems is that they

have excluded ethical considerations. Love, in other words, is economically inappropriate and irrelevant. Our modern life is based on the answer to three simple questions: "Does it work?"; "Does it make us happy?" (particularly the electorate); and "Does it pay?" Dr. Schumacher writes, "Call a thing immoral, or ugly, soul-destroying or a degradation of man, a peril to the peace of the world or to the well-being of future generations; so long as you have not shown it to be 'uneconomic', you have not really questioned its right to exist, grow or prosper."[9] We are ruled today by economic considerations whether they happen to be moral or not. If it is uneconomical it is wrong *per se*; if it is economical, it is right *per se*. So we have witnessed the deification of economic theory. But this god cannot save the 800 million under-nourished people in the world. Only Christian economics has any hope of changing our society. R. H. Tawney has put it well in his book. "If it is proper to insist on the prevalence of avarice and greed in high places, it is not less important to observe that men called these vices by their right names, and had not learned to persuade themselves that greed was enterprise and avarice economy."[10] In our day it is just not considered proper any more to ask ethical questions about the way the world's economy is operated.

The main arguments of this book are that we have lost a true understanding of love, partly because we have separated what God has joined together, and partly because we have joined together what God has separated. So far as separation is concerned, we have not only separated love from God himself, but we have separated the two commandments from each other, and we have divorced compassionate considerations from economic life. We have also seen how in sexuality the god called Eros has supplanted Agape as the dominant influence in people's lives. Attempts have been made to combine Agape and Eros and to have the best of both worlds. But the Greek world of thought and the revelation of love given to us in the New Testament are so different they cannot be joined together. Having looked at the way in which compassion has become divorced from economic life we need to make quite sure that the corrected course is governed by Agape love and not Eros. If love does have a proper place in the field of economics, then it is vital that the right kind of love is being manifested and not the counterfeit variety.

An important contribution to this subject has been made by Jacques Ellul. In his book *Violence* he has a chapter with the intriguing title "The Violence of Love".[11] His main contention is that love itself is God's violence, and, therefore, physical violence in the cause of justice is unjustified. If we truly love one another, then violence is out of place. But Jacques Ellul is swift to point out that there are two kinds of love, and it is important to know the difference. "We must not forget," he writes, "that there are two kinds of love: Eros, which seeks to possess and dominate, and Agape, which gives—gives itself too. Contrary to a modern idea, Eros is not one of the legs of Agape. The Christians who preach violence in the name of the love of the poor are disciples of Eros and no longer know the Agape of Christ. Only in the light of Jesus Christ's sacrifice of himself can man be compelled to live as man."[12]

An important point he makes about the work of the prophets in the Old Testament is that, while speaking boldly against the rich, they never incite the poor to take justice into their own hands and to use violence. "The prophets," he writes, "always pronounce God's judgment on the rich; they speak the word against the rich, but at the same time they declare that justice is the Lord's and that trust must be placed in him."[13] In the last century and a half we have seen a significant movement in the Church towards a more radical approach to social and economic issues. There were the Christian Socialists in the nineteenth century, men like Charles Kingsley and F. D. Maurice. There was the strong movement amongst Anglo-Catholics led by men like Charles Gore (to whom R. H. Tawney dedicated his book *Religion and the Rise of Capitalism*). More recently we have seen the World Council of Churches becoming increasingly committed to social action, and in setting up the Programme to Combat Racism we have seen them deliberately identifying with those who believe in the use of force to stamp out racism. In South America we have seen the development of so-called liberation theology, which has come in for criticism from Pope John Paul II. Most conspicuous of all has been the domination of this century by Marxist ideology, which has always been committed to the use of force and revolution to achieve its ends.

One of the major differences between communist ideology and Christian ethics is found in their view of means. Communism stands squarely for the indiscriminate use of means, fair and foul, to bring about the overthrow of the old society and its replacement by the classless society. But generally speaking Christians believe that both the means and the end need to be ethically correct. Jacques Ellul writes, "I do not say that we are forbidden to employ human means. I say that when we do employ them (and we are not condemned for doing so), we take away from the Word that has been entrusted to us all its force, its efficacy, its violence. We turn the Word into a sage dissertation, an explication, a morality of moderation. When we use political or revolutionary means, when we declare that violence will change the social system we are *thus* fighting in defence of the disinherited, our violence demolishes the spiritual power of prayer and bars the intervention of the Holy Spirit. Why? Because this is the logic of the whole revelation of God's action—in Abraham the disinherited wanderer, in Moses the stutterer, in David the weakling, in Jesus the poor man . . . spiritual violence and the violence of love totally exclude physical or psychological violence. Here the violence is that of the intervention of the Spirit of God . . . it is not authentic spiritual violence unless it is only *spiritual* violence."[14]

Agape love is the only violence God allows. It is spiritual not physical violence. It is the violence of the death of Jesus, described by Peter in that most poignant of phrases as 'the just for the unjust'. That is the Agape method. Eros would have the unjust dying for the just; only Christian love has the just dying for the unjust'. So the Christian can never entertain the idea of 'the last resort'. Ellul says, "The Christian knows only one last resort, and that is prayer, resort to God."[15] The whole meaning of the violence of love is contained in Paul's word that evil is to be overcome by good (Rom. 12:17–21). That is the way of Agape love.

Ellul's thesis would I think be challenged by Victor Furnish in *The Love Command in the New Testament*. He writes about the need for a 'community of love' to be called into being and which is "summoned to responsible action."[16] But Victor Furnish sees a difference between our Church today and the New Testament Church.[17] He sees this in two main respects. In the first place eschatology in the New Testament Church was a future expectation, whereas today "the eschatological now is now". And in the second place, "In most parts of the world the Christian community is no longer a persecuted minority", and so it is no longer easy to distinguish between the Church and the world. Victor Furnish seems from this argument to infer that the kind of ethical restraints that Jacques Ellul pleads for on the basis of the statements in the New Testament, that is the whole concept he propounds of the 'violence of love', are inappropriate today for the two reasons already stated. One must challenge his statement about the Christian community no longer being a persecuted minority. I would have thought there is some evidence to the contrary, namely that most of the Church today is a minority, and a large part of it is being persecuted. In fact the circumstances in which we now live are remarkably similar to the New Testament era. And, secondly, while it may be true that eschatology has a rather different application today, our society is becoming increasingly concerned about the future, and apocalyptic vibrations are being felt more and more. In other words, what the New Testament writers contribute on the theme of love is increasingly relevant to our society, not least because it was so relevant to theirs. The non-violent language of the New Testament is the language of true love. It was Agape to a world dominated by Eros, experiencing the same kind of violence and condoning it just as ours does.

We need to look so at love as it relates to politics. Democracy and the politics which goes with it are not doing very well at the present time. One of the main reasons for this is that government can only be sure of getting into power by promising popular policies. People will not necessarily vote for right policies; but they will invariably vote for popular policies. But the more radically society gets into trouble, the more radical the remedies need to be, and that means either that the wrong party gets into power, or the party which can somehow cleverly sugar the pill so that the unpopular policies are disguised. It has become axiomatic in most democracies that politicians are dishonest; they cannot be trusted by the electorate. Thus democracy increasingly gets a bad name for itself. All ideologies share the same fate. They invariably fail to deliver the goods. They start off with initial enthusiasm. They are prepared to put up with much suffering and inconvenience to achieve their ideals. But they all end up in various forms of disillusionment. Communism itself has failed to construct the utopian society. Socialism has degenerated into small-mindedness. It has fallen from its lofty ideals (many stemming from Christian convictions). It has become a soul-less exercise, a device for spreading greed more equitably. In some countries, the trade unions have become the ruling class. Like the barons, kings and industrialists before them they control society. Ronald Higgins has put it, "In the global perspective organised labour has come close to joining the ruling classes."[18]

For many of the great Christian reformers, the normal democratic processes were the proper sphere in which their ideals could be implemented. In this they were right. But those were the days before the universal franchise which characterises our modern democracies. In a sense we need to rise above party politics. Hans Kung writes about the need to be "neither right nor left" nor to mediate between the two; but rather to "rise above them; above all alternatives, all of which Christ plucks up from the roots. This is his radicalism; the radicalism of love which in its blunt realism is fundamentally different from the radicalism of an ideology."[19] He goes on later to describe Jesus' attitude to politics and social action. "Jesus then was not a naive enthusiast in economic matters, making a virtue of necessity and adding a touch of religion to poverty. Poverty may teach men to pray, but it also teaches them to curse. Jesus glorifies poverty no more than sickness; he provides no opium. Poverty, suffering, hunger are misery, not bliss. He does not proclaim an enthusiastic spirituality which suppresses all thought of injustice or provides a cheap promise of consolation in the hereafter. On the other hand, he was not a fanatical revolutionary wanting to abolish poverty by force overnight and thus mostly only creating more poverty."[20]

Basically Christianity is not an ideology. Jesus did not come to present a new set of ideas to us. He came to show us the meaning of love. He revealed what love is. He manifested love. The secret of his revolution was not the love of power but the power of love. Neither violence nor politics can bring in the Kingdom of God. One is not saying that Christians should not get involved in politics nor join the armed forces. On the contrary Christians should become deeply committed to and involved in society. The salt is not doing its job when it is in the salt-cellar, but when it's in the food. But the Christian cannot see in either the use of violence or the inevitable compromises of politics God's purposes being fully enacted.

One of the most helpful books written on this subject has been written by the two famous Roman Catholic leaders, Cardinal Suenens and Cardinal Camara. Towards the end of the book, they exhort charismatics (who are traditionally not over-enthusiastic about social issues), "Let us show the world together that the true love of God is so abundant that it must overflow into love for neighbours."[21] This is another way of saying "do not separate the two commandments." In another moving passage they pray "Grant that our brothers the rich may understand that gold has no money power in the Beyond, that in the land of eternity love alone is accepted as authentic currency."[22]

Jesus taught the importance of this principle in the Sermon on the Mount. For example Jesus said that there were circumstances in which love for one's neighbour should take precedence over love for God (Matt. 5:23, 24). Spicq comments, "It is perhaps surprising to realise that the duty of loving one's neighbour seems to prevail over duty toward God."[23] He goes on to say, "Agape is an active and effective love operating with a singular tenderness . . . love of neighbour requires as total a renouncement as does love of God."[24] In the Sermon on the Mount Jesus gave practical examples of what that renouncement might involve us in. It includes the renouncing of our rights (going the second mile); the renouncing of power (giving our cloak away); the renouncing of revenge (offering the other cheek).

Sir Frederick Catherwood has said, "To try to improve society is not worldliness but love. To wash your hands of society is not love but worldliness."[25] One of our most important tasks is to re-introduce the dynamic of the love of God into our society, from which it has been largely separated for hundreds of years. But it must be Agape love. Only that kind of love can work in our society, and its source is in God himself.

12 AGAPE VERSUS EROS—
FROM APOSTLES TO REFORMERS

"It was part of her magic (the witch) that she could make things look like what they aren't."
(The Lion, the Witch and the Wardrobe: C. S. Lewis)

Some people can't stand history. I love it. The next two chapters are historical, so you have been warned. If you can't stand it, then skip these chapters. I hope you won't because this particular history is important to our subject. As we begin to see how in the past the Church has lost its awareness of Agape love or tried to combine it with Eros love, it will help us to understand our present situation, in which the same process is still going on, and to find a way of restoring Agape love in the place of Eros.

The conflict between Agape and Eros has been evident since the very birth of the Christian Church. Since true love is descriptive of the nature of God himself, it is only to be expected that those forces opposing God should seek in every way possible to distort the true understanding of love, and to substitute the word Eros with all that goes with it. It needs to be reiterated that we are using the word Eros in the sense in which Plato and other Greek philosophers used it, not in its more restricted modern usage as a synonym for sexuality. Eros is a whole system of thought, belief and human behaviour which is entirely different from Agape. It comes from a different source and has different goals and aspirations. But Eros is not just different from Agape. The words cannot co-exist. Eros is anathema to Agape. They are locked in mortal combat in the same way that we see 'flesh' and 'Spirit' in Pauline theology. Outwardly Eros seems so attractive. Its pursuit of truth, beauty and goodness appears to be so laudable. It has many adherents, who seem to have splendid characters and aspirations. But Jesus Christ and the apostles would have nothing to do with it.

132

The New Testament writers abstained from using the word Eros. Their united testimony is a remarkable one. Their silence is audible. It is not the silence of ignorance. They knew well enough what Eros meant and how dramatically opposed it was to the revelation they had of the love of God. Whether they were tempted to use it, we shall never know. Whenever in the past, as we shall see, attempts were made to unite Agape and Eros, much of the understanding and experience of love was lost. Agape brooks no rivals. It co-exists with no one. In the Old Testament the greatest sin that God's peoples committed was syncretism. The Bible word for it is idolatry. It is the desire to have the best of both worlds, to worship and serve God and other gods. This is what the Church has constantly been tempted to do in the field of ethics. To have Agape and Eros is impossible. They don't mix. They start from opposite positions and have totally different objectives.

In this chapter I have been helped by Nygren. His critics are legion. But, nevertheless, he has something important to show us. Perhaps if he had not exaggerated some of his positions more people may have listened to and accepted his basic arguments. Gene Outka pays tribute to this Swedish theologian when he says that "few have ignored or been unaffected by his thesis."[1] It is certainly the beginning of the modern treatment of the subject, and nothing as thorough has yet been produced in the field of historical studies.

Perhaps we can simplify our study by seeing it in the light of John's famous phrase—"God is Love" (*ho theos agape estin*, 1 Jn 4:8). John is adamant, God is *agape*. He could so easily have written God is *eros*, and he would have received the plaudits of the Greek world. Their philosophers' heads would have nodded approvingly. But John, in spite of all his exposure to Hellenistic influence preferred the weaker and much more insignificant word *agape*.

But the following centuries were to see the gradual weakening of the clear stand that the apostles made. Slowly but surely Eros gained the ascendancy, until in Alexandria in the third century a teacher called Origen changed the words of John to "God is Eros." The victory of Eros over Agape seemed complete. Since then the battle has swayed one way or the other. Sometimes Agape has been in the ascendancy, sometimes Eros. But the Church has never been completely rid of Eros. It has repeatedly flirted with it. Today Eros, though not called that as such, strongly influences the Church. Origen in his commentary on the Song of Songs wrote, "When the gnostic finds the word Agape in Scripture he should at once understand it as if Eros stood in its place, for that is the reality concealed under the protective disguise of Agape."[2] When Ignatius earlier testified "My Eros has been crucified," he was clearly referring to his sinful human nature, for which the word Eros was appropriate. But Origen interpreted the word as referring to Christ being crucified and, therefore, uses Ignatius as support for his view that God is Eros. Nygren comments on Origen's writings in this field. "They mark for the first time a real synthesis between the Christian and the Hellenistic view of love."[3]

One of the most interesting and revealing encounters in the New Testament was that between Paul and the Greek philosophers in Athens (Acts 17). Paul made no attempt to be conciliatory. He was uncompromisingly Christian in what he said to them. Some might have accused him of being tactless and bigoted. He was not prepared to give way. He recognised that they were "very religious" (v. 22), but spoke of the very things that would have been most unacceptable to them. He spoke of repentance (they were amoral and saw no need for repentance), judgment (they had no concept of that at all) and resurrection (they believed in the immortality of the soul which made resurrection unnecessary, and their whole understanding of the physical body was such that the resurrection of it was not even to be desired). Some laughed, others were polite, but unimpressed. In 1 Corinthians 13, Paul has a similar confrontation with the Eros concept of love. The Christian gospel derived nothing from Greek philosophy, and any acceptance of its premises cannot but compromise Christian truth. Times have not changed. We still have the same enemies of the truth and need the same loyalty to the revealed truth in the scriptures and courage to proclaim it, if necessary, in opposition to the errors of humanism. Eros is the ethical foundation of humanism. Some plants like the beautiful oleander are good to the eye but poisonous to the taste; so it is with humanism; so attractive at first glance, but poisonous when it has been assimilated.

In the Apostolic Age love is primarily seen in two relationships. The first is God's relationship to his people. He loves them. The second follows from it, namely, our relationship to each other. We love one another. Our love for God is eclipsed altogether by God's love for us. When we examine the use of the word *agape* and its verbal form (*agapao*) in the New Testament, there are nine times more references to God's love for us than to our love for God, and nearly as many to our love for one another. Our relationship to God is seen as one of faith and obedience to a loving God. Such an emphasis is very different from the Eros concept of love.

The first period of history for us to look at is long and involved and stretches from the Apostolic Age to the Reformation. During this period, through the influence of some of the Church Fathers, particularly the Alexandrians Clement and Origen, and later still the impact of Augustine of Hippo, we see the gradual decline in the dominance of Agape and its replacement by Eros. In practical terms this means that the biblical emphasis on the love of God is reversed. Instead 'the love of God' becomes much more our love for God than God's love for us. Augustine called this *caritas*. His influence was to dominate the centuries that followed, and still does today. His most famous saying was *dilige, et quod vis fac*, which is usually translated "Love and do what you want." Many today understand this as referring to our love for our neighbour; namely that our behaviour towards one another should be governed by the one rule of love, so that provided we are loving towards others we can do what we want. But that was not what Augustine had in mind. He was referring to our love for God, which to him was the determining factor in all ethical questions.

For example, one of the most famous of Augustine's sayings was "If you want to know a person ask him what he loves." He meant by this that love for God is the most important factor in life and it is this love for God that determines everything else and tests the real quality of a person's life. Alas, it was later to be used as a justification for that most unholy enterprise, the Crusades, and that most wicked institution, the Spanish Inquisition. So it was taught that the most loving thing to do for God to a heretic is to torture him so that he returns to the faith. The most loving thing I can do for God is to restore the Holy Land and rescue it from infidels. Love for God became the justification for some of the most inhumane treatment of people, the torturing to death of men and women and the putting to the sword of whole cities.

We need to remember that the Greek culture into which the Christian gospel was to be poured had been intensely cultivated by Eros-religion. Eros was the word used to describe men's religious longings. It was as intensely a religious word as it was philosophical. It summarised the religious expectations of the Greek world. It expressed a universal longing for salvation. But Greek salvation began in the heart of man. Eros describes man's longings for God. The root of man's problems was not, as the Old Testament taught, his sinfulness, but his humanity. His salvation lay in his being released from his body and all its concomitant restrictions in order to soar up to heaven. Eros sees man's basic urge as being like a balloon filled with hydrogen and ready by its very nature to rise up to the clouds. But it is held to the earth by guy-ropes and bags filled with sand. So the problem is solved by casting off the guy-ropes and dropping the bags of sand one by one. The balloon rises serenely and naturally. Eros sees man as immortal or heaven-bound. Only his humanity restricts him. Cast off that humanity and all will be well. Man's salvation lies within himself.

But the Christian gospel of Agape is totally different. It does not take this optimistic view of man's inherent goodness. Rather it sees man as hopeless and helpless, completely incapable of saving himself. Far from having an immortal and imperishable soul, he can by negligence lose his soul. His deliverance does not come through release from the body but from God, who became man in order to deliver us not so much from the prison of the body as from bondage to sin. Christians believe in the resurrection of the body and the essential goodness of matter. Eros is a religion, whose direction is *man to God*. Agape is *God to man*. Eros lifts man up to God. Agape describes God coming down to man. Eros, far from being a description of sensual love (as it has now become), is a religion which delivers man from his senses and takes him to the real world of heaven. Eros is a kind of spiritual gravity, only in reverse lifting man up to heaven to receive his deserts, acceptance as a divine being. Agape is God coming down to undeserving and rebellious men to save them from what they deserve, damnation and judgment. Agape upset all the Greek scale of values. The Cross, as Paul put it, was for the Greeks foolishness.[4] They could only laugh at it. The Resurrection was unnecessary and the resurrection of the body undesirable. Nygren has a useful table in which he contrasts Eros and Agape.[5]

EROS	AGAPE
Desire of good for the self	Self-giving
Man's effort to ascend	Comes down from above
Man's way to God	God's way to man
Man's achievement	A free gift
Salvation which is achievement	Salvation from God
Egocentric love	Unselfish love
Seeks to gain life	Lives by God's life and, therefore, dares to lose it.
Will to have and to possess, resting on a sense of need	Freely gives and spends for it rests on God's riches
Primarily human love	Primarily God's own love

137

Eros—*contd*	Agape—*contd*
God is the object of man's love	Man is the object of God's love
When it is applied to God is a love fashioned on human love	Agape when it appears in man is a love that takes its form from God's own love
Is determined by and dependent on the quality of its object, its beauty and value, hence it is not spontaneous but 'caused', called forth by the value of its object	Agape is sovereign and independent with regard to its object and is poured out on the evil and the good; hence it is spontaneous and uncaused and bestows itself on those who are not worthy of it
Recognises value in its object and therefore loves it	Loves and creates value in its object

Quell and Stauffer in their study on the word love have another interesting comparison between Agape and Eros.[6]

Eros *is promiscuous*, whereas Agape *makes distinctions*, choosing its object and holding to it.

Eros is *impulsive*, whereas Agape is a free spontaneous will-ful act.

Eros is the love of the *lowly* for the high. Agape is the love of the *high* for the lowly.

Eros uses others to achieve happiness. Agape does good to them.

Agape bears that mark of *particularity* which indicates it comes from a divine source. Agape love is righteous love. It is not legalistic, but neither is it antinomian. Agape's origins lie in the stern morality of the Old Testament, not the amoral liberalism of the Greek and Roman worlds. Because Agape is not impulsive like Eros, but rather has as much to do with the human will as with human emotions, it is something which can be commanded, and frequently is in both the Old and New Testaments. Jesus' summary of the Law was in terms of two commandments to love, and the only new commandment he gave to his disciples was "that you love one another" (Jn 13:34). Agape, in its essential nature, flows *downwards*, God to man. Eros rises *upwards*, man to God. Agape's main concerns are for righteousness and truth. Eros seeks for human freedom and pursues beauty and goodness for their own sake. Eros is hedonistic (pleasure-seeking), Agape desires obedience to the will of God and his glory above all else. It is not surprising in our pleasure-seeking age that Eros is the dominant influence in both Church and world.

When we examine the theologians and saints who have most influenced Christianity in two thousand years we shall see how Greek philosophy has constantly played its part in the background. The Church through its leaders has from time to time compromised the gospel message with injections of Greek philosophy. One aspect of this has been the rivalry between the followers of Aristotle and those of Plato. Thomas Aquinas was the principle influence in the Western world in bringing about the restoration of Aristotelian philosophy—and combining it with Christian thought. Morton Kelsey, particularly in his book *Encounter with God*, has been a modern advocate of Plato in opposition to Aristotle, because of Plato's openness to the world of the spirit. Kelsey claims that Christian convictions about the reality of the spirit world was helped by "some of the most sophisticated thinking the world has ever known".[7] Here he refers to Platonism. He goes on to claim that one of the reasons why the Christian world was able to maintain this belief (in the spiritual or supernatural) "was because Christian convictions had the thought of Plato for a foundation."

But in fact Christianity owes nothing to Greek philosophy, and the invasion of its thought has only proved disastrous when it has taken place. The apostles, to whom was given the supreme revelation of God in Jesus Christ, refused to explain that revelation in terms of Greek philosophy. Because they had to use the Greek language it was expressed in Greek words. The absence of Eros in their vocabulary was, as we have seen, proof that they saw love in a different light from that of the Greek masters of philosophy.

139

The significant difference between Christianity and all other religions does not lie principally in its understanding of the Spirit (although here too its understanding is distinctive) but in its understanding of matter, man and the physical world. In this sense the Incarnation is a much more important doctrine than that of Pentecost and the Spirit. It is true that today Western man has become so materialistic that the evidence for an experience of the spiritual dimension has a special significance. But that should not blind us to the fact that the chief dividing line between belief and unbelief lies somewhere else—in the nature of the incarnate Christ and his call to us to make him Lord. At that point, no Greek philosopher can help us—any more than Plato can really help us to understand the spirit. Again, one has to say that Christian understanding of both spirit and man derive from the Old Testament not from Greek philosophy, and whenever the influence of Greek philosophy has intruded, it has blurred the Christian understanding of God, man and human behaviour.

Nygren has another diagram which helps us to understand the difference between Agape and Eros.[8]

Agape	The Relations of Love	Eros
Fundamental	God's own love	Absent
Used freely	Man's love to man	Used with reservation
Used with reservation	Man's love to God	Used freely
Absent	Man's love for himself	Fundamental

Let me explain the diagram. In the centre column we see the different relations of love—God's love for us, our love for one another, our love for God and self-love. As you can see at every point Agape and Eros differ. Fundamentally, Agape describes God's own love for us. John writes, "In this is love, not that we loved God but that he loved us"

(1 Jn 4:10. But Eros has no place at all, for what is fundamental to our understanding of love.

Next in importance for the Christian is brotherly love.
The ideal and practice of it is enjoined frequently on God's
people in both the Old and New Testaments. Eros, however,
has little to say about it. As far as man's love for God is
concerned, the references to it are few and far between in
the New Testament, but in the world of Eros it is used
frequently. Self-love is totally absent in the Bible but it is
the heart of the Greek understanding of Eros.

On the diagram you will see two arrows. The one points
downwards. Agape begins with God's love for us and comes
down from heaven to earth. That is its direction. Eros
begins with self-love and works its way *up* to heaven.

To be blinded to these crucial differences is to be blinded
to a true understanding of Christian doctrine, particularly
in terms of salvation, and Christian behaviour. Man has no
intrinsic merit of his own, nor ability to save himself or live
righteously. Christian ethics can only be properly understood in relationship to a true grasp of the Christian doctrine
of God and man.

In order to study the period between the apostles and the
reformers we are concentrating on some of the main con-
tributors to the Agape-Eros contest during this long passage
of history.

1. The Apostles

We have already seen that the apostles had a clear and
united view of the important place of Agape in the revelation
to them of God; their total neglect of the word and philosophy of Eros is testimony to their rejection of it. Paul in
1 Cor. 13 confronts the Hellenists. In verse five he says
that *agape* "seeketh not her own" (A.V.). That in a nutshell was the rejection of the Eros concept of love, which
as we shall see Augustine was later to revive. In another
passage Paul opposes gnosticism—"knowledge"(*gnosis*),
he says "puffs up, love (*agape*) builds up."

141

Nygren suspects John of hellenistic influence and accuses him of "particularising" brotherly love in its application to Christians rather than to the world or to one's enemies.[9] It is true that John does not mention our love for our enemies as such, but in his gospel he records so many instances of it, particularly in his description of the final hours of Christ's life on earth that we cannot possibly believe that he did not see love extending all the way as Jesus taught. John's emphasis, particularly in his first epistle, is on love within the Church rather than love for unbelievers. But that is surely a matter of emphasis rather than an essential point of difference between him and, say, Paul and Luke. Luke, of course, is particularly insistent on God's love for the world—the sinners and the outcasts of society. But that does not mean to say that he does not at the same time believe in the importance of brotherly love within the fellowship of believers.

2. Marcion (d. 160)

Marcion's claim to fame is two-fold. So far as this study is concerned he was the first major figure after the Apostolic Age to major on Christian love. In the second place he was the first major heretic. His contribution is interesting. His main thesis, that Christianity is a religion of love, was probably timely. Love was not a conspicuous feature of the Christianity of Marcion's day. Being, probably, the son of a Bishop, he knew the Church well enough. He had success, and gathered a large number of followers because he was saying something that needed to be said. However, the theological basis upon which he built his doctrine was hopelessly adrift and was well and truly demolished by men like Irenaeus and later by Tertullian and Hippolytus. Unfortunately, it seems from the evidence we have that some of the true understanding of Agape was lost in the battle; that the Church to some extent threw the baby out with the bathwater. The primacy of love, in other words, went down the plughole with Marcion's unfortunate theology.

For Marcion God is love and nothing but love. Love was for him, as it was later for Augustine, the centre of Christianity. But he went on to separate, as situational moralists do today, law from the gospel. For him there was no law at all. The God of the Old Testament was a God of law. He tyrannised man, and it was Jesus Christ, another God, who rescued man from that tyranny and set him free from the Law. Paul was the only author of the New Testament who really understood this, so Marcion accepted much of the Pauline literature as the only reliable biblical material. Such an exotic view of God was unfortunately not only disastrous for Marcion and his followers but also for a true understanding of Agape, for in attacking Marcion his opponents attacked Agape also. The result was that the stress on Agape itself became regarded as heresy.

3. Irenaeus (130–200)

Irenaeus was the Bishop of Lyon in France. His most famous writing was against heretics, of whom the chief target at that time was Marcion. In many ways he was the first great Christian theologian after the apostles, and since he had heard Polycarp speak, who himself had known the apostle John and possibly some of the other apostles, he had an interesting and unusual link with the Apostolic Age.

The basis of Irenaeus' understanding of love was that it *gives* rather than *desires*. Thus in his writings he repudiated the Eros concept of love. For Irenaeus God did not create man in order to satisfy his own needs, but to have someone on whom to lavish his beneficence. In answer to Marcion's separating of law and gospel to find room for love, Irenaeus retorted that it is precisely love that binds the two together. He sees this in both the Old and New Testaments and so rejected Marcion's idea of two Gods.

143

Irenaeus' theology was deeply incarnational and so he sees love as coming down from God rather than basically rising up to him.

4. Clement of Alexandria (150–215) and Origen (185–254)

These two men exercised a strong influence on the Church particularly in the East. Origen was a pupil of Clement. Eros received a kind of official re-admission to the Church through these two writers. Alexandria became the centre of religious syncretism, in which Christianity and gnosticism were seen as friends rather than enemies, as partners rather than as mutually exclusive. For Clement the Law was provided for the Jew to bring him to Christ, whereas for the Greeks philosophy was God's provision. This of course contradicts Paul's understanding of it. Clement placed 'mere faith' as the lowest form of Christian experience— above which was Christian *gnosis*. If the husk was 'faith', the kernel was *gnosis* (knowledge). Thus there were first and second class Christians. Clement placed Agape in the highest position of Christian experience—a position which those with 'mere faith' had not yet attained. Only through *gnosis* could they reach the dizzy heights of Agape. We shall see later that the mystics tended to follow similar lines with their 'ladders'. Clement assumed the love of God for us, but put his chief emphasis on our need to love God. His emphasis on loving God was so strong that he virtually left out neighbourly love altogether. In fact in one place Clement spiritualises the word neighbour to mean Christ!

His pupil Origen took over much the same kind of thinking. Unfortunately, we have lost a great deal of Origen's writings; but it would seem from what has been left that Origen took the thought of Clement even further in the same direction. He was dominated by the Eros understanding of love and was one of the earliest inventors of 'ladder theology' which was to dominate the thinking of many of the mystics later. It was Origen who brought the concept of Eros full circle with his statement that "God is Eros."

5. Augustine (354–430)

There is no questioning the remarkable contribution of Augustine of Hippo to Christian theology and literature. His influence was one of the most profound of all Christian thinkers and writers. Nevertheless I believe Nygren is right to blame Augustine more than any other writer for synthesising Agape and Eros, and so ensuring the dominance in effect of Eros to the ultimate detriment of Agape. There is no question that in Augustine's theology the love of God predominantly means our love for God rather than God's love for us. Karl Holl may be a little harsh, but there is some truth in his accusation that Augustine was "one of the corrupters of Christian morality". Augustine's training and background was in Neo-Platonism, and his writings always seem to bear this mark. Although Augustine rightly saw the place of Agape in the doctrine of grace and predestination and gave a high place to Agape, he wanted the best of both worlds and included what Nygren calls the Eros motif alongside the Agape.

For Augustine all love is acquisitive. Conversion to him is seen in terms of love—the changing of the direction of our love from the world to God. Love, in other words, for Augustine, was something that all people share in. What makes love good or bad is not the kind of love, or where it comes from, but who it is directed towards. If it is directed at God it is *caritas* and acceptable; if towards the world and other unworthy objects, it is *cupiditas* and, therefore, false and sinful. Love itself is neutral and common to all people.

Although there is something in this, it really does treat love as Eros rather than Agape. It falls into the Eros category, that is its direction is Godward and it is acquisitive, whereas Agape's direction is manward and is unselfish, concerned only with the good of the object of that love.

In his teaching about love for the world he distinguished between *Frui* and *Uti*. *Frui* is a love which *enjoys* its object; *Uti* is a love which *uses* its object. For Augustine both enjoying the world (*Frui*) and using God (*Uti*) were wrong. He wrote, "Good men use the world in order to enjoy God, whereas bad men want to use God in order to enjoy the world."[10] This kind of distinction would be unacceptable to most people today. In many respects we would see nothing wrong in enjoying the world, and many things wrong, especially if we are environmentalists, about using the world. But what we understand by the world and what Augustine understood would be somewhat different so we are not being completely fair. Nevertheless the important point is to see that Augustine's preoccupation was with *caritas*, which meant to him man's ascent to God in terms of love, which is the Eros motif rather than the Agape.

One of the most important areas of his teaching was to create a grave misunderstanding in the theology and ethics of love, the unfortunate results of which are still with us. He had no independent place for neighbourly love. To him the two commandments were virtually one. We are to love our neighbour, but really we are loving God in our neighbour. We have seen that the Alexandrian School of Clement took this line also. The thinking behind this is from Eros. Thus Augustine wrote that "Christ does not strictly love us as we now are but loves us in consideration of what we may yet become."[11] He has no room for an unmotivated spontaneous love. Love is acquisitive and so God could not really love the sinner, only the person he would become by the grace of God. If God cannot love the sinner as he is, neither can we. The only object open to us is to love what we see of God in our neighbour. This is Eros love. It is love for the good and the beautiful and rejection of the bad and ugly. But Agape love is love for all men whether they are good or bad, beautiful or ugly. It creates goodness where there is evil. It does not wait until the goodness appears. For Augustine love for one's neighbour is so dominated by his emphasis on love for God that he sees it as a ladder to climb towards God. Thus in effect one is using one's neighbour to enjoy God.

Nygren points out in conclusion that Augustine was building two positions at the same time, which in fact were on a collision course. The collision took place at the Reformation. In his teaching on *caritas* he was building a structure of ethics which the Reformers were going to have to demolish. But at the same time he was building a structure of the grace of God, especially in his controversy with Pelagius, which the Reformers were going to make much use of to confront the Catholic teaching of their day. It was a strange combination.

6. The Mystics

One of the greatest frauds ever perpetrated was the publication of the writings of 'Dionysius the Areopagite' around A.D. 500. Dionysius was supposed to have been the disciple of the apostle Paul mentioned in Acts 17:34. Actually he lived around A.D. 500 and was a disciple of Plotinus and Proclus. Here essentially was Neo-Platonism with a thin Christian veneer. The unknown author's attempt to deceive Christianity was so successful that this spurious work was regarded and revered as genuine for over a thousand years, and enjoyed almost canonical authority as being written by a disciple of Paul. The works of this man were first challenged at the Reformation but not finally shown to be counterfeit until the end of the nineteenth century.[12]

Few frauds have caused such widespread harm as this one. It is particularly relevant to our subject because these writings (four books and ten letters) profoundly influenced the Church's teaching throughout the Middle Ages. They have been described as "The charter of Christian mysticism,"[13] and in the Eastern Churches his works were regarded almost as a *Summa Theologica*. They were one of the foundation stones of medieval theology. The object of these writings was to achieve the kind of synthesis that we have been referring to between biblical truth and Neo-Platonism, or Agape and Eros. The New Testament according to 'Dionysius' was for "simple people", but Dionysius' teaching was the deeper mystical secret wisdom. Eros comes forth from God and is a kind of ecstasy. It is the final union of the soul with God, for "God is Eros." The seekers after this (the first class Christians) had to go through several stages—purification, illumination and finally union. 'Dionysius' tries actually to dispose of Agape, which is embarrassing for his Eros teaching. He taught that Eros is more divine than Agape.

The sixty-four thousand dollar question is how could the Church be so taken in by this kind of teaching and deceived by such fraudulent writing? The only reasonable answer is that by this time the Church had so wandered from the scriptures and had been so taken over by the Eros concepts of Neo-Platonism that it was ready to accept this kind of teaching and welcomed it with open arms.

Anders Nygren is critical of the widespread development of mystical theology in this period, which depended a great deal for its acceptance and authority on these phoney writings. But it would be unfair to dismiss mystical theology solely because of its links with the fraudulent writings of this unknown person. I also believe that Nygren is unfair in some of his criticisms. There was much that was good in this period—even if at times it is based on unsound theological premises. Bernard of Clairvaux is a good example of a man deeply influenced by this teaching, whose massive contribution to the Christian Church needs to be recognised. Nevertheless he is at least in some measure a victim of the insidious Neo-Platonism of his day.

This period was dominated by the concept of ladders stretched from earth to heaven. One can trace it back much further to St. Benedict (480–550), for example, who had a ladder of humility with twelve rungs to it. Only at the top is a man ripe for the divine Caritas. Johannes Climacus, a sixth century monk from Mount Sinai, also had a ladder he called the ladder of Paradise. Jacob's ladder (Gen. 28:12) was often the biblical model. Climacus' ladder had thirty steps. The thirteenth was Agape, so there was a long way to go before getting to the top. What might be called 'ladder theology' became increasingly a kind of merit table, like the pop charts of modern popular music. You rose by merit from one step to the next. Nygren is fair in his criticism when he points out that the merit table can only be ascended by grace. Without grace there is no merit. Augustine said, "When God crowns our merits it is nothing but his own gifts that He crowns." Although grace is essential if there is to be merit, there is also no blessedness without that merit.

Nygren has made a clear distinction for us between the medieval concept of grace and the reformed position. "In the former case, grace is the divine assistance man needs in order to be able to ascend to God; in the latter, it is the gracious condescension of God. In the former grace and fellowship with God are two different things, grace is the means, fellowship with God the end; in the latter they coincide; grace is God's gracious will in virtue of which He enters into fellowship with us sinners . . . In the former, grace is the power which sets in motion man's upward-directed love, his Eros; in the latter, it is the same as God's Agape."[14]

7. Martin Luther (1483–1546)

Richard Lovelace has rightly written "Ladders are always intimidating."[15] Classical mysticism sets the poor disciple on the bottom rung and bids him climb, albeit by grace. No wonder at times he is tempted to jump off, for the whole thing is so effortful. It is interesting that though Jacob's ladder (at least to Jacob) was stretched from earth to heaven (there was a stressful disciple if ever there was one!), Jesus' ladder seems to be from heaven to earth. Jesus said to Nathaniel, "Truly, truly I say to you, you will see heaven opened, and the angels of God ascending and descending upon the Son of Man" (Jn 1:51). The true ladder was thrown down from heaven for us—like the rope ladders thrown over the sides of ships to rescue people from a ship that is sinking. *But we don't ascend the ladder, the Son of God comes down it himself.* Agape is not the top rung, but every rung is Agape, from top to bottom.

Martin Luther was one of the first to refute 'Dionysius'. He was so steeped in Scripture that he knew that this man could never have been a disciple of Paul or of Christ. Jokingly he says that Paul could never have had such an uninspired disciple. But Luther was above all a ladder destroyer.[16] He turned the whole concept inside out. "Yes," he said, "there is a ladder." But it is not ours to heaven but heaven's to us. *Ipse descendit et paravit scalam* he wrote. In Christ God has come to meet us; Christ is the heavenly ladder and the 'way' furnished by God. Indebted though he was to Augustine in other areas, particularly that of pre-venient grace, Luther knew that the false understanding of love came primarily from the same source.

13   AGAPE VERSUS EROS—
FROM REFORMERS TO PENTECOSTALS

"Love in action is much more terrible than love in dreams."
(Dostoevsky)

We need now to fill the gap between the reformers of the sixteenth century and the pentecostals of our own day. If some are still wondering why we need to go on looking at past history, especially when we are considering such a practical subject as love, I hope they will see how important this study is. Through it we should be able to understand more clearly our present position, the true meaning of Agape love, and where false ideas have originated. The debate is still much the same, and so are the issues. But it is vital for us to understand what these issues are. We can learn much from the past when we are able to see the way the arguments have gone and the outcome of them. It is more difficult to do this in the thick of the contemporary debate.

The Reformation was a watershed, and the periods which followed it are not easy to assess even centuries later. Before the Reformation, Christendom was reasonably united. There was the East-West divide, but there was a coherence about the Christian Church in what it believed and how it behaved which was shattered by the Protestant Reformation. At the same time the new thought, or Renaissance, had a profound effect. Anders Nygren's *Agape and Eros* ends with his treatment of Martin Luther, but that was by no means the end of the story. We shall divide this period into five main streams of spirituality, and see how they have related to the Agape v Eros debate.

1. Pietism.
2. Evangelicalism.
3. Christian humanism.
4. Christian radicalism.
5. Charismatic Christianity.

151

1. Pietism

This word can be used in two ways. First, in the historical sense to describe a movement in the Lutheran Church which was to affect other Churches also. But secondly, it is now used almost exclusively in a derogatory sense to describe Christians who have little or no social conscience and are primarily concerned about so-called 'spiritual matters'.

When the word was first coined in the seventeenth century it was not chosen by the Pietists themselves, but was a label stuck on them derisively by their opponents and critics. The Pietist movement was started in the seventeenth century by a German called Jakob Spener (1635–1705). It began (like other revival movements) with a call to revivify the Lutheran Church. When Spener was living in Frankfurt he started what he called the *Collegia Pietatis*, which was what we today would probably call a prayer meeting. He was a pioneer in giving the laity an active role in the Church and this (as it still does even today) offended the clergy, who opposed him openly. His emphasis was on the inner religious life of the individual and has had a deep and on the whole beneficial effect not only on the Lutheran Church, but on the whole of Protestant Christianity.

Spener's movement was a reaction against cerebral Christianity. Pietism was to continue in the Moravians, led by men like the Count von Zinzendorf; Methodism, led by John Wesley; the Holiness movements; the great revivals associated with men like Charles Finney, D. L. Moody and R. A. Torrey; and the Keswick movement. In the Scandinavian Churches its influence can be seen in the revival movements, the so-called 'inner-missions' and men like Grundtvig in Denmark and Ruotsalainen in Finland. Their sentiments are enshrined in the hymns of men like Paul Gerhardt and Charles Wesley. The modern pentecostal and charismatic movements also have their roots in this tradition.

But the spring from which these waters came was unquestionably the mystics of the medieval church. John

Wesley himself took a great deal of trouble to get some of their writings translated and published in England. He acknowledged his debt to them. It would not be amiss to label all these movements as Protestant mysticism.

But how did this relate to the Agape–Eros debate? What the Reformation did was to restore the Agape principle, that love is mainly that which comes down from God rather than something that rises up to him. Mysticism tended to be confused about this. At its best it emphasised God's love for man—and man's response in faith and obedience. But at its worst it made people so concerned with their own inner life that they had little or no regard for the community or the social needs of people. Because of the particular emphasis of the reformers on Justification by Faith, Prevenient Grace, and man's sinfulness (or as Calvinists would say, depravity), the whole importance of the love commandment, as it relates to people and their love for each other, tended to be ignored or weakened. Some of the reformers, particularly Luther, questioned whether people were capable of love, in spite of the many references to it in the New Testament. The over-concentration on the love of God for man and man's response to it inevitably led to the weakening of the commandment to love one's neighbour. The reformers secured the truth that the love of God is Agape love rather than Eros love, although as Nygren points out they never used the Agape–Eros terminology. But in effect they narrowed the concept of love unnecessarily.

One aspect of the post-Reformation period was the slow but irrevocable development of a social conscience. The tendency to minimise the second commandment was gradually overcome, until today, at least in some areas of the Church, the pendulum has swung so far in the opposite direction that the Church is in serious danger of neglecting altogether the first commandment and separating the commandment to love one's neighbour from its source in God's love for mankind. Thus the two commandments have again been separated.

Pietism played an important part in bringing this about. It is true that pietism tended to stress individual piety. But if we apply the word pietism to them as it is now understood it is a libel. For pietism *was* concerned about the social implications of the gospel in a way that mainstream Protestantism at that time was not. The Count von Zinzendorf was Spener's godson and much influenced by him. It was the Count who set up the famous community at Herrnhut in Saxony, which Wesley visited in 1738, the year before his heart-warming experience. The Methodist revival was extremely 'groupy'—and, although its main impact was in the earliest period of the Industrial Revolution, it had a clear and undoubted social concern which has continued ever since in Methodism.

It is wrong for us to think that pietism and social concern were or are necessarily mutually exclusive. In fact they have often flowed together, and only in the more extreme and immature areas were they divorced from each other. We must not forget that mysticism flowed and flourished from monastic centres which were the welfare state of their day, and from a society which had a real social concern, albeit in the straitjacket of feudalism. When feudalism broke up, the gap was hard to fill, and in some senses has never been filled adequately. It was this absence of an adequate social structure which contributed largely to the horrendous effects of the Industrial Revolution, sweated labour, child exploitation, and the inability of society to deal with the mounting casualties of the system. Here was the seed-bed of socialism, which in its earliest years was motivated by Agape love but was increasingly taken over by those motivated by Eros. This meant that social concern was increasingly secularised and dominated in the end by humanism and outright atheism.

Medieval mysticism, which at first glance seems so remote from socialism, was steeped in community consciousness. And it is no accident that the first trade union martyrs were Methodists living in Tolpuddle in Dorset.

Pietism, therefore, was an important factor in the bridging

of the gap between the two commandments of love. Brotherly love played a vital part in its development. Some of the various pietistic movements had their equivalents in the Roman Catholic Church and in Eastern Orthodoxy. In both these churches mysticism has continued to play a crucial part, although, particularly in the Roman Catholic Church, some of this has found expression in devotion to the Virgin Mary. There is not time to analyse this in relation to the Agape–Eros conflict, except to say that some of this devotion stems from Eros rather than Agape, and some Roman Catholics are the first to admit it. One wonders whether some at least of this popular devotion would have come into being had there been in Catholicism a properly balanced understanding of Agape. It may be that the absence of that, and particularly of a healthy understanding of Christ's love for us, has been a major factor in the promotion of the devotion to Mary in the Roman Catholic Church.

2. Evangelicalism

Evangelicalism has never been too friendly to pietism. The early Methodists were more persecuted by the evangelicals, particularly the Calvinists, than by the Established Church, which tended more to ignore them. The famous evangelical Rector Walker of Truro would not allow John Wesley in the town, and another West Country parson, Augustus Toplady (1740–1778), the author of the hymn "Rock of Ages", defected from Wesley's influence in 1758 and often made scurrilous attacks on him. Pietism has always tended to be Armenian and that has not endeared it to Calvinistic evangelicalism. Bishop Ryle, the first Anglican Bishop of Liverpool, and a staunch Calvinist, was very antagonistic to the Keswick Convention when it started in 1875. Evangelicals also have been amongst the most aggressive opponents of both the pentecostal and charismatic movements.

Evangelicalism has had a long history, and continues to

grow in its influence. Its roots are deeply founded in the Reformation, so it has tended, with its scriptural emphasis on Justification by Faith and gospel preaching, to reflect the reformers' attitudes to the love commandments, that is to emphasise the first to the detriment of the second. It has tended to individualism and to reflect a conservative attitude to life. It tends also to see love as the fruit of obedience rather than obedience as the fruit of love. Its message and ministry has been marred by a harsh and judgmental attitude to its opponents and those with whom it disagrees. Its greatest danger is legalism, and its stress on law has often deprived it of the attractiveness of love which would have drawn more people to its ranks. Its antagonism to Roman Catholics in previous centuries has been at times a deplorable feature of its witness. Its own inner tensions and squabbles have weakened its testimony.

But throughout the centuries there have been prominent evangelicals who have been men and women of love. Its tendency is still to leave social concern to the radicals, but this needs to be seen in the light of the fact that some of the greatest social reformers in the past were staunch evangelicals. Particularly one remembers the so-called Clapham Sect and men like William Wilberforce (whose Bill in Parliament abolished slavery) and the Earl of Shaftesbury.

Richard Quebedeaux in his book *The Young Evangelicals* has shown how rapidly modern evangelicalism is changing.[1] One important aspect of this is the increasing commitment to social action, which was reflected for instance in the Lausanne statement in 1974. It is probably true to say that *some* of the leadership is moving in that direction, but the overwhelming evidence shows that evangelicalism, being such a culturally conservative body, still largely reflects the traditions of the past and a suspicion of anything like socialism or communism. The Bible Belt is still an unshakeable citadel of orthodoxy and regards changes such as these as evidence of defection rather than divine inspiration. Its understanding of God's Agape love and its faithfulness in preaching it, has been the most glorious feature of its witness.

3. Christian Humanism

What we have seen in the past, namely the attempt by some of the Church Fathers to harmonise Christian and Greek thought, was nothing to what happened at the Renaissance when Europe was flooded with humanistic literature and humanist teachers, who claimed Christian authority for what they were teaching and doing. The effects of this are still with us.

One of the most important influences at the Renaissance was a Florentine called Marsilio Ficino (1433–99). In some senses he was the father of Christian humanism, and it needs to be remembered that his teaching was accepted by the Church which ordained him and made him a Canon. He was an unashamed disciple of Plato and also the teachings of the Neo-Platonists. In his *De Religione Christiana* he synthesised Christian and Greek mysticism. But the importance of Ficino is the new emphasis he put on *man* in his temporal existence. Here was one of the seeds of what we shall later see is the modern cult of personalism. Nygren comments, "For Ficino . . . man is made, in a way such as never before, the centre of the universe. In a word it is a question of the human God."[2] In his "Letter to the Human Race," Ficino begins with the exhortation "Know thyself, O divine race in mortal dress." It is the human god whose worship he proclaims. Selfism triumphed, and since then it has spread throughout Christianity, undermining and poisoning much of its message and life.

Mr. Blackham, Director of the British Humanist Society, in a book called *Humanism*, says quite candidly "Christianity was in principle irreconcilable with Greek philosophy as faith is with reason or the human with the divine."[3] He is right in the first statement, wrong in the last two, and therein lies the difference between Christianity and humanism. As Christians we can say that Christianity is irreconcilable with Greek philosophy in part because the human and the divine are *reconcilable*—and reconciliation has come through the incarnation and through the Cross, which the humanist, like the Greeks of Paul's day, regards as folly.

Humanism remains the most subtle of counterfeits. Christian humanism, as it relates to our study of love, has always been an Eros system and has little place for the Agape concept of divine love.

4. Christian Radicalism

The roots of Christian radicalism go back also to the Reformation but are not to be found in the reformers themselves. The word radical means getting to the roots, and the term is used today to describe those who are looking for changes in society, its traditions and structures, so as to facilitate social justice. The Reformation was a time of radical social change and the shifting of power. Martin Luther and others, involved as they were in radical theological change, were arch-conservative when it came to attempts to bring about what we today call revolution. Luther sided strongly with the forces of law and order against the social radicals of his day. His doctrine of the two Kingdoms is not easy to understand because of its subtlety. But to be fair to Luther he did seek to make love the heart of all his ethics. I am grateful to Gordon Rupp, an authority on Luther, for his comments in a letter to me: "We have to think of Luther not as a theorist but as one writing in the very narrow and small scale context of his Wittenberg and Germany, but it is quite clear to him that God rules the whole of human life, the spiritual Kingdom of Christ and the word and the earthly Kingdom of natural man where the secular magistrate has authority. But it is all important that there is only one rule of God and this is always in terms of the great commandment of love."[4]

It is not surprising, therefore, that modern communism does not turn to Luther for its model, but to Thomas

Müntzer, who was hailed by Marx's colleague Engels as the apostle of the real People's Reformation. The Müntzer records are now lodged in the Lenin Library in Moscow. This man, whom Gordon Rupp calls "the Saxon Guy Fawkes", was a revolutionary par excellence.[5] But there were others, also, and the Anabaptists, Quakers and other smaller groups were pioneers of Christian radicalism. Moltmann in his book *The Open Church* writes that we need to look closely again at the 'second division' reformers. Moltmann writes, "It seems to me that the future of the Reformation does not lie on the right wing with its Catholic tendencies but on the so-called left wing . . . They were called 'Schwärmer' (fanatics) and 'baptists' and 'sectarians' and they were rejected. But they sought in truth 'the radical Reformation'. After the 'reformation of doctrine' through the gospel they wanted the 'reformation of life' through love."[6]

Christian radicalism finds many expressions today. On the far Left of the Church it is associated with so-called liberation theology[7] and the radical social activism of the World Council of Churches. It has vocal supporters in all Churches. On the far Right it finds expression in the new independent Churches of the Third World, many of which are pentecostal, the non-denominational Churches of the evangelical word and of the charismatic movement. In Britain they are mostly called 'House Churches'.[8] Christian radicalism has also found expression in the establishment of Christian communities. Some of these, like the Baptist one at Bugbrooke in England, have followed the pattern of other long established radical communities like the Hutterites.

But the changes in society in the last 250 years have created the market for Christian radicalism. I am referring to the Industrial Revolution, colonialism, and the great World Wars. It was the Industrial Revolution which created new forms of inequality and social problems which are now present on a global scale; it was largely colonialism (allied with the iniquitous slave trade) which made the race issue critical, and the two World Wars created as we have seen new questions of conscience. The Church during this period moved so slowly from its agrarian culture that it was unable to adapt to these radical social changes or to put forward Christian answers to them. Coupled with that has been the decline of the influence of the Church in this period. The rapid progress of science especially in the twentieth century has also put great pressure on the Church to explain itself, which it has largely failed to do.

It has been all these kinds of changes that have created the milieu for Christian radicalism. At least there are some who are showing a concern for the world's social and economic problems, the race issue, the issues of justice and the inequalities between the West and the Third World, and suggesting Christian solutions. That these views have fallen on deaf ears is also true. The bulk of the Western Church is still impervious to all this.

But what has this to do with love? All that we have already said about the changes in the world needs to be matched with what has happened in the Church concerning its beliefs. The last 150 years or so have shown a slow but seemingly irrevocable retreat from the old truths, and from confidence in the veracity of the Bible. One of the main ways by which Christians maintain their rootedness in Judaism rather than the fountains of Greek and Roman thought, lies in their acceptance of the scriptures. But throughout this period there has been a move away from the scriptures and an increasing openness to other avenues of truth, and it is in the area of Christian radicalism that this is most apparent. The result has been that Christian radicalism, although in essence expressing Christian concern and compassion for the poor and underprivileged, and setting forward radical remedies for the world's problems, has in fact drifted further and further away from the Christian foundations upon which its message should have been based. To put it simply, in rightly pressing for a real expression of the second commandment, it has cast itself adrift from the first. In concentrating on the importance of loving one's neighbour it has neglected the need to love God. Works have prevailed over worship, the social over the divine.

If love is to be genuine then it has to be rooted in God, and that means also that it has to come from the revelation of God that we have in the Old and New Testaments. Much that one sees in Christian radicalism is no different from humanism. There is little uniquely Christian about it. This is why it has had such little effect on the Churches, and has been almost totally ignored by the world. Christian radicalism needs to go back to its Christian roots. Its desire to demonstrate Christian love is evident. But if that love is not rooted in God himself it easily becomes Eros rather than Agape.

5. Pentecostalism

Pentecostalism, and its sister movement in the historic Churches—the charismatic movement—is a comparative novelty. It has still to celebrate its first centenary. Its longest roots stretch down to the Pietists of the seventeenth century. The inspiration for these movements has always tended to be the revival movements and the holiness emphasis on a second experience of grace. In the Roman Catholic renewal movement there seems to be a recovery of elements of the mystical tradition of the Church; and this as we have seen was itself one of the roots of pietism.

Although evangelicalism has traditionally been suspicious of pentecostalism and in some instances strongly opposed to it, pentecostalism has always tended to be strongly biblical, and mostly fundamentalistic in its interpretation of the scriptures. In the past it has been anti-Catholic and anti-intellectual. The charismatic movement is somewhat different, as one would expect. It is not particularly fundamentalistic, though biblical in its teaching. It is certainly not anti-Catholic and broadly speaking not anti-intellectual, although an element of it sometimes is.

There are some features of pentecostalism which suggest

161

that love has not been one of its strong points. Its fissiparous tendencies are well known. It has split into innumerable Churches and groups, often competing with one another. Its unity is fragile. Its attacks on the other Churches and its unwillingness to co-operate with them is a feature of its life. Its understanding of the Agape love of God has been clear and figures prominently in its evangelism, and accounts in some measure for its success and growth. It has not presented the kind of judgmental gospel which is still to be heard and seen amongst some evangelicals.

Pentecostalism has often been criticised for its lack of social concern, which is not wholly just. Its remarkable success in areas of society which the rest of the Church has largely failed to reach is evident, and social and economic changes have taken place as a result. But in the sense in which the term 'social action' is used today, pentecostalism has tended to be largely indifferent and at times openly hostile to it, at least in the West. There is a different story to tell in the Third World as Walter Hollenweger has documented so well. Dr. Hollenweger has written a short but deeply moving account of the Kimbanguist Church in Zaire which is a striking example in our century of a Church which expresses its life in concern for the social as well as the spiritual and has suffered as a consequence.[9]

The charismatic movement, because of its more diffuse nature, and because its roots are much more widespread than the pentecostal, has proved more open and concerned about the issues raised by the Christian radicals. But there are some leaders, and I would count myself as one of them, who believe that a greater concern and commitment to the issues of social and economic justice is needed. The charismatic movement cannot be a vehicle of the love of God if these matters are left to the economists and politicians.

14 MRS. BERGMEIER'S BABY

"After all," said the Duchess vaguely, "there are certain things you can't get away from. Right and wrong, good conduct and moral rectitude have certain well-defined limits."

"So for that matter," replied Reginald, "has the Russian Empire. The trouble is that the limits are not always in the same place."

(From Reginald H. H. Munro)

Mrs. Bergmeier was a German woman who was put in a concentration camp by the Russians at the end of World War 2. She was separated from her husband, who was a POW in Wales, and the rest of her family were in Germany. How was she going to get out of the camp and be reunited with her husband and family? She found an unusual way out of her dilemma. She discovered that pregnant women were regarded by the Russians as a liability in the camp and were invariably sent home. So she duly obliged the lust of a prison guard, was released and had a happy reunion with her husband. Mr. Bergmeier was very understanding, and the baby when it was born was accepted with joy by them all. A visit to the confessional was unnecessary because nothing had been done wrong. At least according to situation ethics.

This example of sacrificial adultery is quoted by Joseph Fletcher in his book *Situation Ethics*. It is perhaps the most famous and apt example of what this ethical system teaches. Love for the situationalist is the *only* norm of human behaviour, and the most loving gesture Mrs. Bergmeier could make was to allow herself, for the sake of her husband and family, to become pregnant by the prison guard. Or was it? This chapter is about situationalism, although one is tempted as we shall see to call it 'concentration camp ethics'.

As the reader will become increasingly aware I take a

hard line on situation ethics. In doing so I would not want anyone to think that those who expound this position are lacking in care or concern, or that they are advocating lawlessness or moral anarchy. I am not impugning their motives. They believe themselves to be expressing the ethics of Christ himself. Nevertheless I believe they are greatly mistaken in the views they hold. It is, as I understand it, the re-assertion of 'law' which this age most obviously needs, a message which has never been popular, and is so quickly dismissed in our day. I do not believe that situation ethics helps modern man to answer the many serious moral questions which have been raised by our society; on the contrary this concept of ethics tends to confine him in the grey areas of decision-making, when more of the black and white needs to be seen. Of course there are exceptional cases, and it is easy enough in citing them to knock the legal position. Nevertheless, as I see it, the Law is much more than moral advice which one can take or leave; in the majority of cases it should determine the moral issue once and for all.

Situationalism is not the prettiest of words. It's the kind of word that sociologists invent. But we are stuck with it. I used to play games when I was a boy with someone whom I found impossible to beat. Whenever I started winning he would change the rules to his own advantage. Situation ethics can be a bit like that. It is a kind of do-it-yourself ethical kit. You make it up as you go along, and this perhaps explains its popularity. But it is a real mixture, and we shall have to do some careful sifting, for there is much to commend in it, as well as much to criticise.

In the first place it follows such diverse characters as Marcion and Augustine in seeking a reconstruction of ethics which restores the primacy of love to Christianity. For situationalists 'love only is always good' and 'love is the only norm'. Although, as we shall see, these are altogether inadequate propositions, nevertheless they are an attempt to bring us back to love-centred ethics, and that is wholly commendable. Fletcher has unusual ways of describing this love. He calls it, "agapeic calculus", or "the strategy of love". Another famous exponent of this view of ethics is Dr. J. A. T. Robinson, author of *Honest to God*. In another book he has stated, "In Christian ethics the only pure statement is the command to love: every other injunction depends on it and is an explication or application of it . . . apart from this there are no unbreakable rules."[1]

Second, situationalism is unreservedly for 'people'. It is concerned about people rather than things. Fletcher accuses the legalist of being a *'what* asker' (what does the Law say), whereas the situationalist is a *'who* asker' (who is to be helped).[2] A clear concern for people is a thoroughly commendable emphasis in this system of ethics. H. R. Neibuhr wrote that "God nowhere commands love for its own sake."[3] It is for the sake of *people*. Paul Ramsey has called situationalism 'personalistic', and I believe this is something to be thankful for rather than to condemn. For this is clearly part of the ethics of Jesus, and was a widespread emphasis not only in his teaching and life, but in the life of the Early Church.

Third, this school of thought for all its faults is clear and precise. I give it full marks for lucidity. This cannot always be said of modern moral theologians, who tend to be obscure and confusing. People were able to understand the ethics of Jesus, but found the complicated casuistry of the scribes and pharisees infuriatingly obscure. In Joseph Fletcher and John Robinson the situationalists have two clear-headed scholars, who say what they mean, and mean what they say.

Fourth, there is an honesty about Fletcher's approach which is refreshing. It is a notoriously difficult area in which to be transparently honest. Ethics, particularly today, is a veritable minefield. To be really honest is not easy. I believe that situationalism is basically wrong; but at least we can say that it is honestly wrong.

Fifth, the system is a very thorough and timely exposure of legalistic pharisaism, which is still with us, and needs to be confronted as strenuously today as it was by Jesus in his day. Fletcher teases the legalists. Didn't Jesus do the same?

Sixth, there is something natural or obvious about situationalism which makes us all, at least in a limited sense, followers of the system. Professor C. F. D. Moule in a letter to me expressed it like this: "It strikes me that many of the critics (of situationalism) forget that what is under discussion usually turns out to be Christian *decision-making* rather than a Christian *system*, and that even the strongest anti-situationalists find themselves driven to make individual *decisions* (whatever their *principles*) situationally."[4] I believe that this is true. Fletcher himself calls it all "The ethic of decision."[5]

Last, situation ethics is realistic. There is nothing simplistic about it. Unlike some Christian ethical constructions, situationalism is very much set in the modern world, and there is no doubt that decisions about right and wrong are harder to make today than at other times in history. Fletcher and others are right to eschew over-simplifications, although as we shall be seeing, their position could in some ways be criticised as just that. Typical of our modern dilemma is the story which Fletcher tells about the beautiful spy he talks with on the plane, who is working for her country in its secret service, and has been prepared to sleep with men in order to discover their secrets. Many Christians would be horrified at such a suggestion. But would it be any different if instead she had lied (as all spies have to as part of their trade), or slit someone's throat, as James Bond does so often without a trace of guilt? I am not suggesting that adultery is ever God's will. I am only suggesting that it is much harder today to make ethical decisions. Sex and politics have always been mixed in one form or another. We have only to remember Henry VIII and his political intriguing. Perhaps Fletcher has been reading too much Ian Fleming, but the world of 007 is not a neat and tidy one, and we are foolish if we think there will always be easy and slick answers to all ethical problems.

So much for the commendable features. On no account should we minimise the importance of situation ethics. It is probably true to say that, although most people in the world have never heard of it, many are adherents to it. It is probably ethical code number one. In the book *Norm and Context in Christian Ethics* (edited by Gene Outka and Paul Ramsey) Christian ethics are divided into three main schools of thought.[6] The three words, principle, rule and virtue describe these schools. Situationalists come under the first category, those who take the view that love has a built-in moral compass—as J. A. T. Robinson describes it—to intuitively home in on ethical questions. The second view is taken by men like Paul Ramsey, V. A. Damant and Roman Catholic moral theologians, which is the assertion of rules as broadly speaking definitive in moral issues. The third view is that the disposition of the agent cannot be left out. This is the view of Paul Lehmann and to some extent Bonhoeffer. I have listed in the Notes the main proponents of these views.[7] Actually, Frederick S. Carney puts the three together, and I find his approach the most satisfactory. Perhaps the problem we have created for ourselves is in isolating love from its partners. This is the major thesis of this book.

But we need now to describe exactly what situation ethics is. Fletcher summarises his teaching in the form of six propositions, and I will list these now before we go on to comment on them.

1. Love only is always good.
2. Love is the only norm.
3. Love and justice are the same, nothing else.
4. Love is not liking.
5. Only the end justifies the means, nothing else.
6. Love's decisions are made situationally, not prescriptively.

There it is in its stark simplicity. Fletcher himself describes his teaching in a book to which he is a contributor and edited by Gene Outka and Fletcher's chief critic Paul Ramsey.[8] Here is what he says: "Ours is a revolutionary era, one in which the change that is a continuous feature of civilisation is abnormally rapid due fundamentally to the 'New World' of thought and practice opened up by science and technology. Theologising is never carried forward in a vacuum. Theology works in a socio-cultural context just as all human enquiry and reasoning do. And in sensitive response to the world revolution, a new Reformation is taking shape—new theology, new evangelism (like Harvey Cox 'doing the truth' rather than Barth's 'proclaiming') and new morality."[9] He goes on to explain what this new morality is: "Only love is absolute, and it is this anchorage which makes it possible for situationalism's relativisation of all rules to be genuinely relativistic, and not merely chaotic and random and sheerly unrelated . . . *we could for love's sake break any of the commandments* . . . most of the people who affirm and recite the Ten Commandments are hypocrites—especially if loving concern is really the first-order commitment in their ethical approach." Then he concludes with the statement, "*It is better to be a hypocritical legalist than an honest one*," which is a typical statement of a situationalist.

Having stated what situation ethics are, we need now to turn to comment on them. We shall begin with a few general criticisms before looking at each of the six propositions one by one.

In his book Fletcher accuses Christians of being obsessed with sexual ethics. This is a little unfair in the light of the numerous mentions of sex he makes in his own book. Mrs. Bergmeier's baby is typical of his use of illustration. The fact of the matter is that we live in a world that is obsessed with sex, the ethics of which are continually being debated. Nor is it much good decrying this, as sex does have a large and determinative influence on the lives of everyone. Where, however, Fletcher obscures the subject is when he uses his other favourite illustrative device, the concentration camp situation. When the two go together (as with poor Mrs. Bergmeier) you have the argument well and truly set up.

But it is not helpful to treat all ethical matters as if they are the same. One has to admit that there are some areas where one is bound to be hesitant in applying immutable principles. The area of war is a good example of this. Issues like pacifism have always divided equally convinced Christians, and it would be impossible from the scriptures or the traditions of the Church to find any opinion which could be used as definitive. But in the area of sexual morality it is different. Both Bible and Church tradition have been unanimous in their views on many areas of sexual ethics. Adultery, for example, is clearly a sin. Of course you can say that modern man knows better. But you cannot say that there has not been a long and continuous view which has been taken by the Church all down the centuries on these issues. To suggest, therefore, that because we cannot be clear on the ethics of war, we cannot on the subject of sexual ethics, is confusing. Some ethical questions have clearer answers than other, and need to be taken on their own merits.

Fletcher sees situation ethics as the ethics of the hour. This is true to the extent that many people, without often being aware of it, are situationalists. It appeals very much to modern man's pragmatism. It seems eminently practical and gives every man a chance of doing his own thing in the ethical field, a kind of ethical do-it-yourself. But is it really what our world needs at the present time? I think not. Some aspects of situationalism would have been appropriate in, say, the nineteenth century when there was an excessive and sometimes harmful emphasis on legalistic ethics. This was the heyday of the legalist whom Fletcher is most anxious to condemn. But we live in a totally different age—one which has largely overthrown law's restraints, an age in which permissiveness is rampant. Antinomianism is every-where strong. In his quest for freedom, modern man questions any moral restraints at all. Situationalism does not condone his licence. Love, for them, is the determining factor, but since modern man has little or no idea of the real meaning of that word this is not much help to him.

It was Paul who spoke of the Law as a custodian to bring us

to Christ. Although that applies in the historical sense to the role of the Old Testament in relationship to the coming of Christ in the New, it can just as much apply today. It is only as the Law of God becomes understood by people that they can begin to grasp why Jesus came and what he did through his life and death. The world needs to hear the Law—with a view to its turning to Christ. A striking modern example of this has been the visits in 1979 of Pope John Paul II to Ireland and the United States. He could so easily amongst the green fields of Ireland have spoken pious words about loving one another. This would have made no impact at all. Instead he said, "Thou shalt not kill," and the whole world press sat up and took notice. It was not terribly diplomatic—but millions got the message. We have to recognise that love is an ambiguous word—kill and adultery are not. When the Pope went on to the United States he did the same thing. Standing amongst what he delightfully called in his broken English the 'skyscroppers' in New York, he cried out, "Thou shalt not covet." It was enough to shake Wall Street and its sacred Dow Jones Index. They got the message all right. "Try to love your neighbour better," would have missed the mark entirely. There is no way our amoral society can grasp the truth if we talk vaguely about loving one another. It all depends what you mean. But everyone knows what unlawful killing and covetousness are.

This leads on to another general criticism of situationalism. Joseph Fletcher (and others for that matter) make a lot of much quoted ethical problems, in order to try to convince us that the law should play little or no part in decision-making. For example, what happens if a man is caught speeding while rushing to a hospital with his wife in the back of the car about to have a baby? Should the law give him a ticket or fine him? What he does not discuss in the book is the fact that although the law is often called "an ass", there is a whole field called equity, which deals with these very situations. The law is not to be enforced to its letter if by so doing injustice is caused. In England, Lord Denning has upheld its principle—namely that laws are not an end in themselves but there to see that justice is done. But what situationalism tends to do is to make a law of the exceptions and to use them to undermine the Law itself. Because there are occasionally situations in which one may have to compare two needs (in this instance the need to preserve life with the need for safety on the roads), it would be ridiculous to say that you cannot have laws at all, only the law of love. Situationalists tend to make new laws out of the exceptions. Karl Barth called this "The case of the curious exception" (*Grenzfall*). Emil Brunner called it occasionalism.[10] But to allow for the occasional exceptions does not give us freedom to overthrow the law.

And finally, I find in Fletcher another kind of dogmatism which only seems to mirror the very legalism he is at such pains to reject. Someone has said that there is nothing so dogmatic as the person who is against all dogma. His propositions have an absolutism about them which seems to contradict his new attacks on the setting up of absolute guidelines to decision-making. One has sometimes to question his discussion of love in the light of his attacks on those he regards as his detractors. He makes very short shrift of them. He obviously dislikes all those whom he calls pious or fundamentalists, and is all too prone to preface his remarks with the words "no serious-minded person" when he must know that there are good and honest people who hold to those particular views. To say that they are not serious-minded is rather unfortunate.

Now we need to turn to the propositions. In each instance, I have given a counter-proposition.

Proposition 1.

Love only is always good.[11] Counter-proposition: *God only is always good.*

The major criticism of this statement is that it tends to make love into God. Many have warned us about this including C. S. Lewis. "The truth," he writes, "that God is love may slyly come to mean for us the converse, that love is God."[12] Actually Fletcher says the same thing in his book, "The Johannine proposition is *not* simply that God is love, but *God* is love with the emphasis with God. The Christian does not understand God in terms of love; he understands love in terms of God as seen in Christ. We love because he first loved us."[13] He goes on to say that "Faith working through love (quoting Paul) is the essence and pith of Christian ethics."

But the version of God presented to us in the writings of situationalists is inadequate. It is impossible to give a true account of *Christian* ethics without a clear vision of God himself. In other words theology and ethics must go together, and although this makes life difficult for the moral theologian, he must always be a theologian as well as a moralist. But the deductions of situationalists sometimes bear little relationship to God himself. There is some examination of the New Testament, but the Old is so neglected one is tempted to wonder if they are not making the same mistake that Marcion did when he condemned the Old Testament as an account of an enemy-god from whom Christ came to rescue us. But this is the tendency of those who relegate the Law to a minor role.

Fletcher goes so far as to say that we should "reject all revealed norms or laws but one command, *to love God in the neighbours*."[14] But there is no such law. It would seem, therefore, that he rejects revealed law and replaces it with one that does not exist. Nygren rejects this concept which is common today and is Fletcher's affirmation here. He puts it like this, "The 'love God in my neighbour' idea has no basis in the gospel teaching; when Jesus speaks of the first and great commandment, and the second as like unto it, he makes two commandments, each with its own scope. Love to one's neighbour is not a special case of love to God, nor is the second commandment a repetition of the first; its addition means that love is now directed to a different object. The neighbour who is to be loved is neither an arbitrarily constructed ideal of my neighbour

172

(as he may one day be), nor God in him, but my neighbour himself."[15]

What is more serious is Fletcher's rejection of the Ten Commandments and the dilettante way in which he expounds the scriptures. He finds, for example, the first commandment "unnecessary" on the basis that monotheism cannot be commanded. So far as 'swearing' is concerned, he writes that "we ought to obey it unless some real good can be gained by violating it." Law is placed firmly under love. "They cannot be partners," he writes, "at best love only employs law when it seems worthwhile."[16] He pleads for an ethic "more radical than Paul or Jesus."

We have already tried to cover the area of the relationship between law and love. But Fletcher never discusses what the prophet Ezekiel meant by the "writing of God's laws on our hearts". And what about the fact that even love is a commandment? In one place he says that "love can make a lie good."[17]

One of the examples which John Robinson discusses in his own book on ethics is that of a politician who lied regarding a relationship he had had with a woman. Some have suggested that he was right to do so to protect his wife and family. What actually happened was that the truth came out and he had to resign, and never again returned to politics. His wife forgave him, and he was able to reconstruct his life and render valuable service to the community. The danger with any system of ethics that puts the major stress on the situation (as in this instance) is that it takes little or no account of the spiritual principles at stake, and does not allow for what God can do either to change the situation, or to bring to good effect the actual telling of the truth, in this instance through the wife's willingness to forgive and to help her husband re-build his shattered life.

But in all this the Holy Spirit also tends to be left out. Fletcher hardly ever mentions the part the Holy Spirit plays in ethics. As we have already noted Oscar Cullmann has something very important to say about this in his book *Salvation in History*. It is worth repeating. He writes, "In

Paulinism the Law is not abolished as the formulation of the divine will. But's its radical fulfilment is possible for the first time only through the *Pneuma* which is received in faith and which impels us to love our neighbour . . . *it is the Spirit that enables us to fulfil the Law.*"[18] Cullmann sees salvation-history as the only explanation of how law remains, yet in some parts (e.g. circumcision) is abolished. The absence of a place for the work of the Holy Spirit is a serious discrepancy in situation ethics.

Proposition 2.

Love is the only norm.[19] Counter-proposition: *God's love is the only norm.*

This proposition standing on its own, is an ambiguous statement because it all depends on what you mean by love. Fletcher's own exploration of the meaning of love does not inspire confidence. His only definition of Agape is weak. He defines it as "goodwill at work in partnership with reason".[20] Michael Ramsey exposed this mistake when he wrote, "It is on a deductive theory from the concept of love, and not upon a full examination of Christ's teaching that the conclusion is being drawn that 'nothing of itself can be labelled wrong.'"[21] Lord Ramsey's integrity as a theologian would lead him to question many of the assumptions which Fletcher makes, tending as he does to work back towards the nature of God from a position of love, when instead it is vital to begin with God and find out about love through what we know about God himself. David Field in his book *The Returns of Love* writes about this, "Replacing all other absolute standards by the single command to love is not only unfaithful to the New Testament teaching, it is also patently inadequate as an unsupported prop for moral vision in the best of us."[22]

Fletcher's understanding of love tends to be rather cold. He actually says, "Calculation is not cruel."[23] On sexual ethics his statements are at times crude. "The Christian ethic," he writes, "is not interested in reluctant virgins and technical chastity."[24] He blames such notions on what he calls "occult accretions", namely romanticism and puritanism. "Sex outside marriage is not wrong unless they hurt themselves, their partners or others."[25] The situationalist ethic as applied to abortion is that "No unwanted or unintended baby should ever be born."[26] Such an extraordinary statement leaves rights entirely in the hands of the parents. God is not consulted at all—neither is the baby for that matter.

John Robinson has a favourite expression—'the bank of experience'. By this he means that decision-making can be arrived at by drawing on our experience. But every situation is different, and many people have to make serious moral choices who have had no previous experience. How can you tell young people to draw on the bank of experience when they don't have much, if anything, in the bank? It is not too difficult these days for a girl to become pregnant on her first date. What experience of life have young people to help them? And what good is it to say to them, "Love is the norm"? The way the word love is used today would be tantamount to a summons to an immediate sex experience.

Proposition 3.

Love and justice are the same, nothing else.[27] Counterproposition: *They are not the same, though they overlap.*

Situationalists are nearly always committed to a clearly defined social gospel. They are normally concerned about justice. Justice is to them love distributed. As you can see from other parts of this book, I am also committed to the same social gospel as they are, but not the same system of ethics, and I do not believe they necessarily belong together at all. A simple indication of the inadequacy of this particular proposition, as it relates to the rest of the situationalist's arguments, is that it is hard to separate justice from the Law. It is true that law does not establish justice but justice establishes laws for its own enforcement and application. Nevertheless, there is a close and important link between the two. You cannot tinker around with the Law on the one hand and try to replace it with love, and at the same time say that love and justice are the same. Of course love and justice have an important and vital relationship, but Fletcher takes it a stage further by saying "They are not partners, they are one and the same, because they both go out to others."[28] Love relates to a whole lot of other things, which equally go out to others, such as truth, charismatic gifts, wisdom, etc. But it is not helpful to say that because of this they are one and the same.[29]

Proposition 4.

Love is not liking.[30] Counter-proposition: *true but irrelevant.*

The difference between loving and liking has often been debated. The old distinction between the two words was that you could love a person but only like a thing. I suppose you could like a person, but the unpardonable use of words was to speak of loving things—like strawberries, for example. I can remember the interminable debates we used to have in order to establish the fact that Christians, although they had to love everyone, were under no obligation to like everyone. There the matter was usually left. This meant that I could actually dislike people, although I still had to love them.

But I have come to the conclusion that the distinction, in relationship to Christian love, is irrelevant. We are perfectly free to like or dislike strawberries or anything else for that matter. That is a matter literally of taste. But the very thought of 'tasting' people like a wine merchant tastes Burgundy or Claret is in itself a departure from the principle of love. Can we really imagine Jesus discussing with anyone whether or not he liked Peter or any of the other disciples? There may be features of people we dislike—their B. O., their accent, their dress or their mannerisms. But to make distinctions between people on the basis of liking or not liking seems to me to be unloving by any description. To say to a person "I love you but I don't like you" is a contradiction in terms. Surely we must like what we love. When we love our enemies, we are not loving their sinful actions or attitudes. We neither like nor love that aspect of them. But we love them as *people*, and that must surely include liking.

Proposition 5.

Only the end justifies the means, nothing else.[31] Counter-proposition: *both means and ends are to be in love.*

Here Fletcher reveals his misunderstanding of the scriptures. For example, he postulates that since God *allows* evil for our good, the end justifies the means.[32] But this would only be true if God *caused* the evil. Again he quotes approvingly Isaiah 4:1 (where it speaks of seven women taking hold of one man to take away their reproach), whereas in the passage there is no comment on the morality of the situation—it is only a statement about what will happen.[33]

In this part of his book, he reserves his most stinging attacks for those whom he calls "petrified legalists". He quotes Lenin approvingly in support of this proposition.[34] One would have thought the architect of the Russian Revolution and Founder of the Russian Marxist State would not be the kind of person one would turn to for advice on morals. The cruellest and most destructive ideology of our century has as one of its most important principles the proposition that the end always justifies the means; hence the creation of a state devoid of any ethical restraints. It is no good Fletcher saying "Love could justify anything." If the means are unloving then love cannot justify them. If, however, they are loving then what's the problem? They don't need justifying by anyone.

177

Proposition 6.

Love's decisions are made situationally not prescriptively.[35]
Counter-proposition: *the situation is only one of a network of factors all of which need to be considered in decision making. The situation is not necessarily the most important, and is often the least.*

One of the constantly recurring themes of the exponents of the new morality is that people prefer the safety and certainty of legalism to the freedom of situationalism. In the book *Brothers Karamazov*, by Dostoevsky the Grand Inquisitor says that most people do not want freedom, they want security . . . they want law not responsibility; they want the neurotic comfort of rules not the spiritual open places of decision-making.[36] This may have been true in the nineteenth century, but we should seriously challenge whether it is a relevant comment on our *present situation*— and if we are to play the situationalist game, we must ask them to keep the rules also. Is our present age one which, according to Fletcher, "wants to lean on strong unyielding rules"?[37] I would have thought the exact opposite is the truth of the matter, that there are more people who are anti-nomian than legalistic and that Fletcher is much of the time confronting a diminishing minority rather than a dominant moral force in either the Church or the world.

I believe John Robinson makes the same mistake, when he writes, "Life would be very much simpler if as a Christian one could say that certain things are in all conditions and for all persons always and absolutely wrong."[38] I would want to reply "Would it?" There is surely a world of difference between knowing what decision to take and actually making it. Which is simpler for a young man or woman—the conviction that sexual intercourse is only permissible within marriage, or the modern view that leaves the door wide open for other kinds of behaviour? It is a difficult way of life in our permissive society for young people to say no when most people around them are saying yes.

178

The situationalists emphasise, as their name suggests, the situation and in this respect are as rigid and dogmatic as the legalists they so quickly scoff at. Situations can and do change. They are never absolute—always a relative factor in decision-making. Take the situation of Mrs. Bergmeier. I know Christians who would have dealt with it differently. They would have said something like this: "The thought of committing adultery is out of the question because God has made this an absolute rule. I must stick by God in this, knowing that he understands and will work everything together for good. I will pray for that will to be done. God's will could be that I stay separated from my family as a time of trial for my good and theirs; since God is faithful he will provide the way out and will see that my husband and my children will be taken care of. Meanwhile I can be a witness by my faithfulness and bring blessing with God's help to people in this camp. My example of patience and forgiveness in a prison situation will bear fruit, as it did with Joseph in the Old Testament and with Paul in the New. On the other hand, God could intervene and change the situation. A new commandant could come who might change the rules and release all married women. Even a 'mistake' might happen and I could be accidentally released because of a typing error," etc. Thus, we should never allow the *situation* to govern our decisions.

Situationalism's most serious error is that it leaves a miracle-working God out of the situation. The possibilities I have suggested are nowhere mentioned in Fletcher's book. On any showing it is better to follow firm laws than the law of slippery situations.

I want to conclude briefly with a few further general but important criticisms. Some may feel I have spent rather too much time analysing and criticising situationalism. I believe this is both necessary and justifiable because this is where ethics are focused at the present time. *It is the new morality*. But it needs to be carefully and seriously challenged. Its effects have been harmful in our present situation. This is not to assert a new legalism, but freedom through obedience to the revealed will of God through his un-changing laws.

Criticism 1.

Although the situationalists claim that their ethics are communal they are, in fact, largely individualistic. Fletcher, for example, claims that situation ethics is "neighbour centred first and last . . . love is for people".[39] But the situation emphasis inevitably tends to leave lots of people out who are not in that situation. Fletcher, for example, seems to favour abortion under circumstances where the mother is going to suffer in some way or another. But abortion decisions cannot be limited simply to the mother. What about the father? There have been recent legal actions by fathers wanting to restrain their wives from having abortions. What about the community, which will lose one of its members as a result? What about the example to the community at large? What about the conscience of the surgeon carrying out the abortion? And, most important of all, what about the child who is going to be deprived of a place in the human race, and what about God himself who is the giver of life? To narrow the whole thing down to the mother in the situation is to deprive the decision of these other vital factors.

Criticism 2.

There is a misunderstanding and not infrequently an almost pathological dislike of law itself. Fletcher writes that love "only employs law when it seems worthwhile".[40] As we have already seen in chapter five, there are important senses in which law is not only God-given but has a built-in human factor that cannot be so lightly dismissed. I believe Victor Furnish is right when he says "Paul rejects the Law as a way of salvation but he does not reject it as a norm for the conduct of one's life. It remains for him an instrument of God's will and purpose if it is correctly interpreted."[41]

Criticism 3.

Situation ethics stands or falls on the principle of human reason and is a product of humanism rather than Christianity. It assumes man's intrinsic rationality—for it is man who figures the angles. In actual fact, man is seldom as rational as Fletcher assumes, and almost never so when the chips are down and he is in the situation for which he has to make a decision. Father Ceslaus Spicq writes as if love actually displaces rationality, "The Christian is no longer a *reasonable* man who appreciates another's good qualities and adjusts his own attitude accordingly, but a being made entirely of love, given body and soul to his neighbour, touched by whatever touches him . . ."[42] We need to recall again Paul's pithy but devastating statement, "Knowledge (*gnosis*) puffs up, but love (*agape*) builds up" (1 Cor, 8:1). Luther puts it crudely, "Whoever wants to be a Christian should gouge out the eyes of reason. Reason is the devil's bride, a lovely whore."[43] Reason is not a reliable guide, or emotions either, when, for example, modern people find themselves in situations away from their husbands or wives which test their marital fidelity. God's Law is a more reliable guide. "Flee fornication" is brief and simple advice, but not much help to those who do not recognise fornication as sin and chastity as binding on all.

Criticism 4.

Situation ethics assumes man's integrity, a fatal assumption for any of us to make. Like poor Mr. Higgins in *My Fair Lady* the new morality makes out that everyone is a nice guy in the final analysis. No wonder Fletcher and others mock any notion of the fall of man or even that sin is a problem at all. Man, to them, seems intrinsically able to cope. They fail to realise that man is basically manipulative, deceitful, rebellious, hard and unbending, at least until the Holy Spirit has drawn him to Christ, and in most cases for a considerable period afterwards. Man is not only incapable of making rational choices, he cannot really be trusted to do so. The danger when you want something badly enough is to do anything to get it and justify any action on the way to getting it. The pragmatic (it's O.K. if it works) approach to ethics is dangerously unreliable.

Fletcher quotes the person 'healed' through an experience of sexual misconduct.[44] To justify the act on this pragmatic ground is fairly typical of situation ethics but it raises a whole host of questions. Although it 'worked' one could quote in answer a thousand and one examples when sexual misconduct far from 'healing' people has made them sick. How are you to know what is going to happen and what the results will be? Is it really a responsible choice that one could reasonably leave in the hands of anyone? But I would seriously challenge what this 'healing' really amounted to and what were the long term effects of this misconduct and whether such behaviour could ever really be called loving. The fact it 'worked' says nothing about the morality of the decision at all.

Criticism 5.

The new morality assumes that there are only three approaches open for consideration:

1. The legalistic (for law)
2. The antinomian (against law)
3. Situational[45]

The ethics of Jesus Christ are definitive for all his people. He was clearly not a legalist. His life and teaching were in sharp contrast to the scribes and pharisees who were the legalists of his day. He certainly was not anti-nomian. He said "Think not that I have come to abolish the Law and the prophets; I have come not to abolish them but to fulfil them" (Matt. 5:17). That is not the language of an anti-nomian. As my comments in this chapter suggest, I do not see him either as a situationalist. There is a fourth way, and that is the way I have explored in this book. The way of true love.

Although the new morality does not itself raise all the issues that Nygren does in his book *Agape and Eros*, nevertheless I see it as further evidence that the battle continues and that situation ethics is a product of *Eros* rather than *Agape*, of humanism rather than Christianity. Fletcher virtually admits this when he writes, "What is important to note is that the distance is not so great or so wide between the secular humanist and the rational love-ethics of Christian situationists. Their ultimate commitments differ, but their immediate methods are the same."[46] That observation is precisely why I have felt bound to reject this ethical teaching.

15 SELF-LOVE, AGAPE OR NARCISSISM?

> This Narcissus of yours
> Cannot look in the mirror now
> Because he is the mirror himself.
>
> (Antonio Machado)

Our Western society has become newly aware of its narcissism. In the United States one of the 1979 bestsellers was the book *The Culture of Narcissism* by Christopher Lasch, with the sub-title, "American life in an age of diminishing expectations".[1] *Time* magazine wrote of this book, "Lasch is on to something quite real." Some have actually called the 70s "the narcissistic decade". Certainly it was a time of despair and helplessness, emotions which turn people in on themselves. People tended to live only for the moment; there was no future anyway. Their eyes were fixed on their own private problems; in the words of Lasch, they became "connoisseurs of their own decadence".[2]

The question arises, "Should we love ourselves?" Is self-love justifiable, or is it another form of narcissism? If Agape essentially means love for others, how can it ever be self-love? In the last chapter we looked at situationalism, which, with all its good points, is still an unreliable guide to ethics. In this chapter we are looking at another false understanding of love, which we are going to refer to as personalism, or the heresy of self-love.[3]

When we turn to personalism we find something quite different from situationalism. Situationalism is a rather academic exercise, though brilliantly presented by men like Joseph Fletcher and John Robinson. Personalism is omnipresent. In the Western world it has become a multi-million dollar industry, offering to meet a need previous generations did not know existed. It caters for what has become known as the 'me generation'. It is so obviously self-centred that one wonders why so many millions have been taken in by it.

The blindness of so many to its sham pretentiousness speaks for the decadence of so much Western life—it is another manifestation on a large scale of Eros religion.

But before beginning to analyse what personalism is, we need to stress that there is good in it, just as there is in situationalism. Basically where these forms of false love go wrong is not what they affirm, but what they ignore. Truth if it is to be truth must be the whole truth, and these forms of love, in presenting only a part of the truth, distort it and provide us with an inadequate description of love.

Dr. Paul Vitz has written a very thorough critique of personalism (or Selfism as he calls it). His book is called *Psychology as Religion, the cult of self-worship.*[4] The seed-bed of personalism is the field of psychology. Situationalism is mainly about the ethics of decision-making. But personalism is about people and how they are supposed to tick. We are dealing, therefore, with something wider than situationalism. The theological locus is the area of self-love, often called self-actualisation or self-realisation by psychologists. The theological question is "Is there a third commandment—love yourself?" Personalism has thrived in an age which has made psychology into a religion, and made man the object of its worship. As such, it is a product of Eros rather than of Agape.

But there is good in personalism, of that there is no doubt. The rapid growth of psychiatry serves an urgent need in our modern society. While our bodies have been in reasonable shape in our stressful communities, our minds have not. The soulless suburbs, mindless T.V., wasteful affluence, the ravages of total war, and irresponsible parenthood, have created rootlessness and emptiness, which have driven millions to psychiatrists' couches and compulsive drug dependence. Richard Holloway has described it: "Our countrysides are increasingly turned into vast food-producing factories, silent and dead, except for the neurotic bickering of imprisoned chickens. Man presides over a weird sub-lunar landscape, sterilised and rationalised by his own triumphant intellect."[5] On sexuality he observes,

"We know how to manipulate and stimulate our bodies with the same clinical objectivity we bring to everything else; and in so doing we have created an emotional desert, a vast consumer society of throwaway marriages and loveless encounters, in which we use and discard and demean each other, never really penetrating to the mystery of the other. We are as alienated from each other as we are from the natural creation."[6] In this weird landscape and emotional desert personalism has thrived on the widespread fascination for psychology. Psychology has discovered something about persons, but not enough about God, and so for many the desert is still a desert.

Personalism, as its derivation implies, is for people. It cares for people. It tries to heal them. It attempts to get them to relate together. It has spawned many theoretical approaches and techniques. We could mention Group Dynamics, Transactional Analysis, and Gestalt Therapy. In the more directly Christian field, there is Clinical Theology, Inner Healing of Memories, Prayer Counselling and others. There is good in all of them and people are helped and healed through them. But this area needs to be carefully analysed because of its likeness to the cult of self-worship which is so popular in the Western world at the present time. These techniques can easily be a mild palliative; but if theologically they do not do justice to the meaning of God or of persons, they will fail to fulfil the promises they hold out to our sick society.

Before we can proceed further we need to distinguish between self-love, which is an acceptable part of what it is to be human in God's sight, and its aberration which is so common in our own times. We have to begin with the theological question, "Are we to imply by the statement that we are 'to love our neighbour *as ourself*' that there is in effect a third commandment—namely to love oneself?" This is the big question, and we need to relate it to the words of Jesus, "If any man would come after me, let him *deny himself* and take up his cross daily and follow me" (Lk. 9:23).

Nygren deals carefully with the matter of the so-called third commandment in his book *Agape and Eros*. It is a crucial issue, for this text "You shall love your neighbour as yourself"—is the gospel of personalism and its chief justification amongst Christians. Nygren asserts that the idea of self-love, as it is expounded on the basis of this verse, "is alien to the New Testament, and has grown up out of a wholly different soil . . . self-love is man's natural condition; it is also the basis of the perversion of his will to evil.'"[7] He goes on to explain the commandment, "Every man knows how by nature he loves himself. *So*, runs the commandment, thou shalt love thy neighbour; thou shalt love thy neighbour as much as by nature, thou lovest thyself. When love gains its own direction, when it is turned away from the self and directed to one's neighbour, then the natural perversion of the will is overcome. Thus so far from love of one's neighbour presupposing and including self-love, it excludes it and overcomes it." Bultmann has put it excellently, "It is consequently meaningless to say (as, indeed, can only be said on the basis of a *humanistic ideal of ethics*) that love for one's neighbour must be preceded by a justifiable self-love, a necessary degree of self-respect because we are commanded 'thou shalt love thy neighbour as thyself'; hence self-love is presupposed. Yes, it is in truth presupposed; but not as something which man must first learn, something expressly required of him, but as the attitude of the natural man, *which is simply to be overcome*" (italics mine).[8]

In one sense we could say without fear of being misunderstood, *man does not need to be commanded to love himself, he does that anyway.*

As we have seen self-love does lie at the basis of much of Augustine's understanding of love, and the fruit of that is still with us and at least one explanation for self-love ethics in modern Christianity. Victor Furnish is another writer who denies the third commandment. "Divine love alone," he writes, "is to be regarded as the measure and meaning of love's claim. This truth is only obscured if self-love is included as a third commandment, or in some other way made parallel with the commands to love God and thy neighbour."[9] Nygren warns us that it is through this doorway that Eros has again trespassed into the territory of Agape.[10] Eros is egocentric love. The love that seeks to have its needs satisfied, without regard to the will of God. Self-love is fundamental to Eros, but absent in Agape. Karl Barth had grave misgivings about even using the term self-love for love must always have an object, he said.[11] With a touch of humour he writes about self-love: "God will never think of blowing on this fire, which is bright enough already." He goes on to reject the so-called third commandment: "It is true that this self-love is the visible and tangible reality of the one who loves his neighbour. The commandment itself recognises and establishes it to be true. *But the commandment: thou shalt love thy neighour is not a legitimation but a limitation of this reality*" (italics mine).[12] It is clear that we must reject self-love as the third commandment.

A strong advocate of the importance of self-love in recent years has been the Roman Catholic psychiatrist Dr. Jack Dominian. In his book *From Cosmos to Love* he pleads to the Church for greater understanding of his own profession: "It is my contention that there can be no genuine and authentic Christian renewal unless the advances made by the psychological sciences become widespread and well-known, which will facilitate a great deal of human healing."[13] Whilst there is truth in what Dr. Dominian says, it must also be matched with a sound theological understanding of the nature of man. For the Christian, the biblical understanding of man is of supreme importance and what the psychological sciences say does not always square with it.

The importance of raising this at this juncture is because it relates very closely to the whole question of self-love. We need to look at what Dr. Dominian says, because it is fairly typical of the approach of personalism. For example, he writes: "The most challenging aspect of the Judeo-Christian faith is that it is a faith which by its own terms of reference *leads humanity to God via love*" (italics mine—here is the

Eros motif again).[14] He goes on: "It is my contention that the greater our understanding of loving, the nearer we are to the mystery we call God and that the psychological sciences have made fundamental contributions to this knowledge which Christianity has yet to grasp let alone assimilate." Here again we see symptoms of Eros. We see, for instance, that, according to Dr. Dominian our understanding of God comes from our understanding of love. We have already seen that the truth lies in the opposite direction, namely that our understanding of love comes from our understanding of God.

When Dr. Dominian goes on to develop the whole question of self-love he makes even more sweeping statements. "The most basic tenet of the Judeo-Christian faith of loving our neighbour as ourselves has not only been hardly developed as yet, but in fact there is not the remotest hope of really succeeding in loving our neighbour in a sustained manner until we first have learned to know the meaning of loving ourselves."[15] Dr. Dominian's thesis on self-love in this book needs to be seriously questioned; and even if this is, as he asserts, the most basic tenet of the Judeo-Christian faith, his understanding of it seems to come neither from Judaism nor from Christianity, but from the Greek concept of Eros, and is closely related to gnosticism. "We cannot give," he writes, "unless we first possess. We cannot receive, certainly not love, unless we have a sense of being."[16] It is this kind of thinking which was rampant in the Greek world of Jesus' time, and Jesus himself confronted and denied it. Jesus did not say, "Receive and then give," but "Give and it will be given you." Paul described Christian love as "seeking not its own" (I Cor. 13). Dr. Dominian puts it even more strongly when he writes, "The commandment of loving others as ourselves can only be implemented firstly by a love of self . . . which paves the way for our capacity to love others."[17]

Walter Trobisch makes the same point as Dr. Dominian and claims that the Bible endorses it. "We find the Bible confirms what modern psychology has recently discovered.

Without self-love there can be no love for others. Jesus equates these two loves, and binds them together, making them inseparable."[18] The only biblical evidence the writer supplies for this sweeping statement is the second commandment, "Thou shalt love thy neighbour as thyself." But Walter Trobisch fails to distinguish between self-love and self-acceptance. The title of his book reveals this. He calls it *Love Yourself* with the sub-title "Self-acceptance and depression".

It seems that the Bible nowhere says that we are to love ourselves. In other words there is no third commandment. But what the Bible constantly affirms is that we are to accept ourselves, our humanity, our sexuality, our earthiness, our mortality. To be strictly accurate, the Bible mostly assumes this rather than expresses it. We should see it as a natural expression of our humanity rather than a contrived explanation of it. In other words it is more or less taken for granted. Our problem is that it cannot be taken for granted today. In the Psalms we find the Psalmist talking to himself in the most friendly fashion. "Hello, soul," the Psalmist says, "how are you doing today?" Here is no rejection—or feeling that he is talking to something intrinsically evil. In the relationship between David and Jonathan we read, "Jonathan loved him *as his own soul*" (1 Sam. 18:1). When Paul discusses marriage in Ephesians 5 husbands are urged to love their wives "as their own bodies". He goes on, "He who loves his wife loves himself. For no man ever hates his own flesh, but nourishes and cherishes it, as Christ does the Church . . . Let each one of you love his wife as himself." Of course, the word used here is *agape* and the whole passage on marriage is prefaced by the description of Christ's love for the Church. So marital love is to be a reflection of the model of true love, which is Christ's love for the Church.

It is here that we have to make an important distinction. If by self-love we mean that we accept ourselves—that we are male if we are male, and female if we are female; that sex is natural, and to be attracted to the opposite sex is normal. That we accept that we are tall if we are tall or short if we are short; fat or thin, rich or poor, married or single, black or white—and then thank God he has made us the way we are, then it is O.K. When the painter wanted to leave out Cromwell's prominent wart, he was told that he was to paint the famous man "warts and all". Self-acceptance means 'warts and all'. That is what Paul is meaning in his beautiful description of the marriage relationship. Josef Piper in his essay *Zucht und Mass* writes, "There are two opposing ways in which a man can love himself: selflessly or selfishly. Only the first is self-preserving, while the second is self-destroying."[19] The modern word for the latter is narcissism. The Greek myth tells the story of a young man called Narcissus who saw his reflection in a lake. He fell in love with himself and fell into the water only to be drowned. Narcissism is extremely common today. It helps to fill the vacuum caused by the absence of true love. But it is false and in the end self-destructive. Walter Trobisch points out, "Self-acceptance is the exact opposite of narcissism, it is actually a prerequisite for a step in the direction of selflessness."[20] Trobisch uses the word self-love freely in this sense, but I am rather inclined to agree with Barth that the word is best not used at all; there is so much false love of self that man should not be given the slightest encouragement in that direction. But a great deal of our problem today is with people who hate themselves, or cannot seem to accept themselves. That is as unhealthy as the wrong and sinful kind of self-love which Jesus and the apostles so obviously rejected.

There are three particular compound words in English which include 'self'—self-assertion, self-acceptance and self-mastery. The first is the hallmark of personalism, and indeed of our Western culture. The second, rightly understood, is a more helpful term for self-love, since *agape* is always a word for others, never for oneself. In the second commandment ("Thou shalt love thy neighbour as thyself") it is used in relationship to our neighbour, and Paul uses it in the context of the marriage relationship. But it is the final word, self-mastery, that is the most important. It confronts the modern ideologies of self-expression which have caused so much damage to our society. When Paul was listing the qualities of a Christian leader one of them was self-control (Titus 1:8). There is nothing wrong in enjoying oneself. But to control oneself is important and this is where love is seen to its best advantage. Spicq writes about this, "Jesus intended to show . . . the perfect self-mastery he expects from his followers. Only *agape* has this power of ruling a person completely because it is inseparable from renouncement and sacrifice. No one can love his neighbour as a Christian should unless he is willing to give up his own pleasure, his own comforts and *even his own rights*."[21]

We need to recall that when Irenaeus was battling against the false ideas of Marcion, who wanted to restore love to its place of pre-eminence, one of the main planks of his argument was that Christian love is a love which *gives* rather than *desires*. He wrote about God that he "has not created man in order to satisfy his own needs but to have someone on whom to lavish his beneficence".[22] In many ways the very word self-love is a contradiction in terms, at least if it is *agape-love*. Whereas it is true, as Irenaeus says, that God shows his love towards us by lavishing his beneficence on us (and it certainly should be true that we do the same to our neighbour), it would be inappropriate as descriptive of our love for ourselves. That is why I believe we should refrain from talking about self-love and talk more about self-acceptance and self-mastery. Since the true meaning of love can only be found in God, we are only free to use the word in association with God's nature—the way God loves should be the way we love. The famous saint, Bernard of Clairvaux, constructed an interesting kind of ladder, stages on the journey of love. It begins with love of self for self's sake; it moves on to love of God for self's sake; then it arrives at love of God for love's sake; and finally love of self for God's sake.[23] Nygren is probably right to see traces of Eros in this description or categorisation; but if it is there at all it seems very innocent.

In principle it is a remarkable insight into the progress of the Christian from self-centredness to the right under-standing of self-love.

Here perhaps is another way of seeing the distinction which is so important between self-love which is wrong and unhealthy and self-acceptance which is sound and whole-some. The love of self for self's sake is the former, while the love of self for God's sake is the latter.

This kind of distinction may also be helpful in considering the controversial issue of homosexuality. One doubts very much if the word *agape* can ever really be used to describe the homosexual relationship. Is it not in some respects a form of narcissism? In the book *Returns of Love*, Alex Davidson (as a homosexual) says this to his male friend, "These other wants are related, of course, but what I want most is *you*, not as a plaything nor as a picture, but as a person. Now this, whispers the tempter earnestly, is much less carnal, much more lofty a sentiment. Yes, say I, but equally selfish, still wanting, still demanding . . . I like to claim that I could draw the line between the 'loftier'. . . and the more 'carnal'. . . but the operative word on both sides is desire and the attitude throughout is 'I want'."[24]

The very nature of man is very much involved in all this, and here there have been in the Church two opposite traditions. There has been the one, which stems from Augustine and can be called mushy Catholic for want of a better phrase. This starts on the premise that man is basically a loving person, that love is basic to man and that all people love. Fletcher expresses it this way in his book *Situation Ethics*, "The situationalist says to the non-Christian 'your love is like mine, like everybody's, it is the Holy Spirit'."[25]

It is simply put in a popular book called *To Live is to Love* by a Roman Catholic priest called Ernesto Cardenal. He was one of the leaders in the Nicaraguan revolution against Somoza and was made a member of the Revolutionary Government after the Dictator had been overthrown. The book has a long introduction by Thomas Merton. It starts, "All things love each other."[26] In one place he writes, "We find God's initials in all nature, and all creatures are God's messages of love addressed to us, they are flashes of his love. All nature is aflame with love . . ." etc.[27] I am not a naturalist myself, but I have to confess this is not how I see much of God's creation. Certainly the Bible never gives us the creation as an example of love. The snake for instance is always an example of evil and treachery. But it is when the writer turns to man he says some quite extraordinary things; I quote: "The insatiable desire of dictators, of kings, of power, money and property, is the love of God."[28] The whole book expounds the same theme. Now it may be a rather extreme example of this view of man and creation, one would have to say rather unrealistic, but it is the continuation of the Eros type of love which we are able to find traces of throughout the history of the Church.

But when we turn to the harsh Protestant reformers we find them going to the other extreme. Cranmer's book of Common Prayer takes a very dim view of man: read the Commination Service for starters. Luther said that self-love was to be annihilated. Loving oneself he described as a vicious love which had to be destroyed (*vitiosus amor*). Even man's highest ideals are polluted by sin. "Can unselfish fruit be gathered from the tree of selfishness?" he wrote.[29] Luther wanted to see love eliminated from the context of man's relationship to God, except in the sense of God's love of us. Man is so wholly under sin, he *cannot* love properly. In the Heidelberg Disputation in 1518 Luther referred to human love as "acquisitive".[30] Calvin, with his view of human depravity, went even further than Luther, and Cranmer's Holy Communion service in the Book of Common Prayer never really lets the sinner off the hook. To the end of the service there is a constant confession of unworthiness.

So we have to steer a careful course between these two extremes—the optimistic view of man and creation as always loving, and the pessimistic view of man as virtually incapable of loving at all. In one sense it is only the Holy Spirit who can give to each one of us the necessary discernment to know how we can be self-affirming without being self-asserting. How we can be regenerated by the Spirit of God so that we become God's children by his grace, so that the humanity we have can be freely and unashamedly expressed to the glory of God; and how the self, so easily contaminated by pride and selfishness, can be mastered and controlled by the love of God. If Paul by the grace of God was able to write, "The love of Christ controls us" (2 Cor. 5:14), then it can be our testimony too by the same grace that is available to us in Christ.

The Roman Catholic scholar Raymond Brown has written, "The last years of this millennium are likely to be dominated by the continuing quest for the self-expression of the human person." The longing of man for human freedom in the social, economic and sexual fields as well as that of his human personality has found expression in a variety of ways from the emergence in the 60s of the drug culture, to feminism and the gay movement in the 70s, and all the way round to movements for racial emancipation and political liberation. Human rights are in the centre of the stage. To meet this human need our consumer society has provided a vast amount of literature and, of course, the organisations to cater for these needs.

In 1980, while visiting the Word of God Community in Ann Arbor, Michigan, I was given the book which I have already mentioned by Dr. Paul Vitz, *Psychology as Religion*. I am grateful to the author for his permission to quote from it. The author is a Christian psychologist, at present Associate Professor of Psychology at New York University. Passing through phases of superficial Christianity and a long period of atheism and agnosticism, he came to faith in Christ. He recalls in his book moments in the middle of class lectures when he "suddenly became aware that I was saying things I didn't believe." He writes, therefore, as a man who has studied the psychological sciences thoroughly and discovered how anti-Christian much of this area is. From there he went on to see how phoney and anti-Christian much of what I have called personalism is.

If you go to the average book store and look for popular books on this subject you will almost certainly see books by Erich Fromm (b. 1900). Although there are others who have written along the same lines, men like Carl Rogers, Abraham Maslow and Rollo May, Fromm has always exercised a particularly strong influence. Fromm is an unabashed humanist, and, as we shall see, his whole concept of love comes from the Greek concept of Eros rather than the Christian of Agape. In his book with the significant title *Man for Himself*, he writes, "Not self-renunciation nor selfishness but the affirmation of his truly human self, are the supreme values of humanistic ethics."[31] He is explicit in another passage in the same book when writing about love for one's neighbour: "It is something inherent and radiating from him. Love is not a higher power which descends upon man nor a duty which is imposed upon him; it is his own power by which he relates himself to the world and makes it truly his."[32] In the same book in a very significant admission, he writes, "If the dogma of man's innate natural evilness were true then my position would be untenable."[33] Here is the crux. Personalism in both its humanist and, as we shall see, Christian aspects, denies the essential sinfulness of human nature. It is more concerned to affirm man than trust God. Fromm's position is made clear by the title of another of his books, *You shall be as Gods*.[34] These are actually the words of Satan (Gen. 3:5) to Eve. So Fromm and other humanists have fallen for Satan's lies rather than God's word. For Fromm, and other secular psychologists, man is God. And for Christian humanists it is not surprising that the roles of God and man are reversed. God is relegated to the circumference of the circle and man placed in the centre. Although God is there in the system, the view of God is so distant from that revealed to us in Christ and the scriptures that it is misleading and harmful.

Fromm and the others are comparatively unknown compared with those who have popularised their writings and ideas. The two most famous of the popularisers are Eric Berne, with his book *Games People Play*,[35] and Thomas

Harris with *I'm O.K., you're O.K.*[36] Their basic approach is—"You were born to win." Their emphasis is on self-assertion. As Vitz says, "The public appetite for this sort of approach seems insatiable."[37] All these writers have spawned a whole network of psychological systems which now involve literally millions of people particularly in North America. The most famous perhaps is called T.A., which stands for Transactional Analysis. There is also Gestalt Therapy, and more recently, a purely secular approach, but much along the same lines, E.S.T. or Erhard Seminar Training. The last is now a multi-million dollar operation with its aim to *'experience living'*. The emphasis is on self— "YOU are the supreme being . . ." they say. Another adage, "The sole purpose of life is to acknowledge that you're the source, then choose to be what you know you are. It'll all flow from there," which is a re-hash of the existentialism of men like Sartre.

Paul Vitz locks into all this the cult of self-help sex. Alex Comfort's *Joy of Sex* (1972)[38] was enormously popular and influential. John Money, following Alex Comfort, advocates what he calls recreational sex in place of what he calls procreational. Vitz summarises these sex popularists as "Sex in the service of the ego."[39] In 1972 Nena and George O'Neill introduced 'swinging sex' in their book *Open Marriage.*[40] In this book they openly advocate group sex or sharing sex openly with other partners. Unfortunately their own marriage was dissolved two years after the book came out, and in spite of all these modern theories about getting rid of your inhibitions and enjoying yourself the divorce rate has continued to climb.

But there are much more sinister aspects of this, which show how Eros has penetrated deep into the heart of modern Western Christianity and perverted it. Vitz quite rightly takes us in his book behind Fromm to the main source of the development of selfism.[41] It was Ludwig Feuerbach's book *Essence of Christianity* (1841) which had such a devastating effect on Christianity in the nineteenth century. Feuerbach was a left-wing Hegelian. Engels, Marx's friend, was enthusiastic about this book and there is little doubt that it influenced Marx, Nietzsche, Huxley and Freud. In this book he writes, "God is the projected essence of man: what therefore ranks second in religion, namely *man*, that must be proclaimed the first and recognised as the first . . . man's God is man. This is the highest law of ethics. This is the turning point of world history." It was Feuerbach who first coined the phrase "religion is as bad as opium" to which Marx gave his own subtle twist in saying "Religion is the opium of the people." Secular personalism stems primarily from this single source, and from it has flowed so many of the evils of today. Man began to believe and act like a god, and most of our present ills come from this act of rebellion against the Creator and Redeemer of mankind.

But how did all this get into Christianity? Vitz points to the work of two famous and popular American Christian writers, Harry Fosdick and Norman Vincent Peale.[42] If you thumb your way through their writings you will see how closely they echo the thoughts of Fromm and the popularisers. Together they set out to give popular expression to self-realisation or 'becoming a real person'. They were supremely optimistic about men and about society. Fosdick saw modern progress and Christianity as natural partners. In his book *As I See Religion* he describes Christianity as being about "the divine origin, spiritual nature, infinite worth and endless possibilities of each personality".[43] Here we detect immediately the signs of Eros. His enormously popular book *On Being a Real Person*,[44] which is still in print after twenty-nine editions, is intended as a Christian answer to the humanistic writings of Fromm and others. But it is yet another example of syncretistic Christianity. It takes something which is intrinsically un-Christian, and attempts to Christianise it by dressing it in Christian clothes. We have seen down through Church history how there have been those who have tried to marry Agape and Eros, to have an amalgam of the best of Greek thought with Christian ideas. Fosdick substituted the word integration for the word salvation. The chief commandment for him was "Get yourself together, be a real person." The fundamental sin is to be chaotic and unfocused. Vitz described Fosdick's concept of self as "thoroughly anti-Christian".[45]

When we turn to Norman Vincent Peale we see the same approach though he tends to use another method, one which, in the pragmatic atmosphere of American society, has for many years proved popular—case histories or testimonies. If it has 'worked' for others, it will work for me, is the conclusion that the reader is meant to take. As early as 1937 Peale was writing, "The greatest day in any individual's life is when he begins for the first time to realise himself."[46] But it was his book *The Power of Positive Thinking*, which came out in 1952, which not only made him famous, but also introduced to literally millions of people a Christianised version of selfism. One has only to cast one's eye down the chapter headings to see where he was taking people. "How to create your own happiness;" "Expect the best and get it;" "How to draw upon that higher power." It is all very akin to another popular teaching in North America—that prosperity is promised to God's people, and if you pray and believe enough God will make you rich.

The kingdom of God is to them vitally linked to the Dow Jones Index. Peale begins his most famous book with the words, which sum up the gospel of personalism, "Believe in *yourself*! Have faith in *your* abilities . . . self-confidence leads to self-realisation and successful achievements." Several generations have been fed with that kind of stuff from both Christian and secular sources. But the sum of human greed and self-destructiveness continues unabated.

An important point for us to grasp is that this approach to self-love could only thrive in countries like the United States. Can you imagine going to India or Tanzania with such a message? Dr. Vitz asserts that what he calls selfism "is the perfect consumer philosophy".[47] Most countries of the world would laugh at the blatant optimism of the personalists. Elsewhere Dr. Vitz writes, "It is difficult to imagine self-actualisation as a popular concept except in a period of great wealth and leisure." Perhaps a day will come, and it may not be too far off, when the Fromms and Fosdicks will be replaced with the St. Francises and Mahatma Ghandis (if you want to select a non-Christian), and the old popular books which tell us we're O.K. (it really is our parents' fault all the time) will be replaced with books like *The Imitation of Christ*, which, with a much clearer perception of human nature, show us how we can live the crucified life, and where our faults really lie.

Vitz gives a terrifying summary of where all this has taken people. He calls it *existential narcissism:* "It follows," he writes, "from a modern approach to living often chosen in adult life. Its end is the psychological death (in some cases the physical death as well) of the self. Death may come from greater and greater devotion to sensation (sex, violence or drugs) or from retreat into the isolated machine-like world of the careerist ego—cold, calculating, often fuelled by amphetamines. In either case there is an ever-tightening, self-inflicted solitary confinement based on continually repressing the need for love of others . . . there is no escape from the conclusion that the modern self is intrinsically self-destructive."[48] Vitz believes (as I do) that the prodigals will return. Many are doing so now, disillusioned with the false claims of personalism. The uncertainty Dr. Vitz says is not the return of these people, "But whether their Father's house, the true faith, will still be there to welcome and celebrate their return."[49]

We are living in a processed world. We eat processed food. We imbibe news processed for us by the media. Life is presented to us in a processed fashion by television. That is bad enough. What is much worse as we have already noted is that the Church of the West has been preaching a processed gospel. We have processed our theology. We have even tried to process Jesus Christ. The art of processing food is to take certain parts out and add artificial ingredients to preserve, add colour to, or add taste to what is left of food itself. But the additives are never the same as the original, and in not a few cases harmful or even poisonous. We have done this with theology and our presentation of the gospel of Jesus Christ. The gospel stands on its own and needs neither additions nor subtractions. Personalism is an additive, which ultimately poisons rather than heals. It is not part of the gospel message.

Part of the good news for Christians is about the crucifixion of self. "I am crucified with Christ," was Paul's testimony, not "I am self-affirmed in Christ." If personalism is an additive, then the Cross is the truth which has been extracted. All over the Western world we see the sugar-coated gospel; the 'bless me' gospel. Jesus will make you rich, Jesus will take away your pain and grief, Jesus will make life comfortable for you, Jesus will make you secure and actualised. This false gospel is heard in umpteen Christian pulpits. The Cross is sometimes presented as 'what Jesus did for us'; but the Cross as the sign of our life in Christ—hardly at all. During the Jesus movement of the 70s one of the invitations to young people was to take a 'Jesus trip'. Clever though at first sight it was, it is typical of a form of Christianity which really tells people lies, for it only presents the sugar of the gospel. It says nothing about the cost of discipleship, or the Cross which the Christian is called to carry daily. So selfism or personalism has penetrated deep into the Christian Church.

We have today in the West a largely man-centred Christianity. In a word—Eros. Whether this is seen in the radical social gospel, when it leaves the worship of God and Lord-ship of Christ out of its purview; or in the pietism which cares little for the social and economic injustices that people suffer; or the personalism, which is really the resurgence of the old humanism in which man is the measure of all things—it is Eros. Agape begins and ends with God, who is just and righteous. Agape is always filtered through the Cross of Jesus. That is where we see true love demonstrated and enacted, and the love we are to have for one another has also to be filtered through the Cross. Whatever else the Cross means, it is the badge of suffering, and *unjust* suffering at that. Christ died—"the just for the unjust" (1 Peter 3:18 A.V.). The Incarnation itself is the greatest affirmation ever given of our humanity. We need look no further. But that is not the crucial issue—it is what we do with the humanity God has given to us which matters, and the only really true model is Jesus himself. To apply the superficial adages of personalism to Jesus Christ is almost blasphemous. Paul describes the mind of Christ in the sublime words of Philippians 2:5–8, "Though he was in the form of God [he] did not count equality with God a thing to be grasped, but emptied himself, taking the form of a servant, being born in the likeness of men. And being found in human form he humbled himself and became obedient unto death, even death on a cross." Before such words personalism has little to say. Because it has little or nothing to say about suffering, except as something to be avoided or freed from, it has little or nothing to do with the true Christ of Calvary.

In a way it all comes back to the difference between self-realisation and self-surrender. Stanley Jones has helpfully distinguished them for us, "The difference between the emphasis on self-realisation or on self-surrender seems to be this: in self-realisation you try to realise yourself, for all the answers are in you. In self-surrender you surrender yourself to Jesus Christ for all the answers are in him. One leaves you centred on you, a self-centred and self-preoccupied person, albeit a religious person. The other loses his self and finds it. For self-realisation only comes through self-surrender. You realise yourself when you realise Him, and you realise yourself when you surrender to Him."[50]

Personalism has little interest in the holiness of God, or his justice, or that he is a God of severity as well as mercy; and that he requires repentance and penitence from his people: and that he will one day judge the entire human race by Jesus Christ. We must not confuse the truth about the costliness of Christian discipleship with a false idea of asceticism. Paul in 1 Cor. 13 said that asceticism without love is useless: "If I give away all I have, and if I deliver my body to be burned, but have not love, I gain nothing." That does not mean that there is no place for asceticism. But Agape is to be the determining factor. Without Agape, prophecy, knowledge and understanding, faith and asceticism are merely morale boosters or glorified ego trips. Agape like the angels posted at the gates of paradise, stands to guard the way to the tree of life. Eros has no place there at all. Only those bearing the badge of Agape can enter. That badge is in the shape of a Cross.

" 'The rarer action is in virtue than in vengeance.' "
(The Tempest, Shakespeare)

Love and hate, psychologists tell us, are delicately related emotions. The fire of love can in a trice become a conflagration of hate and revenge. What happens when love breaks down? What do we do when we are injured by others? There is a human and there is a divine response to the love-hate conflict. The human is revenge, the divine is forgiveness.

Revenge is one of man's most natural and primitive instincts. The proverb 'revenge is sweet' came into use during the sixteenth century, and many of Shakespeare's plays reveal how the subject of revenge must have absorbed the minds of many people during that century. From Shakespeare to Thomas Hardy revenge has been a principle factor in the development of plots. But when we turn from fiction to fact we see how often revenge has influenced the events of history. When the Iranian Moussavi Garmoudi appeared before cameramen reaching into a box and showing the T.V. audience the burnt human foot of a would-be rescuer of the American hostages, there could have been few whose instinct for revenge was not aroused. When one of the hostages was interviewed after his release he was asked if he would ever go back to Iran; he replied, "Yes, in a B52 bomber."

In marked contrast was the response of the Anglican missionaries, who had also been illegally detained by the Iranians. They wanted to go back in a spirit of forgiveness and love for the Iranian people. When Bishop Dehqani-Tafti's only son Bahram was murdered in Iran the Bishop's wife spoke at his funeral. At times holding on to the coffin for support, she said, "We believe that God will transform this evil and meaningless act and make it a blessing and use it for the strengthening of his Church. Father forgive them, they know not what they do." Then she prayed, "O God, forgive our enemies and those who are evil to us, and do not allow a spirit of revenge and hatred to remain in us." That is authentic Christianity. A young Iranian student, who knew Bahram at university, was converted. *"Khoda hast"*— There is God, she said. With tears in her eyes she added, "Bahram's death has shown him to me."

Revenge is more basic and dangerous than aggression because it is premeditated. *Time* magazine columnist Lance Morrow has written: "The urge for lurid, annihilating retaliation—vindication, satisfaction, the no-good bastard's head upon a plate, fetches back to a shrouded moment when the spontaneous animal reflex of self-protection turned to a savage brooding. The human mind, newly intelligent, began to dream of the barbarously fitting ways in which it would get even. Emanating from hurt and the pain of failure and unfairness, the fantasy of revenge became, it may be, even stronger than the imperative of sex." Self-protection is an animal as well as a human reaction, but it is doubtful whether there are any animals which attempt endlessly to wreak revenge on their enemies as *homo sapiens* does. Animals don't have the long memories men have.

Towards the end of December 1980 a Turkish diplomat was murdered outside his home in Sydney, Australia, by a gang of Armenian terrorists. The reason they gave for killing this man in cold blood was in revenge for the killing of many Armenians by the Turks in 1915. As the poor victim was not even born in 1915 he could not possibly have been responsible for the sins of his fathers. Bernard Levin, commenting on this case in *The Times*, wrote, "Armenian memories are long, then; not that the Armenians are the only ones . . . but I cannot be the first to observe, and to ponder upon, the very great oddness of the fact that the line of hate seems to stretch farther than that of love, the line of revenge than that of forgiveness, the line of

death than that of life."[1] As Lord Byron put it in his poem
Don Juan:

> Now hatred is by far the longest pleasure;
> Men love in haste, but they detest at leisure.[2]

History abounds with the horrors of vendettas. In South
America the Tupinamba tribe used to make their prisoners
of war consort with a woman of their tribe so that they
would have the pleasure when their child was born of
slaying the prisoner and his baby. In New Zealand when a
chieftain was killed in war, hostilities were broken off while
the body of the leader was chopped up by his opponents,
roasted and devoured. Then presumably the slaughter could
go on. Among the Southern Slavs a mother has been known
to lay her infant son down in the cradle to sleep upon the
bloodstained shirt of his murdered father. The child was
thus brought up ultimately to avenge that murder. It became
his bloody vocation.

Our world abounds in repeated instances of revengeful
actions. The Palestinian Liberation Organisation and the
Israelis are constantly seeking revenge on one another, and
on the borders between Eire and Northern Ireland, barely
a day goes by without some civilian being shot dead in
reprisal for another sectarian killing. The whole tragic
history of Ireland is peppered with violence between Roman
Catholics and Protestants, the English and the Irish.
Memories are long in Ireland—reaching at least as far as
the Battle of the Boyne. Lance Morrow writes, "Revenge
has its undeniable satisfactions. It is a primal scream that
shatters glass. But revenge is not an intelligent basis for a
foreign policy. This century has already fulfilled its quota of
smoke and rage and survivors, grey with bomb dust,
staggering around in the rubble, seeking what is left of the
dead they loved."[3]

If nature's instinct after personal injury is revenge, then
the Christian instinct should be forgiveness. Back in the
Old Testament the Law recognised these primitive instincts,
and sought to curb them. This was the origin of the famous

law, "An eye for an eye, and a tooth for a tooth." If someone punched out two of your teeth you had a legal right to knock out two of his—but no more. But revenge implies the taking of the law into our own hands. Francis Bacon called it "wild justice". He went on to say, "Which the more man's nature runs to, the more ought law to weed it out." Thus Bacon sees the law, as in the Old Testament, as the answer to personal grievances, which previously had been settled by the personal vendetta. Revenge is the only justice available in the Wild West until the sheriff arrives to clean up the town. But revenge is seldom just, and never, in spite of what the proverb says, sweet. John Milton recognised this in *Paradise Lost*:

> Revenge, at first though sweet,
> Bitter ere long back on itself recoils.

But in comparatively law-abiding countries, as in Europe and North America, although revenge seldom takes the form of shedding human blood, it is nevertheless extremely common. In our day we resort to all kinds of verbal devices for disguising the nature of revenge. Retaliation sounds better than revenge, and we now commonly talk about "a nuclear *response*", which simply means, "If you hit us with 100 bombs, we'll blast you with 200." It's revenge in twentieth century diplomatic language.

The history of the Christian Church abounds with the most shameful examples of revengeful Christians, who have perpetrated hideous acts in the name of God. The Crusades, the Spanish Inquisition, the Reformation burnings, the wars of religion, have sickened whole generations. And even today many of the worst trouble spots in the world, where there is almost continuous bloodshed, are caused either by conflict between different religions or between parties or denominations within those religions. The instinct for revenge seems as common amongst the religious as the infidels. Even amongst those who are most shrill in their cries for human justice, the note of revenge is seldom silent. Ronald Higgins writes, "It is a peculiar irony that liberals seem especially prone to deny their own share in evil. Their denunciations often ring with a similar blind hatred to that which consumes their perpetrators. They too, if unconsciously, seek vengeance, and simply cannot see that we are all capable of the evil acts they (rightly) protest about."[4]

Now Christians can be very subtle when it comes to the matter of revenge. We are so familiar with the teaching of Jesus about forgiveness and the need to love one another that we know that revenge is out of keeping with that teaching. So instead of wreaking revenge on those whom we think have wronged us or have hurt us in some way or another, we give way to self-pity, or nurse our grievances, or store up our resentments, and we find other ways of revenging ourselves on those who have done evil to us. We ignore them or gossip about them or we treat them as if they didn't exist. H. R. Mackintosh, in his book *The Christian Experience of Forgiveness*, explains that forgiveness differs from the mere abandonment of revenge. "It demands more by far than self-mastery enough to veto retaliation . . . In our resentment at injury we will not strike back . . . the command of Jesus keeps down our hands; but in the private world of feeling we are our own masters and may please ourselves. We have a long memory, and, once wronged, we intend to show the spared offender very plainly that he can never again be the same to us . . . Hence if accident or a good man's guile should bring us into the offender's company, there is that in our demeanour if not our language which openly proclaims that positive reconciliation is not to be thought of."[5] He goes on to say, "To call this forgiveness would be absurd. It is a temper largely composed of scorn, and scorn is one of the emotions on which . . . Christ set his ban."

H. R. Mackintosh is right—this is not forgiveness at all. But what we need to see is that this is another form of revenge. Because we are Christians we cannot shoot people; so we find another form of retaliation. Unlike the more drastic forms of revenge, which are quickly over, this can be spread out over many years. So we can slowly turn the sword in the wound, until we feel ourselves completely revenged. Alas, this is so commonplace amongst practising Christians that one is more surprised when one does not see it, than when one sees another example of it. But it is as unloving and un-Christian as doing actual physical harm to a person.

In 1 Corinthians 13, the hymn of love, Paul says that love is "not resentful". Arnold Bittlinger translates this, "Love does not keep lists." He writes, "We encounter evil . . . in our brother. Humanly speaking it is understandable that we then begin to make lists and reckon up how often we have been treated badly. Certainly we are prepared to forgive if the other requests it, but hardly to the point where we also *forget*. But love keeps no lists, not even in the mind. Love forgets when it forgives. Forgiving without forgetting is not real forgiving, it is hypocrisy . . . Love has no use for a list of the other's misdeeds, for 'Love is not resentful'."[6] If as Christians we do not forget the bad things that have been done to us; or if there are definite strings attached to our forgiving another person (I will so long as they ask to be forgiven), then in God's sight it is not forgiveness at all, but worse than that it is a form of revenge, we are taking the Law into our hands, and that is very offensive to God.

Now Jesus came to change all this. For him it was no longer a case of using the Law to restrict the amount of revenge exacted. In the Sermon on the Mount Jesus introduced a completely new way of looking at the old commandments. "You have heard that it was said, 'An eye for an eye and a tooth for a tooth.' *But I say to you*, Do not resist one who is evil. But if anyone strikes you on the right cheek, turn to him the other also . . ."[7] He went on to talk about the need to love our enemies and to pray for those who persecute us.

There are two fundamental questions which have been raised by what we have written so far. The first is, if there are still immutable moral laws of God, what happens when we break them? And the second one, if love is commanded by God, how can we keep that commandment, especially in the difficult set of circumstances when good relationships break down? There are two tensions here for which there is only one answer—forgiveness. To break God's Law is not the end of the world. There is a way back to relationship with God through repentance and forgiveness: and in the constant flux which our relationships with each other go through, there is only one way to keep them together, and that is to learn how to forgive *and forget*. If we leave out the forgetting, then our forgiving is not like God's forgiving, and so is not genuine.

Forgiveness is the final and indubitable seal on true love. It authenticates it. Its innate simplicity means that its importance is often missed. When confronted with the complicated problems of human relationships it seems almost cheeky, even superficial, to suggest forgiveness as the cure. Yet in many ways, it is the key which unlocks the doors which bar us from reconciliation with each other. It is the final and only invincible answer to love's failures and frustrations. How do we fight people who won't fight back? How can we go on hurting people who go on forgiving and treating us as if we've not done anything bad to them? How can we cope with people who want us to be right when they know we are wrong, and for themselves to be wrong when they know they are right?

Christianity conquered through this message—that God is a forgiving God and his people are forgivers also. The gospel message in a sentence is that 'God receives sinners'. As H. R. Mackintosh has written, "The gospel triumphed by means of its message of forgiveness, in which it had no rival." He goes on to comment, "The faith which ventures on a gospel so great has the future in its hands."[8] Christians will continue to triumph in their Lord to the extent they grasp this essential truth—that Christ came to show us the meaning of true love, to die that it might be released in us, and that its finest quality is its power to forgive. Without forgiveness, love is meaningless. The early Christians did not triumph because they had better ideas than their rivals for the truth, nor because their moral and social doctrines were superior (although they were), but because they had a message about forgiveness. And times have not changed; it is still true today.

When Dr. Dand Rahbar, a highly intelligent Moslem, turned to Christ, he wrote these words to his Moslem friends: "In our search for the truly worshipable we must look in human history for a man who loved, who lived humbly like the poorest, who was perfectly innocent and sinless, who was tortured and humiliated in literally the worst manner and who declared his continued transparent love for those who had inflicted the worst of injuries upon him. If we do find such a man, he must be the Creator-God himself. For if the Creator-God himself is not that supremely suffering and loving man, then the Creator-God is provenly inferior to that man. And this cannot be. Such a man did live on earth . . . his name was Jesus . . . when I read the New Testament and discovered how Jesus loved and forgave his killers from the Cross, I could not fail to recognise that the love He had for men is the only kind of love worthy of the Eternal God."[9] There is no other religion on earth which has begun to approach these sublime heights.

Jesus' teaching was quite clear—if we do not forgive one another, then God will not forgive us. In the Lord's Prayer, the Sermon on the Mount and several of the parables, Jesus taught the importance of forgiveness. It is also one of the keys to answered prayer. "Whenever you stand praying," Jesus said, "forgive if you have anything against anyone; so that your Father also who is in heaven may forgive you your trespasses" (Mk. 11:24, 25). The way to God's forgiveness of us can be blocked by our refusal to forgive one another; and prayer will remain unanswered because of our un-willingness to forgive others. True love is gratuitous and completely self-forgetful and radically opposed to any expectation of repayment. Spicq has put it well—"Christ forbids his disciples to pass any judgment on their neighbour's moral worth or conduct, or even to condemn anyone without first compassionately taking all the extenuating circumstances into account. *If they are forced to judge they must be swift to absolve, hopeful of acquitting and ingenious in finding excuses for the accused so they can clear him.*"[10] All our skills need to be applied to the great cause of forgiveness.

There is a Persian proverb that "Blood cannot be washed away with blood." Revenge, in other words, is never effective. It does not work, though it may give some relief to pent-up anger in the aggrieved party. But radical remedies are needed and in that sense the power of forgiveness always works, even if its real effects may not be felt for a long time afterwards. In that sense innocent blood can wash away the guilt of others, as it certainly did through the death of Jesus Christ—'the just for the unjust'. If you want to test the genuineness of love, look for the Cross; it will usually be there if love is true.

In Africa today there are many striking examples of the power of forgiveness. One of them is the growth of the Kimbanguist Church in Zaire and now in other parts of Africa. Simon Kimbangu was born in 1889 and was converted to Christ and baptised in 1915. In 1918 he was given a vision, which was repeated several times. In 1921 he found he had a healing ministry—and this led to large crowds gathering. Kimbangu soon became the leader of a large and enthusiastic movement which shook the country.

Kimbangu's success led to an investigation by the Belgian Government in the Congo and it was deemed to be a subversive movement since it was undermining the concept of white superiority. Kimbangu fled but later that year gave himself up. He told his followers to accept suffering courageously, never to use the sword and to repay the evil done by the Europeans by doing evil to them. So, after only five months of public ministry Simon Kimbangu was put through a pseudo-trial called later "a juridical monstrosity", and sentenced to 120 lashes followed by capital punishment. The Belgian King commuted capital punishment to life imprisonment. Kimbangu was deported to Katanga where he spent thirty years in prison. He died in prison on October 12th, 1951.

Kimbangu left nothing to his disciples except his Bible. They were persecuted for forty years. About 37,000 heads of families were deported, most of whom died in exile. But today the Church numbers over three million members. The parallels between the life of Christ and the life of Kimbangu are obvious. Walter Hollenweger has written about Simon Kimbangu, "Because he believed, because he trusted the one who had sent him on the way, he rejected the use of any violence. To resort to violence would be for him unbelief or even atheism."[11] From the seeds of his willingness to forgive has grown a large indigenous African Church, which is now a member Church of the World Council of Churches.

St. Chrysostom has given us a fine framework for forgiving action. There are several stages he recommended:

1. Not to take evil initiatives ourselves.
2. Not to avenge another's evil.
3. Be quiet.
4. To suffer wrongfully.
5. Surrender to the evil doer even more than he demands.
6. Not to hate him but
7. To love him and do him good.
8. To entreat God himself on his behalf.

To forgive those who do evil to us is not to condone the evil they do. God will judge and deal with that. When Paul exhorts the Romans "Let love be genuine," he goes on to say, "Hate what is evil, hold fast to what is good; love one another with brotherly affection; outdo one another in showing honour" (Rom. 12: 9, 10). Genuine love always treats sin and evil seriously. It hates that which corrupts and ruins our humanity. But it forgives those whose actions are dictated by that corrupt humanity. As we have seen, Augustine saw the importance of the question, "What do you love?" For him this question was vital for self-knowledge. A man was known by what he loved. But we can equally say that a person can be known *by what he hates*. Hatred of evil is a mark of genuine love, just as the willingness to forgive is the indubitable seal of true love.

A friend of mine, who was Principal of a Missionary Training College at the time, visited Calcutta a few years ago, and called on Mother Teresa. As he was leaving he asked her if she had any words for his students back home. "When you get home," she replied, "just teach your students how to love." The subject of love is perhaps regarded as too simple to include in any college curriculum, or the teaching programme of any church. Anders Nygren, more than half a century ago, said that Christian love "has never, strictly speaking, been the subject of dogmatic treatment".

The neglect of this subject may explain why Eros has so successfully replaced Agape as a governing principle of spiritual life. Thus the gospel has increasingly been stated in terms of Eros, so that some Christians have become rather too absorbed in individual spirituality at the expense of the corporate, in moral idealism and social action which is blind to the experience of God himself, and thus deprived of the only source of true love.

We can sometimes see how this works out in practice in the way the Church has developed its sacramental life. For example, the Eucharist ought to be, in its central aspect, a clear declaration of the reality of Agape, God's love for us. Instead it has become more and more a celebration of man's love for God. So also in the modern practice of Baptism, particularly with those who emphasise 'believer's' Baptism. It has become increasingly a declaration of a person's decision to follow Christ, rather than God's love in saving him.

Basically our trouble is that we desire power more than we do love. Power struggles and place-seeking permeate all institutions, secular and spiritual. But the love of power is incompatible with the power of love. We have tried to make love, when our destiny is to reflect it. C. S. Lewis has described this as "acquiring a fragrance that is not our own but borrowed, in becoming clean mirrors filled with the image of a face that is not ours."[12] The face is Christ's. According to Paul, something happens when we look into that face, we "are being changed into his likeness from one degree of glory to another, for this comes from the Lord who is the Spirit" (2 Cor. 3:18). The recovery of that love, in the power of the Holy Spirit, is the only hope for the world, and the greatest task of the Church.

NOTES

Chapter 2

1 BBC. 1969. pp 346–347.
2 *English History 1914–45*. Oxford University Press, 1965. p 317.
3 John le Carré in his introduction to the book *Philby, the spy who betrayed a generation* calls the 1930s, "the last lot that cared" (p 28). Somewhere between the '20s and '40s there was an ethical watershed. It has never been quite the same since.
4 *Salvation in History*, S.C.M. P., 1967. p 334.
5 *The Commandment of Love in relation to the other Commandments*. Helican Press, 1966. p 451.
6 Taylor, A. J. P. *English History 1914–45*. Oxford University Press, 1965. p 518. To be fair to the Royal Air Force, and particularly the often maligned Bomber Command, in the period 1940–44 the Germans could only be attacked from the air since land contact with the German army was lost after the Dunkirk evacuation. There seemed a moral compulsion to do so, particularly after Hitler's invasion of Russia. Since daylight and low-level bombing were impossible due to the strong German defences, and since precision bombsights had not yet been developed, virtually the *only* target that could be hit with any certainty was a large city centre. The heavy losses in Bomber Command (over 55,000 were killed in action) and the courage of the crews should not be forgotten. For a balanced account of this action see *Bomber Command*, Max Hastings, Michael Joseph, 1979.
7 *Agape in the New Testament* Vol. I. Herder, 1963. p 36.
8 Adam & Charles Black, 1949. p 1.
9 St. Andrew's Press, 1978. pp 66, 67.
10 *Situation Ethics*, S.C.M. P., 1966. p 63.
11 Spicq, Ceslaus. *Agape in the New Testament* Vol. I., Herder, 1963. p 16.
12 Higgins, Ronald. *The Seventh Enemy*, Hodder & Stoughton, 1978. p 269.
13 Jonathan Cape, 1962.
14 '1st September 1939.'

Chapter 3

1 *Divine Imperative*, Lutterworth, 1937. p 84.
2 Ibid. p 86.
3 *Gospel and Law*, Cambridge University Press, 1951. pp 44–45.
4 Ibid. p 83.
5 *On Being a Christian*, Collins, 1977. p 256.
6 Fontana, 1963. p 25.
7 S.P.C.K., 1932. The sub-title is "a study of the Christian idea of love". It was translated by the well-known Anglo-Catholic scholar A. G. Hebert of Kelham, who wrote an important and supportive preface.
8 Letter written April 3rd, 1980.
9 Nygren discusses this in Vol. II, Part 2. p 60f.

Chapter 4

1 Collins, 1974.
2 Ibid. p 33.
3 *Agape and Eros* Vol. II, Part 2. S.P.C.K., 1932. p 232.
4 Ev. Jn. Tract 83.3 PL35. p 1846.
5 Epworth Press, 1952. p 42.
6 *Love* (part of *Kittel's Wordbook*). p 59.
7 Ibid. p 44.
8 One of Augustine's favourite scriptures was the Pauline formula, 'faith, hope, love', which especially is developed in the *Enchiridion ad Laurentium sive de fide, spe et caritate*. Of the three he regarded love as the really decisive factor. Both faith and hope can be present without our relation to God being right. "The devil believes," he wrote, "but he does not love."
9 Cf. Nygren, Vol. I, Part 1. p 32.
10 Ibid. p 78.
11 *The Moral Teaching of the New Testament*, Burns & Oates, 1965. p 329.
12 Cf. Spicq I. p 30.
13 *Ethics and the New Testament*, Penguin, 1973. p 72.
14 *Marcion*, 2 Aufl., 1924. p 20.
15 See *Agape and Eros* Vol. I, Part 2. p 115.
16 See *Agape and Eros* Vol. I, Part 1. p 98f.

17 *New Vision of Glory*, Mowbray, 1974. Particularly chapter 4 'The Myth'.
18 Quoted by Richard Holloway.
19 Article "A sign for unbelievers: Paul's attitude to glossalalia", *New Testament Studies* XIII, April 1967. pp 240–257.
20 1 Samuel 15:9.
21 John 14:15.
22 John 14:23.
23 *Gifts and Graces: Commentary on 1 Corinthians 12–14,* Hodder & Stoughton, 1973. p 91.
24 John 13:1.
25 Meyer, W., *Der I Brief an die korin ther*, Vol. II, 1945. p 186.
26 Bittlinger, op. cit. p 93.
27 Bittlinger, op. cit. p 81.
28 S.C.M. P., 1966. p 87. For comments on this proposition and theme of love and justice see pages 175–176.
29 Routledge & Kegan Paul, London, 1964.
30 Tyndale Press, 1964. p 203. (His comments on 2 John 2.)
31 Hodder & Stoughton, 1973. p 134.
32 Reported in *Russia* by Robert G. Kaiser, Secker & Warburg, 1976. p 11.
33 Ibid. p 215.
34 S.C.M. P., 1955. p 33.

Chapter 5

1 *Theological Ethics*, A. & C. Black, 1968.
2 Galatians 3:24.
3 *Christian Morals Today*, S.C.M. P., 1964. p 23.
4 *Knowing God*. pp 124–125.
5 Quoted in *The Church and Homosexuality* by Michael Green, David Holloway and David Watson, Hodder & Stoughton, 1980. This book was written as an answer to the liberal Gloucester Report, the Church of England Commission on Homosexuality. David Holloway was a member of that Commission. p 100.
6 In *The Cost of Discipleship*, S.C.M. P., p 111. 1959.
7 *The Christian Counter-Culture*, I.V.P., 1978. p 72.
8 S.C.M. P., 1970. p 334.
9 *The Love Command in the New Testament*, S.C.M. P., 1973. p 95.

10 Article "the Basis for Christian Ethics" in the newsletter *Loaves and Fishes*, May 1979. Quoted with permission.
11 *Theology and the Kingdom of God*, Philadelphia, 1969. p 79.
12 *Church Dogmatics* Vol. II, T. & T. Clark, 1957. 2.519.

Chapter 6

1 *Situation Ethics*. p 15.
2 *Knowing God*. p 129.
3 *The Four Loves*, Geoffrey Bles, 1960, Fontana Edition, 1963. p 128.
4 Ephesians 6:1–4.
5 Luke 11:13.
6 *The Four Loves*. pp 48–49.
7 *Agape in the New Testament* Vol. I. p 139.
8 Lion Publishers, 1979. pp 136–137.
9 p 85.
10 *Flesh and Spirit*. p 63.
11 pp 261–262.
12 See *Agape and Eros* Vol. I, Part 1. pp 34–37. "The history of the idea of Christian love cannot rightly be presented as a continuous and uniform development. It is the story of a meeting of two opposite ideas of love, and of a process of blending which makes it next to impossible to distinguish the two strains."
13 *Agape and Eros* Vol. I, Part 1. p 36.
14 Quoted by Joseph Fletcher in *Situation Ethics*. p 103.
15 Herder, 1963.
16 Presses Universitaires de Bruxelles, 1968.
17 Letter 29.4.80.
18 1970.
19 *Flesh and Spirit*. p 64.
20 p 278.
21 See Nygren, *Agape and Eros* Vol. I, Part 1. p 83f. According to him Paul introduced it as a technical word.
22 Bultmann also regards the words of Jesus about "loving our enemies" as the *ipsissima verba* of the Lord. For further discussion of this see Victor Furnish op. cit. p 64.
23 *The Love Command in the New Testament*. pp 60–61.
24 *Agape in the New Testament* Vol. I, p 83

Chapter 7

1   *Ethics*. p 34.
2   *Knowing God*. p 135
3   Ibid. p 134.
4   *Life Can Begin Again*, Fortress, 1963.
5   *Love* (*Kittel's Wordbook*). p 2.
6   *Love—Christian Style*, an Address to the Western Conservative Baptist Seminary (5511 SE Hawthorne Boulevard, Portland, Oregon, 97215 USA), 1976. p 12.
7   *The Moffatt New Testament Commentary*. Hodder & Stoughton, 1946. p 110.
8   *Gospel and Law*, Cambridge University Press, 1951. pp 44–45.
9   p 278.
10 *Divine Imperative*. pp 55 and 83. In this passage Brunner is making an important point, but in doing so has tended to exaggerate the difference between the old and the new. Any reading of Ezekiel, Jeremiah or Hosea would show one immediately that there was a richness of understanding and experience of love before Christ, even of what we might call "Calvary love". But even this was to be eclipsed in the coming of the Son of God.
11 *Ethics*. pp 34–35.
12 *Agape in the New Testament* Vol. I. p 32.
13 p 333.
14 *The Love Commandment in the New Testament*. p 93.

Chapter 8

1   See James Moffatt *Love in the New Testament*, Hodder & Stoughton, 1929. p 23. "The Latin *experior* does not mean 'try' in the sense to 'test'. The *expertus* is the one who has experienced the love of Jesus and thus (alone) knows what it is to love him in return." (Prof. C. F. D. Moule in a letter to the author, March 1981.)
2   Part 1. pp 54–55.
3   Vol. II, Part 2. p 508f.
4   Weimar Auflage 5, p 33, 25ff. Quoted by Nygren op. cit. p 510.
5   Ibid. 36, p 360, 8ff. Quoted by Nygren p 512.
6   Ibid. 18, p 652, 4ff. Quoted by Nygren p 514.
7   *Love*. p 18

8 *Agape in the New Testament* Vol. I. p 115.
9 Quoted by Joseph Fletcher in *Situation Ethics*. p 104.
10 Ibid.
11 Ibid. p 105.
12 *Love*. p 2.
13 Ibid. p 4.
14 *Agape in the New Testament* Vol. I. p 36.
15 Ibid. p 59ff.
16 Ibid. p 61.
17 Ibid. pp 116–117.
18 *The Divine Imperative*. p 322.
19 *The Cost of Discipleship*. p 134.
20 Homilies on the Gospel of St. Matthew. p 281.
21 C.U.P., 1979. p 174.
22 Quoted by John R. W. Stott in *The Christian Counter-Culture*. p 119.
23 See *Agape and Eros*. p 505ff.
24 *Agape in the New Testament* Vol. I. p 105.
25 *Expository Thoughts on the Gospels: St. Luke* Vol. I, William Hunt & Co., 1858. p 237.
26 *Church Dogmatics* Vol. IV. 2.745. p 221.
27 *Love*. p 24.
28 *Agape in the New Testament* Vol. I. p 140.
29 See *Agape and Eros* Vol. I, Part 1. p 133ff.

Chapter 9

1 *Agape and Eros* Part 1. p 70.
2 Ibid. p 69.
3 Ibid. p 71.
4 Ibid. p 72. See also Victor Furnish *The Love Command in the New Testament*, p 206, in which he writes that the truth about divine love as being the measure and meaning of all love becomes obscured when a third commandment is added. This theme is more fully expounded in chapter fifteen of this book, "Self-Love, Narcissism or Agape?" Paul Ramsey deals fully with the subject in his book *Basic Christian Ethics*, Scribners, 1950.
5 *Charismatic Renewal and Social Action: A Dialogue*. Malines Document 3. p 8.
6 Ibid. p 10.

7   Isaiah 1:12f.
8   Amos 5:21f.
9   From talks given in New Zealand, January 1977.
10   *The Love Command in the New Testament*. p 69.
11   *Deliverance from Evil Spirits*, Servant Books, Ann Arbor, 1980.
12   *Agape in the New Testament* Vol. I. p 74.
13   *Apology* 39.7
14   *Agape and Eros* Vol. I, Part 1. p 108ff.
15   *Testament of Jesus*: a study of John in the light of chapter seventeen, Fortress Press, 1968.
16   *The Love Command in the New Testament*. p 148.
17   *Agape and Eros* Vol. I., Part 1. p 90ff.
18   *The Love Command in the New Testament*. p 94.
19   *Love*. pp 57 & 61.
20   Tyndale Press, 1956. p 54.
21   pp 11–12.
22   1 John 5:21.
23   p 89.
24   *Love*. pp 89, 91.
25   *Rich Christians in an Age of Hunger*, Hodder & Stoughton, 1977. p 164.

Chapter 10

1   Collins, 1974. Paperback edition, 1977. p 88.
2   Matthew 4:4.
3   Jeremiah 2:13.
4   *Love*. p 2.
5   S.P.C.K., 1976. p 2.
6   *On Being a Christian*. pp 261–262.
7   December 4th, 1980.
8   *New Covenant* magazine, Vol. IX, number 5, November 1979.
9   *Distinctive Ideas of the Old Testament*, The Epworth Press, 1944.
10   Edited by Rachel Moss, Collins, 1981.
11   Ibid.
12   *Church Times*. December 5th, 1980.
13   Collins, 1971. p 208.
14   *Church Times*. March 13th, 1981.

Chapter 11

1 Speech made on September 12th, 1975.
2 Reported March 27th, 1980. The report comes from a body called the International Union for the Conservation of Nature and Natural Resources.
3 *Christianity Today*. May 2nd, 1980.
4 Penguin Edition, 1938. The book is the Holland Memorial Lectures of 1922, first published in 1926, the year of the General Strike.
5 Ibid. p 52.
6 This is the sub-title of his book *Small is Beautiful*, Blond Briggs, 1973. This was true of the medieval period at least in theory. In practice there was greed and exploitation as well as corruption. But at least it was a period in which people believed there were moral principles to govern economic life.
7 *Religion and the Rise of Capitalism*. p 73.
8 Quoted in *Small is Beautiful* (p 20); as Schumacher comments, "The road to heaven is paved with bad intentions."
9 Ibid. p 230.
10 *Religion and the Rise of Capitalism*. p 72.
11 Seabury, 1969.
12 Ibid. p 167.
13 Ibid. p 160.
14 Ibid. pp 168–169.
15 Ibid. p 170.
16 p 209.
17 pp 212–213.
18 *The Seventh Enemy*. p 229.
19 *On Being a Christian*. p 262.
20 Ibid. p 269.
21 *Charismatic Renewal and Social Action*. p 79.
22 Ibid. p 80.
23 *Agape in the New Testament* Vol. I. p 137.
24 Ibid. p 138.
25 *Is Revolution Change?* I.V.P., 1972.

Chapter 12

1 *Agape and Ethical Analysis*, Yale University Press, 1972.
2 *Commentary on Song of Songs*, quoted by Nygren in *Agape and Eros* Vol. I, Part 2. p 173.

3   *Agape and Eros* Vol. I, Part 2. p 175.
4   1 Corinthians 1:23.
5   *Agape and Eros* Vol. I, Part 1. p 165.
6   *Love*. pp 28–29.
7   *Encounter with God, A Theology of Christian Experience*, Hodder & Stoughton, 1972. p 51ff.
8   *Agape and Eros* Vol. I, Part 1. p 171.
9   Ibid. p 108ff.
10 Quoted in *Agape and Eros* Vol. II, Part 2. p 288.
11 Ev. Jn., Tract 65.2.
12 By two R.C. theologians H. Koch and J. Stiglmayr in 1895. They discovered this independently of one another. They proved that an extensive section of the work is a plagiarism of the works and thoughts of Proclus. See *Agape and Eros* Vol. II, Part 2. p 359.
13 See *Agape and Eros* Vol. II, Part 2. p 358ff.
14 Ibid. Vol. II, Part 2. p 407.
15 *Dynamics of Spiritual Life*, an Evangelical Theology of Renewal, Paternoster Press, 1979. p 19. He gives sound advice when he writes, "It is my suspicion that Christians should always assume that they start each day at the top of the ladder in contact with God and renew this assumption whenever they appear to have slipped a rung . . . true spirituality is not a superhuman religiosity; it is simply true humanity released from bondage to sin and renewed by the Holy Spirit."
16 See *Agape and Eros* Vol. II, Part 2. p 489. Luther Weimar Auflage 16. p 144, 2ff.

Chapter 13

1   Harper & Row, 1974.
2   *Agape and Eros* Vol. II, Part 2. p 449ff.
3   Penguin, 1968. p 110.
4   February 13th, 1980.
5   In his monograph *Thomas Müntzer, Prophet of Radical Christianity*, Bulletin of the John Rylands Library, 1966.
6   S.C.M. P., 1978. p 117.
7   See *Liberation Theology* by Andrew Kirk, M.M.S., 1979.
8   For one expression of the House Church radicalism see *The Radical Christian* by Arthur Wallis, Kingsway, 1981.

9 *Marxism and Kimbanguist Mission, a Comparison*, the in-augural lecture delivered at the University of Birmingham, November 1972. Dr. Hollenweger is the Professor of Mission at the University. Those who know the author's provocative style should not allow their eyebrows to rise too much at the title of this small booklet. It was published by the University of Birmingham in 1973.

Chapter 14

1 *Christian Morals Today*, S.C.M. P., 1964. p 16.
2 *Situation Ethics*. p 50.
3 Quoted by Fletcher. Ibid. p 61.
4 January 24th, 1980.
5 *Situation Ethics*. p 52.
6 S.C.M. P., 1969.
7 View A is followed by John A. T. Robinson (e.g. *Honest to God*, S.C.M. P., 1960), Joseph Fletcher (e.g. *Situation Ethics*), H. A. Williams (e.g. *Soundings: essays concerning Christian understanding*, edited by Alec Vidler, Cambridge, 1962), and the authors of *Towards a Quaker View of Sex*.

View B is the one taken by Paul Ramsey, V. A. Damant and the Roman Catholics. Roughly speaking it is ethics by rules.

View C is nearer to A. It looks to a transformed humanity as a necessary prerequisite owing to the specific action of God in Christ Jesus (e.g. Paul Lehmann, *Ethics in a Christian Context*, Harper & Row, 1963). See also Bonhoeffer, *Ethics*, S.C.M. P., 1955.
8 *Norm and Context in Christian Ethics*.
9 Ibid. p 326ff.
10 Quoted in *Situation Ethics*. p 149.
11 Ibid. p 56.
12 *The Four Loves*. p 12. It has been said: "God is love is not a palindrome. Love is God does not mean the same thing."
13 *Situation Ethics*. p 49.
14 Ibid. p 26.
15 *Agape and Eros* Vol. I, Part 1. p 70.
16 *Situation Ethics*. p 71.
17 Ibid. p 63.
18 p 335.

19 *Situation Ethics*. p 69.
20 Ibid. p 69.
21 Quoted in *The Church and Homosexuality*, Michael Green, David Watson and David Holloway. Hodder and Stoughton, 1980.
22 I.V.P., 1973. p 79.
23 *Situation Ethics*. pp 113–114.
24 Ibid. p 140.
25 Ibid.
26 Ibid. p 39.
27 Ibid. p 87.
28 Ibid. p 88.
29 We see in this argument the attempt on the part of Fletcher to achieve a synthesis which is just not possible.
30 Ibid. p 103.
31 Ibid. p 120.
32 He attacks those he calls "the pious popularisers", and reveals that he does not seem to understand Paul's letter to the Romans.
33 Ibid. p 123.
34 Ibid. p 121.
35 Ibid. p 134.
36 Quoted by Fletcher. pp 81–82.
37 Ibid. p 82.
38 *Christian Morals Today*. p 16.
39 *Situation Ethics*. p 31.
40 Ibid. p 73.
41 *The Love Command in the New Testament*. pp 95–96.
42 *Agape in the New Testament* Vol. I. pp 124–125.
43 Quoted by Fletcher, p 88.
44 *Situation Ethics*. p 79.
45 Ibid. p 17.
46 *Norm and Context in Christian Ethics*. p 349.

Chapter 15

1 Warner Books, 1979.
2 The opening chapter is called "The Awareness Movement", and is a brilliant description of contemporary society. pp 27–70.
3 See *Agape and Eros* Vol. I, Part 1. p 72ff.

4 Lion Publishing, 1979.
5 *New Vision of Glory*. p 68.
6 Ibid. p 69.
7 *Agape and Eros* Vol. I, Part 1. p 72.
8 Quoted in *Agape and Eros* Vol. I, Part 1. p 72.
9 *The Love Command in the New Testament*. p 206.
10 He asserts, "*Self-love* is the very essence of Eros." p 170.
11 *Church Dogmatics* IV I:2:338.
12 Ibid.
13 *From Cosmos to Love, the meaning of human life*, Jack Dominian and A. R. Peacocke. p 43.
14 Ibid. p 42.
15 Ibid. p 43.
16 Ibid. p 45.
17 Ibid. p 75.
18 *Love Yourself*. Editions Trobisch, Baden-Baden, 1976. pp 9–10.
19 Quoted by Trobisch. p 12.
20 Ibid. p 13.
21 *Agape in the New Testament* Vol. I. p 81.
22 Quoted in *Agape and Eros* Vol. I, Part 2. p 180.
23 Quoted in *Situation Ethics*. p 112.
24 I.V.P., 1973. p 79.
25 p 51.
26 *Image Books*, 1974. p 23.
27 Ibid. p 29.
28 Ibid. p 27.
29 Quoted in *Agape and Eros* Vol. II, Part 2. p 498.
30 Ibid. p 505.
31 Rinehart, 1947. p 17.
32 Ibid. p 23.
33 Ibid. p 212.
34 Holt, Rinehart and Winston, 1966.
35 *Games People Play*.
36 *I'm O.K., you're O.K.*
37 *Psychology as Religion*. p 31. How about *I Ain't Much, Baby, But I'm All I've Got,* published in the United States in 1969? This book promises to help you "free yourself through this proven program of self-acceptance, self-enrichment and love."
38 *The Joy of Sex*.

228

39 *Psychology as Religion*. p 34ff.
40 O'Neill, Nena and George, *Open Marriage*.
41 *Psychology as Religion*. p 66ff.
42 Ibid. p 69ff.
43 Harper, 1932. Chapter two.
44 Harper, 1943.
45 *Psychology as Religion*. p 71.
46 Ibid. p 72.
47 *Psychology as Religion*. p 60ff.
48 Ibid. p 125.
49 Ibid. p 135.
50 *Victory through Surrender*, Abingdon Press, 1971. p 8.

Chapter 16

1   December 31st, 1980.
2   Lord Byron's poem, *Don Juan* (Canto 13:6).
3   *Time* magazine. May 12th, 1980.
4   *The Seventh Enemy*. p 192.
5   Nisbet & Co., 1927. p 29.
6   *Gifts and Graces*. p 86.
7   Matthew 5:38.
8   *The Christian Experience of Forgiveness*. p 21.
9   Quoted by Sir Norman Anderson in his book *God's Laws and God's Love, essays in comparative religion*, Collins, 1980.
10 *Agape in the New Testament* Vol. I. p 90.
11 *Marxist and Kimbanguist Mission, A Comparison*. p 11.
12 *Christian Reflections*, Eerdmans, 1967. p 6.

BIBLIOGRAPHY

Although many popular books have been written on this subject in the last one hundred years, from Henry Drummond's famous *The Greatest Thing in the World* to the almost equally famous classic by C. S. Lewis, *The Four Loves*, there is still a scarcity of theological books on this important subject. The three major books on love are all difficult to obtain. Anders Nygren's great book *Agape and Eros* is at the moment out of print. The other two are originally in French and German—namely *Agape dans le Nouveau Testament* by Ceslaus Spicq, and *Die Liebe als Grundmotiv der Neutestamentlichen Theologie*, by Viktor Warnack; and only the former has an English edition (published in the United States).

When one widens out the scope of this subject into the territories of theology, ethics and the social sciences, the literature is vast. What I have done, therefore, is to list, first of all, the theological books of which I have made particular use myself; second, the more popular reading, where one has had to be very selective; and third, the books which I have found helpful in the various related subjects. Here one has had to be most selective of all.

Theological

Barth, Karl. *Church Dogmatics* (particularly Vol. II). T. & T. Clark, 1957.

Bittlinger, Arnold. *Gifts and Graces*. Hodder & Stoughton, 1967.

Bonhoeffer, Dietrich. *Ethics*. S.C.M. P., 1971.

Brunner, Emil. *Divine Imperative*. Lutterworth, 1937.

Burnaby, John. *Amor Dei* (Hulsean Lectures 1938). Hodder & Stoughton, 1938.

Fletcher, Joseph. *Situation Ethics*. S.C.M. P., 1966.

Furnish, Victor P. *The Love Command in the New Testament*. S.C.M. P., 1973.

Houlden, J. L. *Ethics and the New Testament*. Penguin, 1973.

Joly, Robert. *Le Vocabulaire Chrétienne de l'amour est-il original? Philein et agapan dans le grec antique*. Presses Universitaires de Bruxelles, 1968. English translation, S.C.M. P., 1973.

Kung, Hans. *On Being a Christian*. Collins, 1977.

Moffatt, James. *Love in the New Testament*. Hodder & Stoughton, 1929.

Morris, Leon. *Love, Christian Style*. Western Conservative Baptist Seminary, 1976.

Nygren, Anders. *Agape and Eros*. S.P.C.K., 1932.

Outka, Gene. *Agape, an ethical analysis*. Yale University Press, 1972.

Piper, John. *Love your Enemies*. Cambridge University Press, 1979.

Quell and Stauffer. *Love* (part of *Kittel's Wordbook*). A. & C. Black, 1949.

Rahner, Karl. *The Commandment of Love in relation to the other Commandments*. Helican Press, 1966.

Ramsey, Paul. *Deeds and Rules in Christian Ethics*. S.J.T. Occ. Paper 11, 1965.

Robinson, John A. T. *Christian Morals Today*. S.C.M. P., 1964.

Schnackenburg, Rudolf. *The Moral Teaching of the New Testament*. Burns & Oates, 1965.

Spicq, Ceslaus. *Agape in the New Testament* (3 volumes). Herder, 1963. (French edition, Gabalda, 1958.)

Spicq, Ceslaus. *Théologie Morale du Nouveau Testament* (2 volumes). Gabalda, 1965.

Thielicke, Helmut. *Theological Ethics*. A. & C. Black, 1968.

Popular

Becker, Wilhard. *Love in Action*. Victory Press, 1972.

Bigelow, Jim. *Love has come again*. Lakeland, 1978.

Cardenal, Ernesto. *To Live is to Love*. Image, 1974.

Kerr, Cecil. *Power to love*. (An interesting account of love against the background of Northern Ireland.) Christian Journals, 1976.

Lewis, C. S. *The Four Loves*, Geoffrey Bles, 1960. Fontana 1963.

Powell, John. *Why am I afraid to love?*(One of several popular books by this author on this subject.)

Trobisch, Walter. *Love Yourself*. Editions Trobisch, 1977.

Wesley, John. *A Plain Account of Christian Perfection*. Epworth, 1952. (Wesley's teaching on 'entire sanctification', a foundation of which is love.)

Related

Anderson, Sir Norman. *God's Laws and God's Love*. Collins, 1980. (Law and love in the field of Comparative Religion.)

Barclay, William. *Flesh and Spirit*. St. Andrew's Press, 1978. (Another of his superb books, particularly helpful on word studies.)

Cullmann, Oscar. *Salvation in History*. S.C.M. P., 1967. (Not directly on this subject, but important insights into relationship between the Spirit and love.)

Dodd, C. H. *Gospel and Law*. Cambridge University Press. 1951.

Ellul, Jacques. *Violence*. Seabury (U.S.A.), 1969.

Higgins, Ronald. *The Seventh Enemy*. Hodder & Stoughton, 1978. (A chilling book guaranteed to sober anyone.)

Holloway, Richard. *New Vision of Glory*. Mowbray, 1974.

Kelsey, Morton. *Encounter with God*. Hodder & Stoughton, 1972.

Lasch, Christopher. *The Culture of Narcissism*. Warner Books, 1979.

Packer, James. *Knowing God*. Hodder & Stoughton, 1973.

Schumacher, E. F. *Small is Beautiful*. Blond Briggs, 1973.

Suenens, Cardinal (and Cardinal Camara). *Charismatic Renewal and Social Action*. Darton, Longman and Todd, 1980.

Tawney, R. H. *Religion and the Rise of Capitalism*. Penguin, 1938.

Vitz, Paul. *Psychology as Religion*. Lion, 1979.

INDEX

Authors of the main source books, from which quotations have been taken, are in italics. Where a subject has been dealt with in greater detail the page numbers are in bold type.

Agape (the Greek word), 10, 15, 38, **54–64**, 70–1, 81, 89–90, 111, 135, 141, 190–2, 214
Anabaptists, 159
Aquinas, St. Thomas, 139
Aristotle, 11, 16, 60, 139
Auden, W. H., 19
Augustine of Hyppo, 12, 29–31, 33, 56, 87, 135–6, 141, 143, **145**, 149–50, 164

Barclay, William, 16, 60, 63, 119
Barth, Karl, 53, 89, 171, 188
Benedict, St., 29, 31, 148
Bernard of Clairvaux, 31, 75, 148, 192
Berne, Eric, 196
Billing, Pemberton, 15
Bittlunger, Arnold, 36–8, 209
Bonhoeffer, Dietrich, 12, 41, 45, 65, 69, 85–6, 167
Booth, William, 31
Brandt Report, 13, 120
British Council of Churches, 117
Brown, Douglas, 118
Brown, Raymond, 195
Brunner, Emil, 12–13, 21–2, 69, 82, 171
Burnaby, John, 12

Camara, Dom Helder, 95, 130
Cardenal, Ernesto, 193
Carney, Frederick S., 167

Cartland, Barbara, 111
Catherwood, Sir Frederick, 131
Charismatic movement, 34, 152, 159, 161–2
Christenson, Larry, 48–9
Christian humanism, **157**
Christian radicalism, **158**
Christian socialism, 126
Churchill, Sir Winston, 12
Chrysostom, St., 31, 45, 85, 213
Clapham Sect, 156
Clark, Kenneth, 11
Clement of Alexandria, 135, **144**, 146
Climacus, Johannes, 148–9
Communities, 115–16
Cullmann, Oscar, 14, 46, 73, 173–4

Darnant, V. A., 167
Darwin, Charles, 124
Davidson, Alex, 193
Denning, Lord, 170
Dionysius, 147
Dodd, C. H., 22, 67–8, 79
Dominian, Dr. J., 188–9
Dostoevsky, 151, 178
Dürrenmatt, Friedrick, 20

Edwards, David, 119
Ellul, Jacques, 126–8
Emerson, 123
Engels, 159, 197
Eros, **59**

Evangelicalism, **155**
Evans, Dr. Leonard, 9, 96–7

Feuerbach, Ludwig, 197–8
Ficino, Marsilio, 157
Field, David, 174
Finney, Charles, 152
Fletcher, Joseph, 17, 38, 42, 55, 78, 104, **163–83**, 184
Fosdick, Harry, 198–9
Francis of Assisi, 31, 200
Friedman, Milton, 123–4
Fromm, Erich, 196, 198
Frost, Dr. Robert, 9
Furnish, Victor, 47, 64, 73–4, 97, 100–1, 128, 180, 187
Fynn, 28, 107

Galbraith, Professor, 124
Gerhardt, Paul, 152
Gore, Bishop Charles, 126
Greet, Dr. Kenneth, 118
Grundtvig, 152

Harnack, Adolf, 31
Harris, Thomas, 197
Hegel, 13
Heidelberg Disputation, 87, 194
Heller, Joseph, 18
Higgins, Ronald, 20, 129, 207
Hippolytus, 142
Holl, Karl, 145
Hollenweger, Prof. Walter, 162, 213
Holloway, Richard, 33, 185
Homosexuality, 116, 193
Houlden, J. L., 31
House Churches, 159

Ignatius, 134
Irenaeus, 44, 142, **143**, 192
Irish potato famine, 123–4

John of the Cross, 31
John Paul, Pope II, 127, 170
Joly, Robert, 62
Jones, Stanley, 202

Kasemann, Ernst, 100
Kelsey, Dr. Morton, 139
Keswick Convention, 152, 155
Keynes, Lord, 123–4
Kimbanguist Church, 162, 212
Kingsley, Charles, 126
Kung, Hans, 24, 60, 110, 129

Lausanne Statement, 156
Lawrence, D. H., 110
Lebeau, Paul, 62
Lehmann, Paul, 167
Lennon, John, 11, 16
Levin, Bernard, 205
Lewis, C. S., 21, 24, 55–7, 59–60, 104, 108, 132, 171, 214
Lovelace, Richard, 149
Lucian of Samosata, 99
Luther, Martin, 25, 41, 67, 77, 87–8, 90, **149**, 151, 153, 158, 194

McInerny, Dr. Ralph, 112
MacKintosh, H. R., 208, 210
Marcion, 29, 31, 44–6, **142**, 164, 172, 192
Marx, Karl, 124, 127, 198
Marxism, 11, 177
Maurice, F. D., 126
Methodism, 152, 154–5
Meyer, W., 37
Miller, Henry, 52
Milton, John, 207
Moltmann, Jürgen, 159
Montanus, 29, 33
Moody, D. L., 152
Morris, Dr. Leon, 67

Morrow, Lance, 205–6
Moss, Basil, 118
Moule, Prof. C. F. D., 10, 166
Mumford, Bob, 67
Müntzer, Thomas, 159
Mysticism, **147**, 153

Narcissism, 91, **184**
Neill, Bishop Stephen, 78
Neo-Platonism, 145, 147–8, 157
Niebuhr, H. R., 79, 165
Nietzsche, 108, 198
Northern Ireland, 206
Nygren, Anders, 12–13, 16, 25, 29–30, 54, 60–2, 76, 87–8, 91, 94, 99–103, 133–4, 137, 140, 142, 145, 147–50, 153, 172, 183, 187–188, 192, 214

Origen, 61, 134–5, **144**
Outka, Gene, 133, 167

Packer, Dr. James, 41–3, 55, 65
Peale, Norman Vincent, 198–9
Pelagius, 147
Pentecostalism, 29, 33–4, 152, 159, **161**
Pietism, **152**
Piper, John, 85
Plato, 16, 60, 132, 139, 140, 157
Polycarp, 143

Quakers, 159
Quebedeaux, Richard, 156
Quell (and Stauffer), 16, 29–30, 79–80, 90, 102, 104, 109, 138
Quick, Canon, 61

Ramsey, Michael, 174
Ramsey, Paul, 165, 167
Rashdall, Hastings, 93
Rayner, Karl, 14

Reformation, 122, 147, 151, 153, 158, 207
Ricardo, David, 123
Richardson, Alan, 78
Ritschl, 76, 91
Robinson, Dr. John A. T., 42–3, 110, 165, 167, 173, 175, 178, 184
Rockefeller, Nelson, 120
Ruotsalainen, 152
Rupp, Gordon, 158–9
Ryle, Bishop, 88, 155

Scanlon, Michael, 97
Schnackenburg, Rudolf, 30
Schumacher, Dr., 123, 125
Self-love, **184**
Septuagint, 54, 63, 88
Shaftesbury, Earl of, 120
Shaw, George Bernard, 35
Sherrard, Philip, 110
Sider, Ron, 105
Simeon, Charles, 33
Situation ethics, **163–83**
Skemp, J. B., 62
Smedes, Lewis, 59
Smith, Adam, 123
Snaith, Norman H., 113
Solzhenitsyn, Alexander, 12, 14
Spencer, Herbert, 124
Spener, Jakob, 152, 154
Spicq, Ceslaus, 15, 17, 30, 58, 61–62, 64, 72, 78, 80–1, 88, 90, 98, 131, 181, 211
Spurgeon, Charles, 65
Strachan, 63, 68
Stott, John R. W., 40, 45, 121
Sueneus, Cardinal, 95, 130
Sweet, J. P. M., 34, 38

Tasker, Prof., 102
Tawney, R. H., 122–3, 125–6

Taylor, A. J. P., 12, 15
Teresa, Mother, 31, 214
Tertullian, 99, 142
Thielicke, Helmut, 42, 67
Tillich, Paul, 38, 55, 64
Tolpuddle martyrs, 154
Trench, R. C., 63
Trobisch, Walter, 189–91

Vitz, Prof. Paul, 10, 185, 195, 197–
  200

Walker (of Truro), 155
Wells, H. G., 52
Wesley, Charles, 75, 152
Wesley, John, 29, 31, 75, 152–5
Whitehouse, Mrs. Mary, 113
Wilberforce, William, 156
Wordsworth, Bishop, 75
World Council of Churches, 126, 159
Wycliffe, 122

Zinzendorf, Count von, 152, 154